THE STORY OF AUSTRALIA

Don Watson was born in 1949, the same year as Robert Menzies became Prime Minister. He grew up with two brothers and a sister on a small hilly farm near the Victorian town of Poowong which is famous for rare giant earthworms. He went to primary school at Poowong and high school at Korumburra, and played football for Loch.

For most of the past seventeen years he has lived in Melbourne – famous for its football – going to university and lecturing at Footscray Institute of Technology. In the year that Bob Hawke became Prime Minister he gave up his job to write full-time. He has a daughter aged nine.

CONSULTANTS

Professor Manning Clark
Dr Peter Cook
Dr Geoffrey Serle
Dr Anne Summers
Aboriginal Education Consultative Group
Victorian Archaeological Survey

Some of the places that played important parts in the story of Australia

THE STORY OF AUSTRALIA

DON WATSON

Illustrated by Ron Brooks
with Shane McGowan

Thomas Nelson Australia
in association with
McPhee Gribble Publishers

Contents

Map
Acknowledgements
Foreword by Professor Manning Clark

Ancient Australia

Cold-blooded dinosaurs and ancient fossil fish **4** How did people get here? **6**
Does that fish hook go with these charred eel bones? **8**
On the shores of Lake Mungo 2000 generations ago **10**
The past is precious **12** The mystery of the megafauna and the dingo **14**
Who owns the past? **16** Mungo woman **18**

Aboriginal Australia

Moving among spirits **20** The people of the riverbanks **22**
The people of the deserts **24** The people of the far south **26**
Captain Cook did not discover Australia **28**
Aboriginal Australia through English eyes **30**
Sydney Cove, 1788 **32** 'It's like a white man' **34**

1788-1809

The other side of the world **36**
All of Eastern Australia becomes a British possession **38**
A most valuable acquisition **40** Outcasts in their own land **42**
Starting a new life **44** A chance for free men to make their fortunes **46**
Rebellion **48** George Bass **50**

1810-1829

'Hurray for old Sydney and the sky over it' **52**
Beyond the Blue Mountains **54** A city to be proud of **56**
God and New South Wales **58** Van Diemen's Land was a wild place **60**
'Pure merinos' **62** No 'rich and romantic land' **64**
Lachlan Macquarie **66**

1830-1849

Meat three times a day **68** A squatter on the Monaro **70**
The greatest landowner in the world **72**
The massacre at Myall Creek **74** A large and respectable country town **76**
South Australia would be better **78** Tasmanians at war **80**
Caroline Chisholm **82**

1850-1869

Gold fever **84** At the diggings **86**
The Eureka Stockade **88** Foreign devils **90**
Burke and Wills and the Dig Tree **92**
An 'amusement of madmen' **94** A dream of a small farm **96**
Raffaello Carboni **98**

Contents

1870-1889

A supply of cheap labour 100
Dealing with disease 102 Opening up the north 104
A mining town 106 The Ned Kelly story 108
A jewel in Britain's crown 110 Getting there 112
James and Grace Forsyth 114

1890-1909

The Great Strikes 116 Life on the Collingwood flat 118
Bush schools 120
Textile workers and sweatshops 122 New ways of seeing the place 124
A White Australia 126 1900 128
William Lane 130

1910-1929

An Edwardian family 132 Empire and 1914 134
A nation at war 136 Miraculous progress 138
Daisy Bates and the Aborigines 140
Flying machines 142 The battler on the land 144
Billy Hughes 146

1930-1949

The Great Depression 148 The wireless in the loungeroom 150
'For their own good' 152 War in the Pacific 154
Australians prepare for invasion 156
Work to be done 158
Peace 160 John Curtin 162

1950-1969

A house, a Holden and a Hills hoist 164 Australia goes wild about the queen 166
Milking cows and listening to Tarzan 168
The best in the world 170 Watching the box 172
Migrants from Europe 174 The mining boom 176
Albert Namatjira 178

1970 to the present day

Pictures of Australia 180
Vietnam years 182 It's time 184
Living in the cities 186 A family in the seventies 188
The right to the land 190
More hairdressers than steelworkers 192

Picture sources 196
Select Bibliography 198
Index 199

Acknowledgements

Many people helped produce this book. McPhee Gribble Publishers came up with the idea. Hilary McPhee wrote the chapters on prehistoric Australia. Peter Cook contributed much in the way of researching and writing a number of chapters. The consultants were invaluable both in the advice they gave us and in their support for the project.

We want to thank Gary Presland of the Victorian Archaeological Survey, Sharman Stone of the Aboriginal Education Consultative Group and Gaye Sculthorpe of the Anthropology Department of the Science Museum of Victoria for all the advice they provided; also John Mulvaney, Sandra Bowdler, Neville White, Henry Reynolds, Phyl and Noel Wallace were most helpful.

A number of people contributed pictures from their private collections. Thanks go to Ponch Hawkes, Ruth Maddison, Ross Fitzgerald, Archie Glenn, Frank Laffy, Gary Lavers, Michael McKernan, Norman and Mary McPhee, David Potts, Dimity Reed, Lillie Reeves, Gary Smith, Mrs D.M. Thomson, Phillip Toyne, Phyl and Noel Wallace, Doug and Mary Watson.

For other pictures and assistance we are grateful to Narelle Crux, BHP Archives; Scott Murray, Cinema Papers; Kenneth Jacoby, GMH; Fenn Hinchcliffe, Tamara Winikoff, Australian Centre for Photography; Chris Hogarth, Gaye Sculthorpe, Science Museum of Victoria; Barbara Perry, Sylvia Redman, National Library of Australia; Baiba Berzins, Mitchell Library, New South Wales; Rosalie Tuohy, Education Department of Victoria; Siddons Industries; Olga Howell, Australian Information Service; Ronin Films; Mr R.E. Comer, Snowy Mountains Hydro-Electric Authority; Albert Tucker; Dan Sprod, Blubberhead Press; Warni Atma, Kim Bassett, Channel Seven Publicity; Gail McCarthy, ABC Publicity; David Spratt, Melbourne Media Services; Andrew Hooper; Pat Sweeney, Department of Home Affairs; Don Whyte; Australian Heritage Commission; Ross Lansell; Ron Miller, Rosemary O'Shea, Teresa Buck, Division of Natural History Education Service, Museum of Victoria; Alan Thorne; Frank Strahan, Melbourne University Archives; Gary Warren, Department of Geography, Monash University.

Ron Brooks and Shane McGowan we thank both for their pictures and for their enthusiasm for the project. Demos Krouskos did a great deal of the picture research, George Dale was generous with archival material, Keith Robertson and Greg Carroll contributed much to the layout and design, and Jenny Trustrum and Sandra Meredith helped in a multitude of ways.

Foreword

In my childhood I heard and read many stories of the people of other countries. At school and at church I heard of the heroes and heroines of Greece and Rome, and Israel. I do not remember ever hearing a story by the Aborigines, or about the Aborigines, or indeed any memorable story about the people of Australia. I lived in Australia but knew little about the country, its people or its history. That was a great impoverishment. Happily the children of this generation are no longer deprived of knowledge of the country in which they live. Thanks to revolutions in transport and communication they either see it for themselves or see it on the television. Thanks also to a change in the attitude of the white settlers to the Aborigines, they can now read or hear Aboriginal stories. Now Don Watson and McPhee Gribble Publishers have filled yet another gap for children. They have told them the story of people in this country. Like all good historians they have told it as a story, and told it so well that both adults and children will now have a better idea of who we are, and, maybe too, what we are likely to be.

Manning Clark, 1984

ANCIENT AUSTRALIA

Approx.

500 million years ago   Fish in northern Australian waters.

45 million years ago   Australian continent separated from Asia and Antarctica.
Animals and birds and plants start to develop Australian forms.

15 million years ago   New Guinea formed.

2 million years ago   Last ice ages begin.
Giant animals and birds in Australia.

120-50 thousand years ago   People probably arrive in Australia from South-east Asia, but Aborigines believe life was created here in the Dreamtime.

25 thousand years ago   Aborigines arrive in Tasmania.

15 thousand years ago   Climate much drier than now.
Megafauna starting to die out.
Aboriginal people's tool kits include horsehoof cores, flaked tools and stone axe heads.

10 thousand years ago   Sea levels have risen to form Bass Strait, separating Tasmania from mainland.

6 thousand years ago   First signs of dingoes in Australia.
Volcanoes still erupting.
Seas have risen to their present level.
Christians until the late nineteenth century generally believed this was when God created the world.

5 thousand years ago   People's tool kits include small finely worked blades of stone, bone and shell.

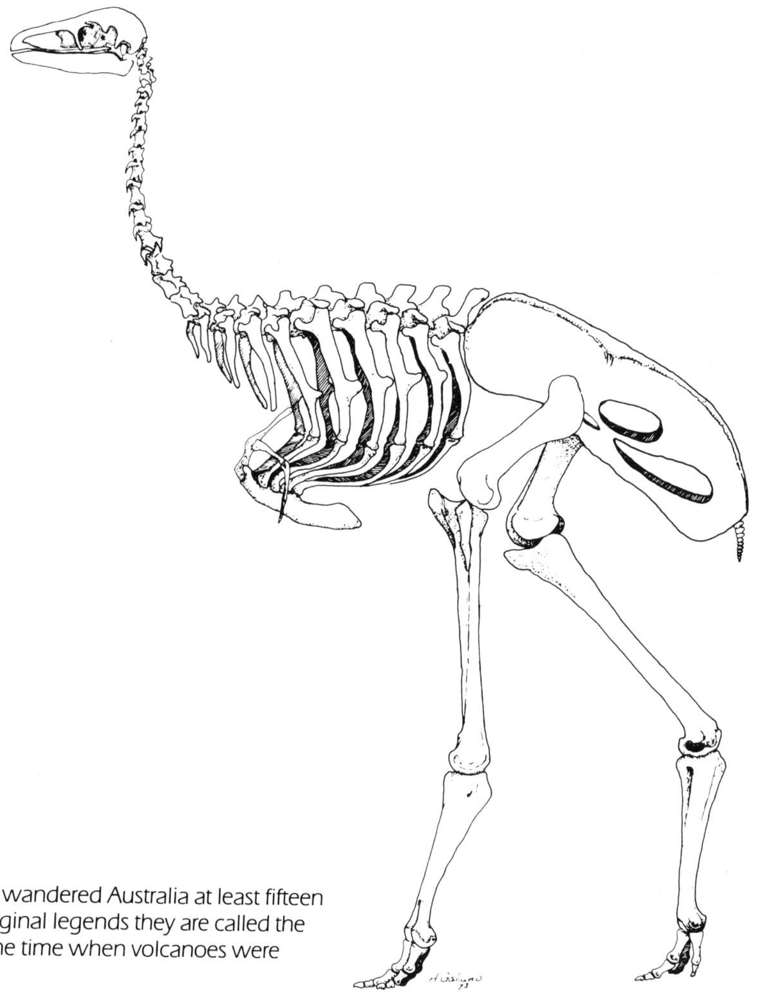

These two metre tall birds wandered Australia at least fifteen million years ago. In Aboriginal legends they are called the Mihirung which lived at the time when volcanoes were still erupting.

COLD-BLOODED DINOSAURS AND ANCIENT FOSSIL FISH

An extraordinary little oasis area at Palm Valley in central Australia. Here the vegetation is much as it would have been two million years ago when central Australia's climate was wet and lush. The palm-like tree, **Livistona mariae**, is one of the rarest, and oldest, trees in the world. Only three thousand still exist.

Australia is many hundreds of millions of years old.

Fossils of ancient fish – about five hundred million years old, the oldest known in the world – have been found in the Northern Territory.

It took the animals and birds and fish we are familiar with today from about five hundred million years ago to about four thousand years ago to develop. During that enormous amount of time many other creatures lived in and around this continent but they have gradually died out.

Australian creatures, like those of every other part of the world, have been affected by very slow but massive changes to every aspect of the environment in which they lived.

One of the most important changes which made Australian creatures different from any others happened during the last forty-five million years. By that time the land mass we call Australia was no longer joined to Antarctica and was separated from much of the land we know as Asia. The animal and birdlife on this continent was then isolated from the rest of the world and would evolve in ways that are peculiar to Australia.

This is why Australian animals seemed so weird to the first Europeans who saw them, and why they still seem 'cute' to American tourists.

Then fifteen million years ago, the northern edge of the land mass began to crumble up against the crust of South-east Asia. The vast pressures this produced meant that New Guinea began to rise to become the cool moist highlands that exist today. New Guinea was still joined on to Australia then, so these mountains were an important area for the development of our species, particularly when Australia was going through periods of great dryness.

The world's climate was always slowly changing which meant that creatures had to adapt themselves to quite different conditions from time to time. Parts of Australia were covered with ice-sheets for long periods which would only have suited the survival of some kinds of creatures. During the times of extensive deserts, cold-blooded dinosaurs would have coped better than other living things. During cool periods warm-blooded mammals thrived.

Plant-life on which bird and animal life depended – if not for themselves then for the smaller creatures they fed on – changed along with the climate.

The last major climatic change that affected Australian vertebrates was the cooling and drying of the continent which started about fifteen million years ago and ended about two million years ago – before the last set of ice ages began.

Much of central Australia became desert and animals that once were adapted to the wet forests of central Australia had to try to compete for food in the new woodlands, grasslands and deserts. Many types of creatures which could not change their living patterns quickly enough simply vanished.

Those that managed to adapt slowly evolved into creatures we think of as distinctively Australian – such as the red kangaroo and wombat – but in much bigger versions than we know today.

The ancient armoured tube-nosed fish lived in the waters which covered north-western Australia four hundred million years ago. The artist, Peter Schouten, was able to reconstruct what the fish would have been like from fossils.

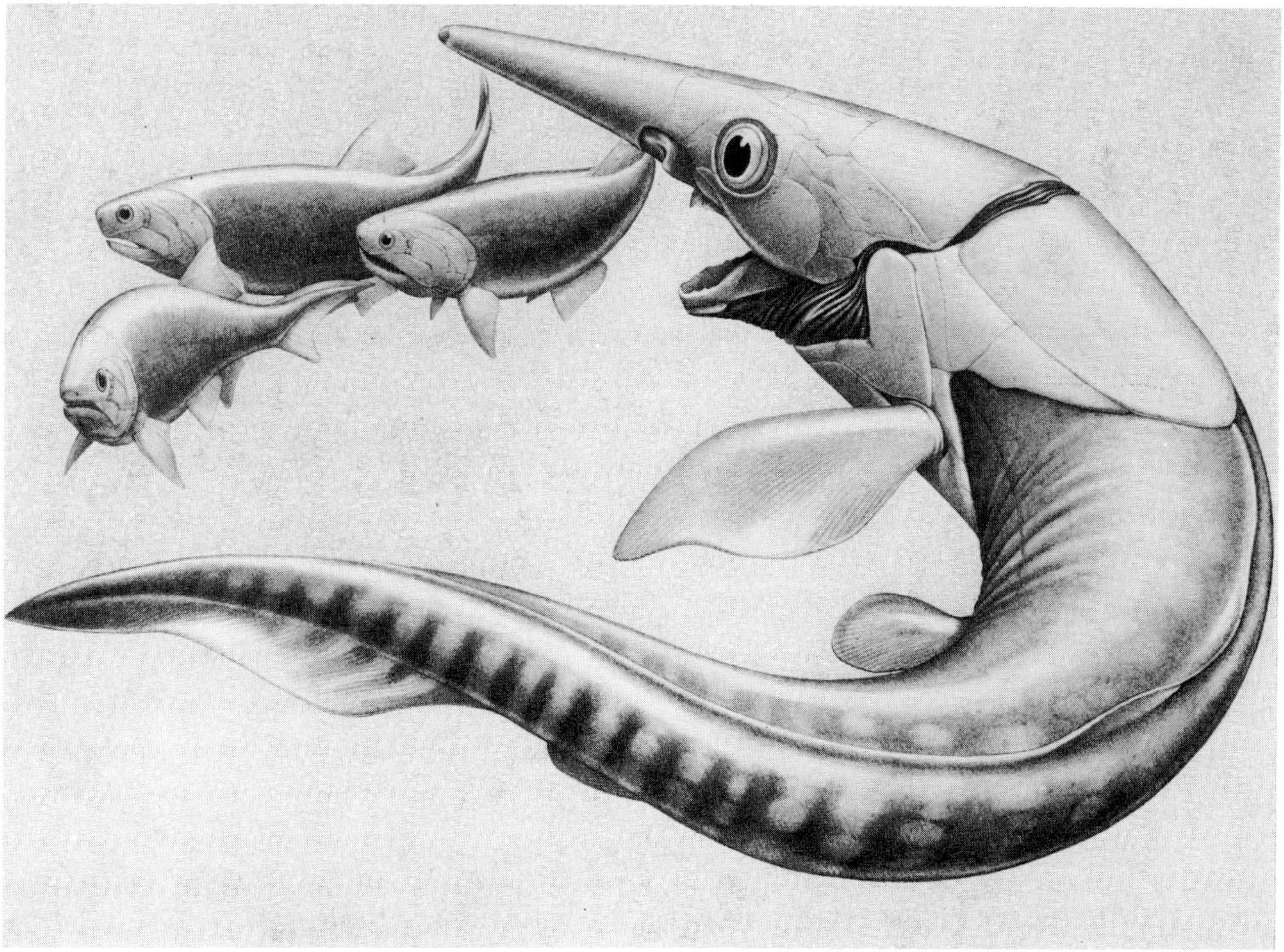

HOW DID PEOPLE GET HERE?

Aboriginal Dreaming legends tell of human life being created in Australia. Bunjil's Cave in Victoria contains an Aboriginal rock painting of Bunjil the Father Creator of life and the land in the south-eastern part of Australia.

A lot of Aboriginal people would say that their ancestors did not 'get here' at all. They would say that human life in Australia started in Australia – in the time of the Dreaming when all life was created.

But most white Australian scientists argue that the Australian Aborigines came from the north at least fifty thousand years before Europeans arrived. It may even be more than one hundred thousand years ago.

Scientists think this because there is evidence of much older human life in South-east Asia and China than has ever been found in Australia. The people of ancient Australia, they say, were migrants from Asia and it is from them that the modern Australian Aborigines are descended.

Fifty thousand years ago the earth's climate was much colder than it is today. The ice caps around the north and south poles were a lot bigger and the level of the seas was lower – maybe one hundred metres lower. Tasmania was joined on to the mainland of

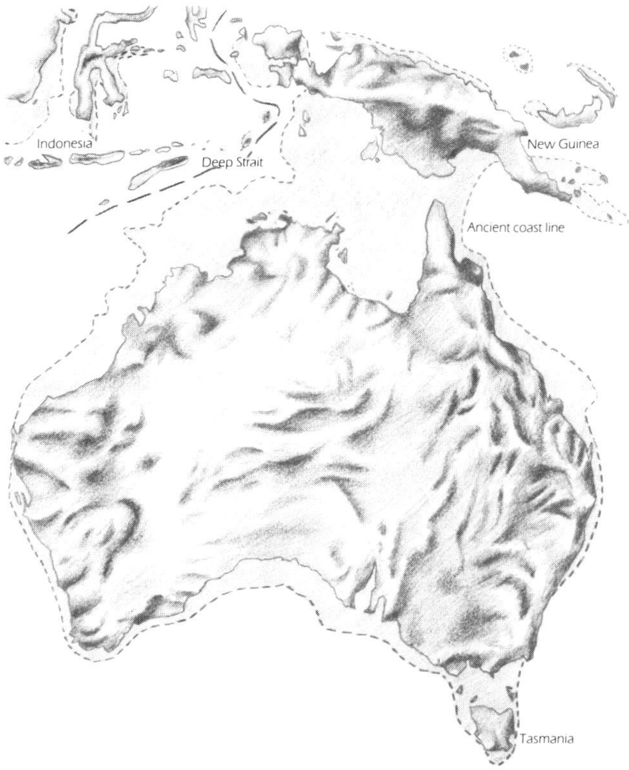

About twenty-five thousand years ago sea levels were maybe one hundred metres lower than they are now. New Guinea, Tasmania and Australia formed one huge land mass. Between Indonesia and Australia was a deep strait about eighty kilometres wide.

Australia. So was New Guinea and the islands around the coast.

Australia was separated from Asia by a deep sea about eighty kilometres wide. So if the first Australians did come from Asia they must have come by boat.

The people who lived on the coasts of South-east Asia and China knew how to make rafts and canoes many thousands of years ago. Perhaps they were accidentally swept on to the Australian coast.

Perhaps they were stranded here but were able to survive because of the knowledge they brought with them. Maybe they came from a similar kind of country and knew what fish and plants to look for. Certainly these people were able to make stone tools. The earliest stone tools found so far in Australia are very similar to those that have been found in parts of South-east Asia.

The Australian continent only got to be its present size about six thousand years ago when the last ice age ended and the seas reached their present levels. The beaches on which the first Australians fished, the land on which they hunted and the caves in which they might have lived have all disappeared under the sea. There are now very few signs left – very few clues as to how the first Australians lived.

Nobody knows yet how they spread through the land.

Did the first inhabitants and their descendants spend thousands of years in the north? Did they gradually spread throughout the land in pursuit of the giant animals they found here? Did they spread within a few hundred years through all the best country round the coasts and the riverbanks? Were there several groups of people who arrived from different parts of Asia at different times?

There are clues being discovered all the time and new questions to be asked as a result. The answers will probably never be final.

Scientists imagine small groups of people crossing the seas by accident from South-east Asia.

DOES THAT FISH HOOK GO WITH THESE CHARRED EEL BONES?

In ancient times a dead fish is covered in silt on a lake floor. Millions of years later rocks have formed and the fossil skeleton is embedded beneath a stream. In modern times archaeologists find the fossil close to the bank of a recent stream.

The only way we can begin to understand how people lived before our time is to study what they left behind.

Some societies leave much – writings and paintings, buildings and roads, iron tools and china plates and monuments to the people and ideas they thought important.

There is not much physical evidence for other societies. Maybe a small number of objects were used for daily living and great importance was placed on religion, ceremonies, singing, story-telling, family networks, drawings in sand and paintings on rock, a close relationship with the land they lived in. These things are much harder to trace and to preserve.

Wood and food and skins and baskets rot away very quickly – sometimes leaving stains in the earth that can be studied. Stone tools and fossils will remain forever as long as the weather doesn't erode them. Charcoal from camp fires and ochre can occasionally be seen in the soil. Bones sometimes remain, especially if they are burnt or carefully buried. Seeds and pollen can be collected from the ground too.

By examining these things it is possible, for instance, to work out how long a campsite was used. Some were used over and over again for thousands of years.

Perhaps this was an especially comfortable place to live for a time – close to water, dry, with plenty of food throughout the year. Or maybe it was a place of great importance, where people gathered for ceremonies and to exchange goods with members of other tribes or clans.

Occasionally there might be a painting or markings on a rock nearby telling us what images were important enough to paint or engrave – although meanings can only be guessed at.

Around the hearth may be scraps of bone from meals – telling what kind of animals these people ate.

Sometimes there are signs of stone tool-making – fragments struck from the sides of stones when they were being shaped, or tools themselves that were lost or discarded. Usually the stone is from nearby outcrops but sometimes tools were made from stone carried from a long way off – telling us it was valuable in some way.

There is usually no sign in the earth of the resin or rushes used to fasten the sharp tools to wooden handles. We have to make guesses from stone tools still in use today, from drawings made by the people themselves or by outsiders observing them.

Pollen and seeds can tell us what kind of plants and trees grew there and something of what the weather was like, and what the people ate.

These remains are of no use if they are not dug up very carefully and their position recorded.

When things are left on the surface of the earth after people move on, sand or dust or grass or leaves quite quickly covers them. When the campsite is next occupied more things are left behind and covered over. A new layer is made on top of the first one.

Sometimes many layers of human occupation can be seen. Sometimes the layers are disturbed by tree roots, burrows, erosion, or a new stream.

But careful digging down through the layers can tell us much about the order of what happened in that place. Which stone tool is earlier than the other? Does that fish hook belong with those charred eel bones? Is this pollen the same age?

All this information has to be carefully gathered and thought about because it is incomplete. Archaeologists and prehistorians who do this work must try to fill in the gaps – without letting their own ideas about how things happen get in the way.

An excavation is in progress in the Nyah Forest area of north-central Victoria during the late 1970s. The signs of human occupation long ago were fragments of animal bone, charcoal, stone tools and clay pellets.

ON THE SHORES OF LAKE MUNGO 2000 GENERATIONS AGO

Forty thousand years ago the Australian continent looked very different from the way it did when the first Europeans settled here.

The weather was cooler. It may have been wetter and more windy than it is now. The mountains of Tasmania and eastern Australia had more snow on them all year round. There were huge freshwater inland lakes and swollen rivers where there are none now.

In western Victoria volcanoes occasionally erupted – as they were still doing until about five thousand years ago.

Huge square-faced kangaroos, large flightless birds, diprotodon – wombat-like creatures the size of rhinoceros, marsupial lions and Tasmanian devils, as well as numerous smaller creatures, were in all parts of the continent as far as we know.

Forty thousand years ago people were living in Australia, too. That is about two thousand generations back.

The earliest signs of human life in Australia so far discovered come from Lake Mungo in western New South Wales. They are forty thousand years old but we know that people would have been here before that.

Forty thousand years ago and for a long time afterwards these lakes were full and brimming over into each other to form a chain of fresh water lakes covering hundreds of miles. Occasional great gum trees grew around the edges amid the lush grasses and rushes.

Aboriginal people often visited the shores of the lakes, and the glow of their small fires would have beamed across the water at night. They camped, and ate there – which we know from the blackened remains of their hearths and food scraps.

Lake Mungo people had a varied high protein diet. They hunted reptiles and marsupials and collected shellfish and emu eggs. They caught crayfish and large fish like Golden Perch and Murray Cod.

Pollen has not been found at Mungo so we don't know what plants were eaten. Grindstones over eighteen thousand years old have been found in other places so that we can guess that seeds were prepared at Mungo as they still are in places today, by pulping them and mixing them with a kind of flour for baking.

Stone was rare but hearths made of preheated mud lumps have been found, and so we know the people baked their food in earth ovens. These mud lumps are among the oldest examples of deliberately fired clay found – the first pottery known in the world.

But the most important information about these people comes from four sets of fragments of human bones.

The bones have been cremated and smashed into fragments and burned again – in some kind of ritual associated with burial of the dead. This is the earliest known cremation and proof that forty thousand years ago the Aboriginal people of Lake Mungo thought deeply about life and death.

Lake Mungo today is dry — one of a chain of lakes with a rim of sand and clay like a wall to the east.

An impression of life at Lake Mungo forty thousand years ago. The artist, Giovanni Caselli, was able to imagine details of the way people lived from the small amount of evidence found in the earth.

THE PAST IS PRECIOUS

Europeans believed God created life about six thousand years ago.

The first Europeans to settle in Australia did not know how old life on earth is. If they thought about it at all, they said it was about six thousand years since life began, a figure they worked out from the book of Genesis in the Old Testament.

Many Christians believed that all black people were descended from the sons of Ham whom Noah had cursed and cast out. Looked at this way, the Australian Aboriginal people were just a few generations younger than Europeans.

Europeans of 1788 could never have believed how old the earth really is, or that the Aboriginal people had been here for more than forty thousand years. And they could not have realized that the Aboriginal way of life had changed greatly over the years.

In the last one hundred years or so we have learnt how ancient life is. We also know more about the Aborigines' long occupation of the Australian continent.

It is only thirty years since ways of accurately dating evidence of human occupation have become possible. In 1955 two shell middens in Victoria were dated at about eight thousand years old – although by then many people guessed that Aboriginal peoples had been here much longer than that.

People are now aware that any evidence of the ancient Aboriginal past is precious. More sites are reported to archaeologists so that they can be excavated and studied. Once they would have been ploughed up or built over.

Hundreds of archaeological sites have now been excavated around Australia. Many more sites on the land's surface – caves, cliff overhangs, coastal middens – have been explored. Between them they are beginning to reveal to us a picture of the last forty thousand years or so.

Stone tools survive longer than any other kind of evidence of human life, so they are carefully studied. But they cannot tell us very much.

It is not easy to tell exactly what certain tools were used for. Although we can learn something from the scratches on their edges and the way they have been worn down, it is difficult to tell how handles were fastened to tools or how the tools were made.

We can learn a lot from observing Aboriginal people today and studying what was written when white settlement began. But over many thousands of years and with dramatic changes in the climate the way people used these tools must have changed.

The tools themselves have altered too. Again and again in excavations of sites older than five thousand years the same basic 'tool kit' turns up. There are the so-called horse hoof cores which were probably used for pounding and scraping. There are tools made from flakes from these cores. They have been deliberately chipped and worn along one edge and were probably used in many tasks, including making wooden tools.

Later additions to the tool kit found in Northern Australia were ground stone hatchet heads which would have been joined to a handle.

About six thousand years ago, after the sea stopped rising, the coastal plains in many parts of Australia

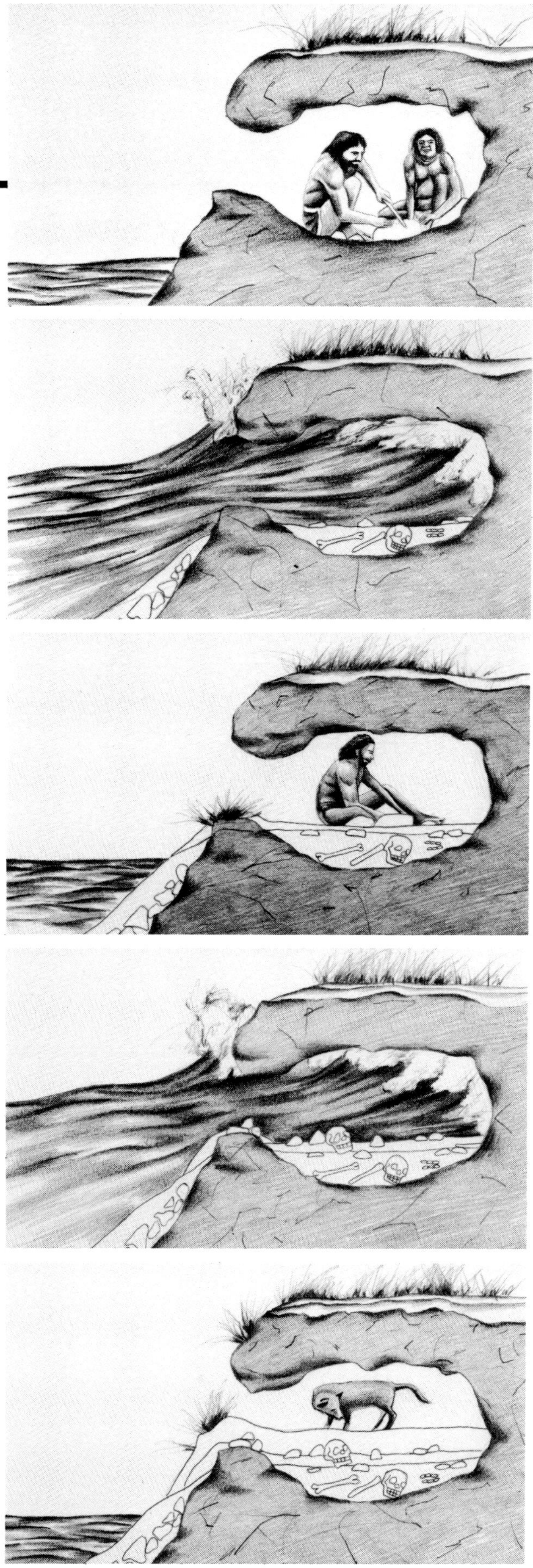

Much evidence of early man was lost as sea levels rose from time to time when the climate was warmer and wetter in between ice ages.

were intensively used by groups of Aboriginals who carried much more complex tool kits. Some of them included beautifully made small blades and more finely worked edge-ground tools of stone, bone and shell.

No one can say for certain why these sudden changes occurred. Are the finer tools a sign that another group of people arrived in Australia with different ways of doing things? A sign of major changes in the way people lived to handle changes in the environment? Or just a few good local ideas that caught on?

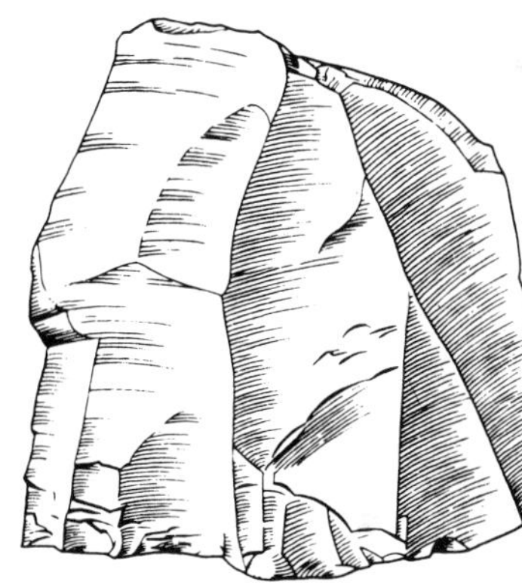

A horsehoof core may have been gripped in the hand and used for pounding.

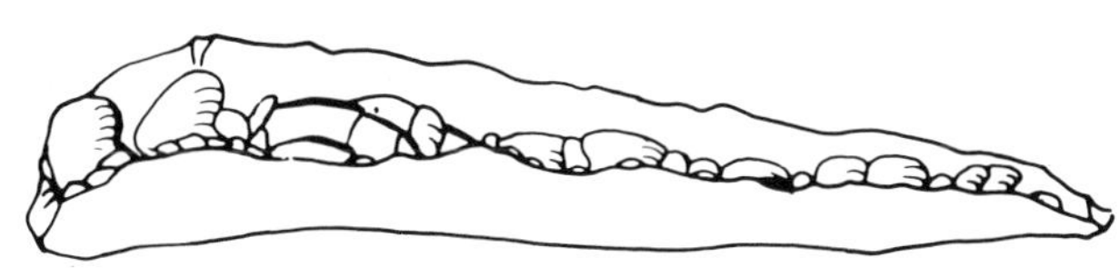

Small blades which have been sharpened along one side. Several of these may have been set in resin to act as barbs at the point of a spear.

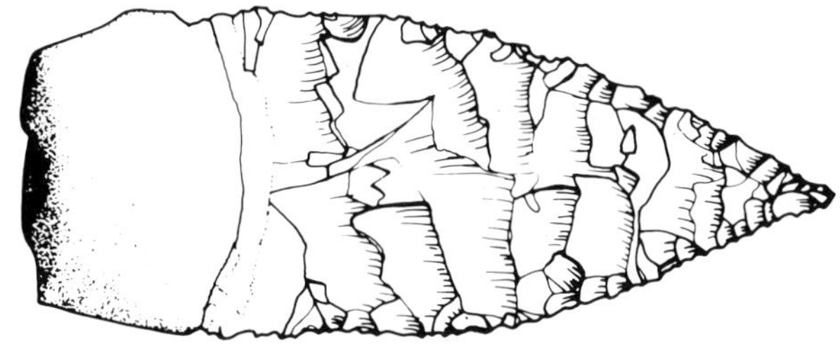

The pointed blades sharpened on both sides would almost certainly have been bound and set in resin on to a wooden handle.

THE MYSTERY OF THE MEGAFAUNA AND THE DINGO

We now know that the giant animals, Australia's 'megafauna', disappeared between about fifteen thousand years ago and thirty thousand years ago. The reasons why they vanished are mysterious.

Certainly the climate changed dramatically during those long ages and some creatures may have been unable to cope. Droughts may have limited their food supplies. Diseases may have spread at times.

People probably hunted the megafauna and could have played some part in their eventual extinction. Fires would have been much more frequent after humans arrived and would have changed the vegetation. There would have been fewer rainforests and more grasslands and forests of trees that are adapted to fire, as eucalypts are – all must have made it harder for giant Australian creatures to survive.

We may never know for sure why the megafauna vanished. Nor why some species rather than others could only survive in smaller forms – the wombat, the echidna, the goanna.

Dingoes are thought to have played a large part in determining which species of native creature survived to the present. Dingoes are efficient hunters of marsupials and would have been fierce competition for other hunting animals they encountered, such as thylacines.

Although the dingo was here when the first white settlers arrived, how and when it came to Australia is not yet known.

There are no signs of the dingo in Tasmania or New Guinea, which means that it must have arrived on the mainland after the landbridges had been flooded by the rising seas.

The earliest skeleton of a dingo to be discovered so

The megafauna might have looked something like this twenty thousand years ago. There were giant lizards and square-faced kangaroos. The largest marsupial that ever lived was three metres long and two metres high, and an early relative of the wombat was the size of a bull.

A skeleton of a dingo almost one thousand years old found at Mallacoota in Victoria.

far was found at Fromm's Landing in South Australia. It is about six thousand years old. This was about the time different kinds of tools, smaller blades and fine points, became part of people's tool kits throughout the country.

Some prehistorians think that the dingo arrived in Australia with a group of people from somewhere else, with different ways of working stone and bone. Certainly we know that, however it got here, the dingo adapted readily to the country and spread quickly through it.

Aborigines tamed dingoes and used them for hunting. European settlers remarked on their fondness for them and described how, when a dingo died, some tribes paid great attention to its burial.

A hole would be dug, lined with bark or dry grass, and the dog settled in the grave as if it were asleep. More coverings were put on top before the grave was filled in. Sometimes fires were lit by the grave as if to comfort the spirit of the dingo.

WHO OWNS THE PAST?

In November 1982 at Robinvale in north western Victoria, three Aboriginal boys were looking for discarded fishhooks and sinkers on the banks of the Murray River. The banks were crumbling in places and the boys came to a place where human bones were being eroded out.

Only ten years ago, white experts would have taken over and made all the decisions about what was to happen next.

This time – and in other recent discoveries of Aboriginal sites – the Aboriginal community in the Robinvale area took charge. They decided that they wanted to know more about what the boys had found, so an archaeologist, Sandra Bowdler, was called in to work with them.

What was discovered was not a burial of two or three skeletons but skeleton after skeleton crammed in, often on top of a previous burial. Although only a few metres of the site were excavated, the bones of ten people, many of them young, were uncovered and examined. The whole site is thought to be a large burial ground used over many years and containing more than two hundred skeletons.

After Sandra Bowdler had completed the first part of the excavation, and it was realized what was there, the Aboriginal people became concerned about what was happening. The rest of the Robinvale Aboriginal community was consulted and they decided that the excavation should not proceed any further, at least for some time.

Scientifically the site is of great importance. There appear to have been many types of burial over a period of one to three thousand years. The bodies have been laid out in different ways.

There are skulls of different thickenesses which raises the question: were several kinds of people buried there, or did the changes in the local diet at some time have an effect on the structure of their bones?

From the number of bones present there would be ways of working out approximately how many people had once lived along the banks of the Murray. And we could have learnt something of how they lived.

The Robinvale burial ground from across the Murray.

The river bank has eroded and human bones can be seen.

These are all important questions, but to Aborigines and some white people, not as important as taking into account Aboriginal concerns.

Some people were deeply disturbed that the bones would lose their meaning, their spirits would be interfered with by the bones being taken out of their sacred earth, measured and tested and kept in plastic bags in laboratories somewhere. They believed that more would be lost than would have been gained if the excavation had proceeded.

Other Aboriginal people argue that the only way they and their children can learn about their ancient past, now that so many changes have come about since the arrival of white people, is to allow the evidence to be studied scientifically.

There is, as yet, no answer to this dilemma. Meanwhile the Robinvale excavation has been carefully covered over and will stay like a sealed time capsule until the time is right to open it again.

Archaeologists and the Robinvale Aboriginal community discuss their work over a drink.

MUNGO WOMAN

In July 1968 a geologist walking on the shores of Lake Mungo in western New South Wales found a cluster of bones. They turned out to be those of a young woman who had been buried there about twenty-five thousand years ago.

Lake Mungo is now dry. Twenty-five thousand years ago it was full of water. Aboriginal people caught huge golden perch and gathered mussels along its shores. They also hunted giant emus, thylacines and other animals which have long since become extinct.

'Mungo 1', as the bones have been called had been small and slender. She was between twenty and twenty-four years old when she died.

After her death her body had been cremated. Then her bones were broken into small pieces, burnt again and finally buried in a shallow grave in the sand.

About a third of her bones and three of her teeth had survived. From them we have learnt a little about the people with whom she lived. It is plain from the way she had been buried that death had a deep meaning for them. This evidence of religious rituals is among the earliest discovered in the world.

The bones of the woman at Lake Mungo also proved that Aboriginal people had been living in Australia a lot longer than the vast majority of people thought. Since this discovery another set of bones at least thirty thousand years old have been discovered at Lake Mungo.

These young Aboriginal women were painted by an Englishman, George French Angas, in 1845 in South Australia.

ABORIGINAL AUSTRALIA

1432 Aborigines in the north may have been visited by Ch'eng Ho and his great fleet from China.

1450 Printing press invented in Europe.

1492 Colombus reaches America.

1498 Vasco da Gama discovers sea route from Europe to India.

1558-1603 Queen Elizabeth I on English throne. Portuguese ships in Australian waters.

1606 Aborigines may have sighted Dutchman, William Jansz, as he sails past the northern coast of Australia.

1642 Aborigines in southern Australia meet Dutch explorer, Abel Tasman.

1688 Aborigines on north-west coast of Australia encounter Englishman, William Dampier.

1700 Aborigines first meet Macassans who begin visiting north coast of Australia.

1718 Britain begins sending slaves to American colonies.

1770 Aborigines meet James Cook in Botany Bay and other places along east coast of Australia.

1775 James Watt perfects the steam engine in England.

1776 American War of Independence begins.

A young Balmbi woman prepares water lily 'cakes' in Arnhem Land, Northern Territory.

MOVING AMONG SPIRITS

The Aboriginal people of Australia are usually described as hunter-gatherers, which means that they lived from the land by hunting animals and birds, by catching fish and gathering plant foods, shellfish and eggs.

To Europeans the Aborigines seemed to live very simply. They had few possessions, were nomadic and, it seemed, had little effect on the countryside. This was only half true.

Aboriginal people hunted and gathered only what they needed from day to day. They did not hoard food. Their weapons were efficient, but they did not kill more than they needed to eat.

There was a good deal of fighting between Aboriginal tribes. Aboriginal people believed that no death was accidental. They believed that if a person died it was because another tribe had worked some magic to bring about the death. So the death had to be avenged.

This helped to control the numbers in each tribe. It was very important that the number of people in an Aboriginal band was not too great for the food supply available.

Hunting the nesting magpie-geese with specially designed three-pronged spears in Arafura swamp in Arnhem Land, Northern Territory.

To help maintain this balance Aboriginal people, like all hunter-gatherers, practised several forms of birth control. To ensure the survival of older children and the group in general, newborn babies were sometimes killed.

When a member of the tribe died, the kinsfolk entered into a long period of mourning. Close relatives expressed their grief by gashing their heads and bodies with stones and wailing and crying for days.

As the Aboriginal people moved through their lands they moved among spirits. They did not build churches to their gods or shrines to their dead. The land itself was sacred.

They were not simply rocks and hills and waterholes they saw. These were sacred places often highly decorated and well cared for – and only known to those who had been taught their special meaning. The rocks were their ancestors turned into stone in the Dreaming – the time when everything was created, including animals and men and women.

While the Aborigines were semi-nomadic their lands had boundaries which were known to all. The size of the tribal lands depended on how rich in food each area was. In areas where food was scarce the boundaries were wide and the people travelled almost constantly. In places where the food was abundant all year only short seasonal journeys were necessary.

To keep up the supply of food the tribes set fire to the bush and grasslands at certain times of the year. Fire created new growth for the animals to feed on.

Over thousands of years this firing must have had dramatic effects on the vegetation of Australia. It was a way of controlling the land. In fact they were 'firestick farmers'.

There were about six hundred tribes or clans in Australia, each with its own language or dialect, its own ceremonial life, its own lands and way of living. Over two hundred quite distinct languages were spoken, although there were some key words that were known among tribes all around the continent.

Hunters in the Western Desert near Mt Fanny in Western Australia.

For each clan there were extremely complicated marriage rules which every member of the clan had to follow.

All Aboriginal people also had to learn about their ancestry. Every person was born into a totem. A totem was some object or animal or bird which was descended from the same spirit as the person. The totem was like a brother or sister. People with the same totem could not marry. In some places, there were strict laws about when and if the totem could be eaten.

Those Europeans who thought that Aboriginal society was simple were wrong. It was very complex, as it still is.

THE PEOPLE OF THE RIVERBANKS

The riverbanks and plains of south-eastern Australia are comfortable places to live – rich in food and natural resources with a climate that is usually gentle.

The many tribes that inhabited these areas did not need to cover long distances in search of food. They often built permanent dwellings from the stone that was abundant in places, inhabiting them for months at a time and returning to them each year.

The rivers supplied fish and crayfish and near the sea shellfish was abundant. There were wallabies, kangaroos, koalas, bandicoots, echidna, possums, emus, snakes, waterfowl, swans, scrub turkeys and an endless supply of eggs, insects and wild honey, vegetables and fruits. The seeds of wild barley grass were ground, made into cakes and baked.

Fishing was planned to take advantage of the seasonal movements of fish up and down the rivers. Streams were sometimes diverted into stone-lined canals across which nets were stretched. Fishing weirs made of small sticks laced with leaves and branches were constructed at favourable points in rivers and lagoons. Long eel pots were woven from twigs and grasses and carried from place to place.

Along the river the people caught ducks and other waterbirds by laying nets and frightening the resting birds so that they would take off and fly into them.

Where the weather was very wet in autumn and winter the people moved from the plains to the river banks and coastal strip. Stone huts with bark roofs were constructed in some areas. In hot weather people often slept in shallow holes dug into the ground and covered with a roof of leaves and branches.

Large mounds of earth can be seen in clusters in many places, particularly in areas where water lay around after rain. It is thought that huts were constructed on these mounds, some large enough to house a number of people.

The people were frequently in contact with other

tribal groups. Goods appear to have been exchanged over a wide area.

For some ceremonies several hundred people gathered for two or three weeks. This was a region that could support many people. Fish weirs and eel traps were probably constructed to feed the people at these gatherings.

A few actual objects or domestic utensils have survived. However descriptions from early settlers tell of many more, including elaborately decorated wooden implements, baskets, bark paintings and possum skin cloaks sewn from many skins and decorated with complex diamond and zigzag patterns.

Body painting was common too – in ochre and grease with adornments made from feathers and plants.

Mats, baskets, nets, twine, girdles and necklaces traditionally made by the Ngarrindjeri people of the Lower Murray River.

THE PEOPLE OF THE DESERTS

Using her digging stick and scooping the earth out in a wooden bowl, a Pitjantjatjara woman digs down to the underground cavern where honey ants nest.

The Pitjantjatjara people have lived for thousands of years in the Western Desert of Australia.

A plateau about three hundred metres high covering an area larger than France and Italy put together, the land is crossed by sand dunes, the rocks and soil are bright red, spinifex and desert grasses grow everywhere and gum trees flourish along the gullies.

A prominent feature of the Western Desert is Gumbubundil or Lake Disappointment – an enormous salt lake which is dry most of the time. Aboriginal people never visit the lake fearing it is the home of cannibal beings.

The Desert people are made up of hundreds of different small groups who speak a variety of dialects but can understand each other. Marriage patterns, family ties and religious ceremonies are very similar throughout the desert.

There are well over fifty edible plants in the Western Desert as well as emus, kangaroos, snakes, goannas, lizards, grubs and insects. The bush tomato is an important food. It is dried, skewered on sticks and soaked before eating. Yams dug from about 30-40 cms underground, are another valuable source of food.

This Pitjantjatjara woman at a waterhole will carry on her head the water she has scooped into a wooden bowl. Behind her are a grinding stone and her digging stick.

The availability of water dominates the way life is lived in the Western Desert. The Pitjantjatjara are careful not to over-use the main sources and take steps to preserve springs and wells by covering them from the sun. Small bands of people move from one source of water to another and regroup when their supplies diminish. They also congregate for ceremonies and exchange but only when the area has sufficient water to support a large gathering.

The tools carried by the Pitjantjatjara are lightweight and multi-purpose. The digging stick carried by the women is essential for finding yams and roots and grubs. Women also carry large wooden dishes and a small smooth stone which is used with large grinding stones for crushing seeds. The grinding stones and other heavy implements are left at campsites.

The men carry spears, a spear thrower, a club and a boomerang. In the Western Desert the boomerang is not used for hunting, but for fighting and as a musical instrument. Small knives made of sharpened stone are carried. These are not usually attached to wooden handles. A wooden spindle is important for making twine from bark, human hair and plant fibres. Twine is twisted into headbands and belts for carrying food.

Pitjantjatjara children in the Musgrave Ranges of the Western Desert.

Very simple shelters are all that are required – for windbreaks and shade in temperatures that can range from over 40° in summer to −4° at night in winter. A low fire is kept burning all night next to the sleepers.

The Pitjantjatjara occasionally fire their land over a small area as they move through it. This flushes out small animals and encourages the rapid growth of grasses and bush tomatoes.

The Western Desert people have been effected by European settlement like Aborigines everywhere else. Metal, glass and cloth have been adopted by the people whenever they have been available. Explorers visited the area early on and information spread very quickly about white settlement in coastal areas.

Apart from these occasional explorers, such as Ernest Giles who twice made the journey from Alice Springs to the west coast in the 1870s, the Aboriginal people of the desert had little contact with white Australia.

Missionaries came later but it was not until the 1950s and 1960s when the British began testing rockets and atomic bombs in the desert that the Aborigines' traditional way of life virtually came to an end.

Today there are no Aborigines who have not been affected by the white invasion of their lands.

THE PEOPLE OF THE FAR SOUTH

Tasmania was still joined on to the rest of Australia when Aborigines first reached the far south of the continent. It is not yet known how long ago they first inhabited the south but it was more than twenty thousand years ago.

When the seas rose and Bass Strait was formed about ten thousand years ago, the Tasmanian Aboriginal people were isolated from the gradual changes that were happening to Aboriginals on the mainland. They developed a way of life suited to the Tasmanian countryside and the size of their population.

There were about three thousand people in Tasmania before European settlers arrived. They were divided into nine tribes spread throughout the island. Each tribe was divided into a group of bands with its own language or dialect, its own marriage laws and rituals and its own lands.

The south-west coast of Tasmania is wild and very cold. Four bands of the two to three hundred

Aborigines of Tasmania, painted some time before 1860.

Fishing off the south coast, as seen by an artist on the Baudin expedition.

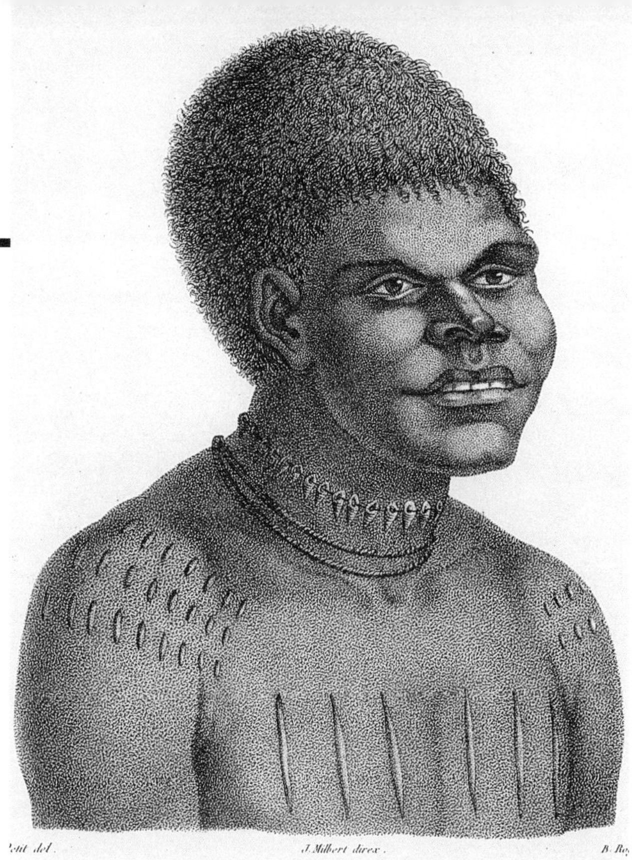

This man, his hair powdered with red ochre, was Bara Ouru. He was among the Tasmanian Aborigines who met two French ships commanded by the French explorer Nicolas Baudin when they landed at Oyster Bay in 1802. Bara Ouru was about twenty-four years old.

South-West people occupied the long narrow heavily forested coastal strip for about 450 kms. Hardly anyone lives there now.

The people moved between local 'villages' of beehive shaped huts close to fresh water and the best food-collecting areas. Seals and seabirds were plentiful and rolled-bark canoe-rafts were used to visit the islands off the coast.

Only a few tools seem to have been necessary in this region. The South-West people had no tools with handles. No boomerangs, spearthrowers, nets or garments that needed sewing have been found. Instead they made one-piece tools, single-skin cloaks, kelp buckets and shell necklaces.

As in other parts of the island, men carried fire and hunted animals with implements made of bone, stone and wood. Their hair was twisted into ringlets, greased and coloured with red ochre. Loops of twisted and ochred sinews ornamented their bodies.

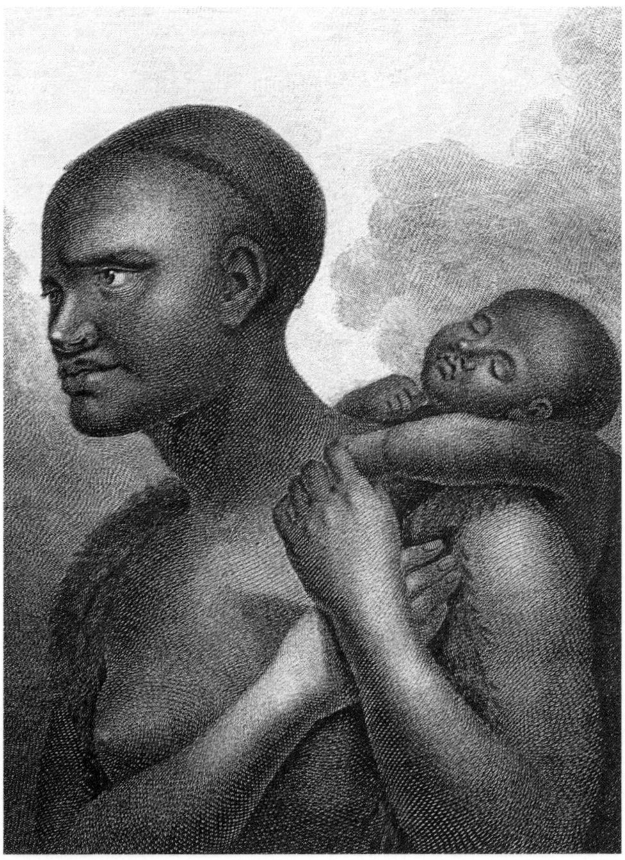

A woman of Van Diemen's Land.

The women carried the children and their few household effects – water containers, baskets, digging sticks and sometimes stone tools and shells. They searched for roots and small animals and plants, and dived to great depths in the icy water for shellfish. They climbed trees to catch possums and made necklaces from shells and baskets from grass and reeds. They cropped their hair short and arranged it carefully according to the customs of the band they belonged to.

Both men and women cut their bodies in patterns of lines and circles and rubbed ochre and grease into them so that high weals were raised on the skin. This probably indicated which band they belonged to.

Tasmanian Aborigines encountered different groups of Europeans for over two hundred years before the invasion of their lands by white people began. Abel Tasman looking for new routes and markets for the Dutch East India Company landed on the island in 1642 and named it Van Diemen's Land.

From then until 1801 there was a succession of explorers, sealers and whalers who visited, recorded, exchanged goods with the Aboriginal people. Some treated them with curiosity, some with respect, but most forced them to work, abused or murdered them.

CAPTAIN COOK DID NOT DISCOVER AUSTRALIA

Explorer George Gray was startled to find this huge European head carved in sandstone in the far north-west of Australia where no Europeans were believed to have been before him.

Captain Cook did not discover Australia. We cannot be sure who did. There is a possibility that a mighty fleet of ships commanded by the Chinese eunuch, Ch'eng Ho, landed on northern Australian shores in 1432.

Arab traders searching for gold and spices in the East Indies might have landed in Australia in the fifteenth and sixteenth centuries. But, if they did, no trace of them has been found.

On the other hand we can be fairly sure that Portuguese vessels reached Australia early in the sixteenth century. There have been a number of signs of their presence. Two Portuguese cannons were found on the coast of Western Australia. In the nineteenth century the wreck of a very old and unusual ship was seen by several people in sandhills near the town of Warrnambool in Victoria. Known as the Mahogany Ship, it is now thought to be a Portuguese caravel which has been buried.

In British and European libraries there are maps drawn by Portuguese seamen in the sixteenth century which seem to give an outline of the coast of Australia.

So it seems quite likely that Portuguese sailors explored much of the Australian coast in their frail and beautiful ships long before the Dutch and the English.

The Dutch sailed along the north and west coast early in the seventeenth century. William Jansz saw the west side of Cape York peninsula in 1606. He was followed by Palsaert, Hartog and others. In 1642 Abel Tasman sailed along the south coast of Australia, including Tasmania.

With most of these European voyages the Australian Aborigines must have seen the ships' sails. But only rarely did they see the people on them.

The animal on the bottom right of this sixteenth century Portuguese page looks very like a kangaroo.

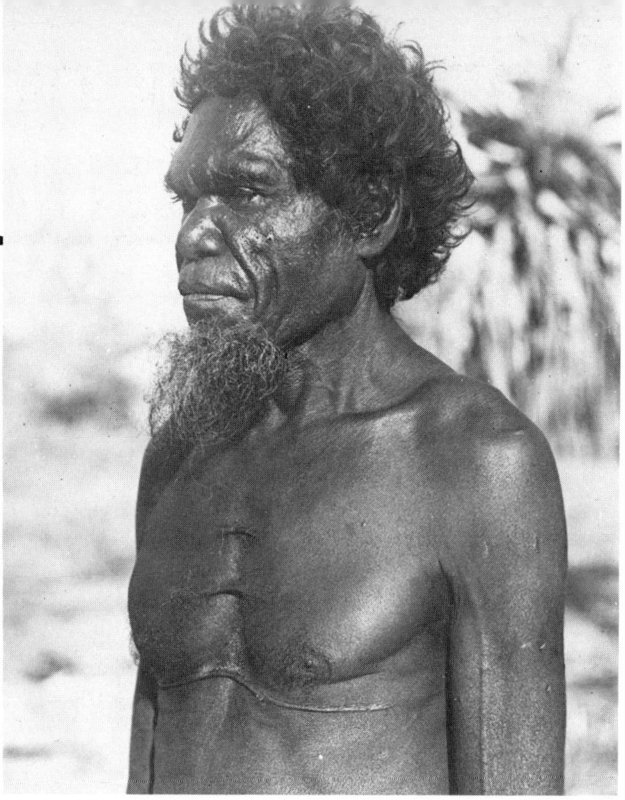

Some Aborigines in northern Australia adopted Macassan-style beards like this man from Arnhem Land.

It was different with the Macassans. They came from Sulawesi (the Celebes in those days) which is part of Indonesia. Around 1700 the Macassans began coming to northern Australia to collect trepang – also known as sea slug, sea cucumber and bêche-de-mer.

Trepang was prized by the Chinese who used it to make soup. Eating trepang soup made them better lovers they thought. The Macassans took the trepang from northern Australian shores and sold it in the markets of Canton.

The Macassans came to Australia in small boats called praus which were made of wood and had crude fibrous sails. They came in December with the monsoon which blows from the north west. There were up to sixty praus in a fleet and about fifteen hundred men. The Macassans worked right through the monsoon, catching the trepang from dugout canoes.

An Aboriginal painting of a Macassan prau.

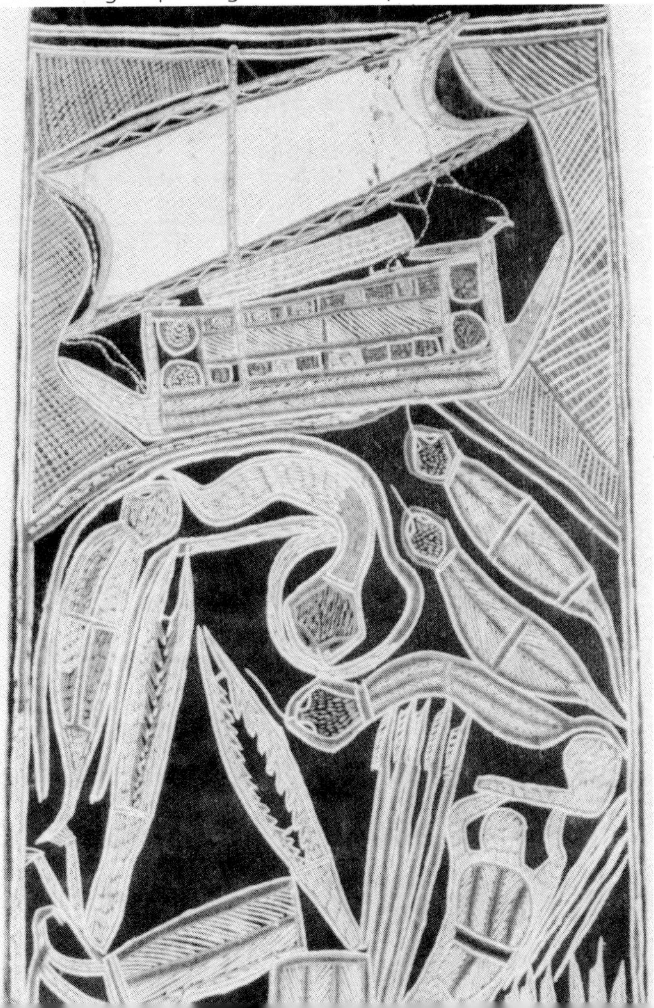

The trepang had to be gutted, boiled and smoked. So the Macassans had to go ashore on the coasts of Arnhem Land, Cape York and the Kimberleys. They set up camps. In May they returned home, their praus blown by trade winds from the south east. The Macassans and the Aborigines got to know each other. The Macassans wanted to be friendly. They wanted to be welcomed back each year.

Sometimes, however, the Aborigines attacked the Macassans. The people of Melville Island were particularly savage towards them. They were very suspicious of intruders, probably because many years before Portuguese ships had come to the island and taken people away as slaves.

However most of the time the Macassans and the Aborigines were friendly. Aborigines sometimes worked on the praus, even sailing to Sulawesi with the cargoes of trepang.

The Aborigines learnt new skills from the Macassans. They copied the Macassans' dug out canoes. From their metal and glass they made axe heads and spear tips. They smoked Macassan pipes and wore Macassan style beards – the Macassans had copied the beards from the Dutch who ran their country. The Aborigines also learnt the Macassan language.

On the rocks the Aborigines drew pictures of the trepangers and they sang and danced about the coming and going of the praus.

ABORIGINAL AUSTRALIA THROUGH ENGLISH EYES

Most of the Europeans who passed close by Australia in the seventeenth and eighteenth centuries were in search of great riches. They were hard and brave men, but like all treasure hunters their imaginations sometimes got the better of them.

These sailors never knew what they were going to find when they stepped ashore in unknown lands. They imagined finding weird people, giants and dwarfs, ferocious cannibals and noble people living in perfect peace. They imagined cities of gold. They even imagined finding the Garden of Eden.

Naturally they were disappointed when they found the west coast of Australia. They were not at all impressed by the desert or the desert people.

William Dampier was an English buccaneer – a pirate. In 1688 he came ashore on the coast near the Kimberley Ranges and stayed there for three months. We don't know what the Kimberley Aborigines thought of Dampier and his men, but we do know what Dampier thought of them. He said they were 'the miserablest people in the world'.

It seemed to many Europeans that Aborigines did not use the land as it should be used, and that they therefore were not to be taken seriously as owners.

To Dampier's eyes the Aboriginal people were ugly. They were little different from brutes, he said. He was horrified by the flies that crawled on them.

As far as Dampier could see, the Aborigines lived on nothing more than very small fish they caught in traps each time the tide went out. He wrote

> . . . the Earth affords them no Food at all. There is neither Herb, Root, Pulse, not any sort of Grain, for them to eat, that we saw: nor any sort of Bird, or Beast that they can catch, having no instruments to do so.

Dampier saw the Aborigines with English eyes which means that he could not see them properly.

For a start he thought that they had no God. He did not know about the Dreaming or the rocks and plants and animals that were sacred to them.

Nor could he see that the Kimberley Aborigines lived on more than fish. Englishmen like Dampier thought that because hunting and gathering was the oldest way of living it must be the least effective. They thought that because the Aborigines lived in the desert they must be underfed.

But unless there was a severe drought in 1688 the Aboriginal people there would have been gathering grass seeds, yams, lizards and small marsupials as well as fish.

They were probably better fed than most English people at the time and, despite the flies, just as healthy.

Europeans thought that because they did not plough the soil, plant crops and store food, the Aboriginal people did not have a right to the land. This was an idea drawn from the Old Testament. Not that it mattered much – Europeans always found an excuse to overrun any native society living on land they wanted.

Europeans could not see that in fact the Aborigines did farm the land. They farmed it with fire. Nor could they see that the Aborigines did not need large ships and guns to catch fish and live in the desert.

Europeans of Dampier's day found it just about impossible to see anything good about Aboriginal society.

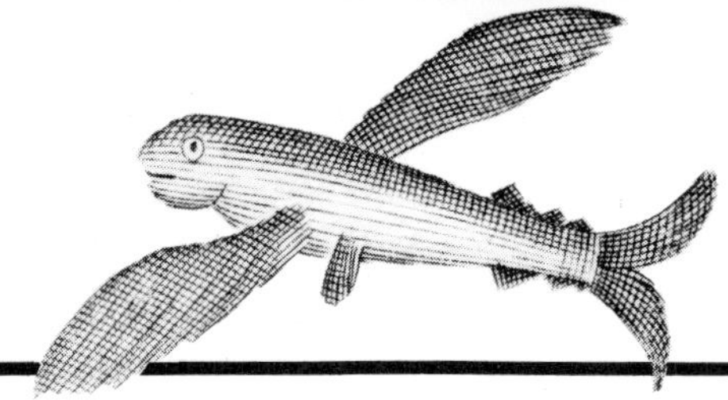

This is what a flying fish looked like to William Dampier.

Sixty years later in the age of Captain James Cook many Europeans thought differently. Cook was one of the greatest explorers and seamen in history. In three separate voyages he explored the Pacific Ocean more thoroughly than any man before him.

Cook wanted to find the Great South Land – Australia. In 1770 he did, after finding New Zealand first. He spent some time in Botany Bay, then sailed north charting the east coast of Australia.

Sometimes when he went ashore the Aboriginal people threw stones at his boats. Sometimes they ignored him altogether. Cook studied their behaviour, as he had the Pacific islanders. They were coastal tribes he saw and, because it was a good season, no doubt they were looking healthy and well fed.

Cook disagreed with William Dampier and other seventeenth century Europeans who had visited Australia. The Australian Aborigines, he said, 'may appear to some to be the most wretched people upon Earth, but in reality they are far happier than we Europeans'. To Cook hunting and gathering provided Australian Aborigines with a life of perfect tranquility.

This was what a lot of Cook's readers wanted to hear. In Europe many people had begun to hate their own society. They wanted to think that somewhere a better way of living existed.

Perhaps Aboriginal society was better. But thinking this did not help Europeans to understand Aboriginal society. What is more, thinking that the Australian Aborigines were happier than themselves did not stop Europeans invading their land and destroying their way of life.

When Cook sailed out of Australian waters in 1770 the invasion was just eighteen years away.

In 1779, a year after the first fleet arrived in Botany Bay, Captain James Cook was killed in Hawaii. Cook had discovered Botany Bay in 1770.

SYDNEY COVE, 1788

Aborigines fishing, cooking and eating in their canoes in Sydney Cove — as Phillip Gidley King of the first fleet saw them.

To the Aboriginal tribes who lived there and knew it in every detail, and to white Australians now, the area where Sydney now stands would have been near perfection in 1788.

The water in the huge harbour and its hundred inlets was blue and crystal clear. Eucalyptus forests ran down to the harbour's edge. The undergrowth, in spring, was brilliant with wildflowers. The landscape buzzed with the sound of millions of insects.

The harbour and the ocean ran deeper inland than it now does. Waves broke on the Manly esplanade, and further up the coast there were sandhills and lagoons instead of suburbs.

Sydney cove extended well up Pitt Street. A small freshwater creek ran down from Hyde Park which was then a swamp inhabited by wildfowl and eels. Bennelong Point on which the Opera House stands was an island.

Unlike those in Europe the trees around Sydney Cove did not drop their leaves in winter. The leaves did not change colour except with the new growth of spring. The large trees were almost all eucalypts. The smaller ones were acacias – wattles and blackwoods. Besides these there was a vast variety of small flowering plants, and weird ones like the ancient grasstrees or 'blackboys' with their single large stems protruding like spears.

Because they had to cope with Australia's droughts even in the poorest soil the trees grew to heights which Europeans found surprising.

It seemed to many of the first Europeans, who never

Kangaroos were a great source of wonder to Europeans seeing them for the first time. But no kangaroo ever fed its joey gum leaves.

went far from the shore, that the Australian bush was all the same. The 'general impression is dismal', said one. 'Unpicturesque', a 'dreary monotony of form and colour', a 'deformity', said others.

European eyes could not make out the detail or the differences in the landscape. They could not get used to the colours. There was never enough shade. Europeans wanted to see an English park.

To see the differences in the landscape and appreciate its beauty Europeans needed to go deeper into the bush and live there. For many Europeans the land also had to be conquered, turned into farmland and planted out with English trees and shrubs, before it could be loved. Unlike the Aborigines they could not bear to live on the surface of the land; they felt a need to sink ploughs into it.

Those eucalyptus trees were more of a curse to Europeans than things of beauty. One European wrote that in the bush there was not 'a single scene' from which a painter could make a 'landscape, without greatly disguising the character of the trees'. He meant that they should be painted to look like European trees.

An undisturbed landscape in New South Wales drawn about thirty years after the arrival of the first fleet.

'IT'S LIKE A WHITE MAN'

An Aboriginal painting of a droving scene in a sandstone rock shelter near Ingaladdi water hole, Northern Territory.

'They had never seen a white man in their lives – this is in the early time. There was one white man who must've got lost and he followed the Murray River down and there was a big camp and a few dark ladies went out to pick the wild-bean – they go out daily to get this wild food every day. When they went out and they looked up the river and they saw somebody moving and they got up and they look again and someone was moving alright and they take it for – they call it the witchcraft man – the witchcraft man must be moving about. They left all their bean trees and they ran home to tell all the people back home in the camp – 'We saw something strange up there – It's like a white man! – a white man!'

'Blackfellow by and by all gone, plenty shoot 'em, whitefellow – longtime plenty, plenty.'

Aboriginal people have always passed their history on from generation to generation in stories. These tell of encounters with white people.

Men of the first fleet pay a visit to some people of Botany Bay.

1788-1809

1788 Aborigines of Port Jackson and Botany Bay meet the first fleet.

1789 French Revolution begins.
First steam-driven cotton factory in England.

1790 Second fleet arrives in Sydney.

1791 Whaling from Sydney commences.
George Vancouver discovers King George III's Sound, Western Australia.

1792 Governor Phillip returns to England.

1793 Reign of Terror in Paris: execution of French aristocrats.

1795 John Hunter, Governor of New South Wales.

1796 First vaccination against smallpox in England.

1797 Spanish merino sheep imported to New South Wales.

1798-9 Bass and Flinders prove existence of Bass Strait.

1800 Phillip Gidley King, Governor of New South Wales.
Napoleon conquers Italy.

1804 Settlement commenced in Van Diemen's Land.
David Collins, Governor.
Convicts rebel at Castle Hill.

1806 William Bligh, Governor of New South Wales.

1807 Bligh bans trade in rum.

1808 Governor Bligh overthrown.

1809 Lachlan Macquarie, Governor of New South Wales.

Convicts of New South Wales in the days before they were made to dress in a uniform which distinguished them from free people.

THE OTHER SIDE OF THE WORLD

No one knows for certain why the British government decided to make a settlement in Australia. There could have been several reasons.

In 1787, when the first fleet of convicts and soldiers left Portsmouth Harbour for Botany Bay on the other side of the world, the jails of Britain were full.

By the eighteenth century the people who had once lived and worked on the land were being steadily driven from it. The land and the wealth were in the hands of a few people.

In the cities the poor lived in squalor, without work or money, decent food, clothing or housing.

Cities like London and Manchester in England, Dublin in Ireland and Glasgow in Scotland were horribly overcrowded, and for a great many people there was no work to be found. This is Whitechapel in London.

A view of London backyards from a new railway line in the mid 19th century. Britain was then the richest country in the world, but these people were among the poorest.

In these degraded conditions it was not surprising that many people lived by crime.

In the rural areas of Britain many people also turned to crime – either to survive or to protest at the way landowners treated them. They poached animals from the estates and sometimes destroyed the crops and machinery of the owners.

Britain in those days included all of Ireland as well as Scotland and Wales. The Irish resented the English control over their land. They tried to drive them out by destroying the property of English landowners.

In Britain property was sacred. The Bible said 'Thou shalt not steal'. The people who owned the property agreed. The government, which was made up of people who owned property, passed laws to try and protect it. In 1778 there were about two hundred 'crimes' which carried the death sentence.

But rather than hang someone for crimes like stealing two shillings, or cutting the strings on sheaves of hay, the people who broke the law were generally

Public hangings were common in Britain, even though judges preferred to send most criminals to Australia. Sometimes people were trampled to death by the crowds who clamoured to see the execution.

sentenced to transportation instead.

Since the days of Queen Elizabeth I, the British had been getting rid of troublemakers by banishing them abroad or putting them to work rowing the galley ships. The British liked to make convicts work for them while punishing them at the same time.

In 1718 the British government decided to send convicts to their colonies in America. Colonies are lands which Britain and other European countries, such as Spain, France and Portugal, had taken over and used to grow products they wanted.

Britain needed men and women to do the work. They used slaves brought from Africa – and convicts. Between 1718 and 1770 about 30,000 convicts were transported to the British colonies in America.

In 1776 the Americans fought a war with the British and won their freedom to govern themselves. Britain no longer had a place to send convicts. Until a place could be found to send them they were confined in the hulks of old ships on the River Thames.

Some convicts were shipped out to places like Central Africa, but the climate there was so terrible most of them died. In 1786 the government decided to send convicts to the east coast of Australia, to Botany Bay – the place Captain Cook had visited in 1770.

This seems an expensive solution to the problem. Running a gaol nearly twenty thousand kilometres away would cost the government a lot of money.

The British, however, might have seen other advantages in starting a settlement at Botany Bay.

Possibly they planned to grow flax to make sailcloth for ships, and to harvest the tall pine trees on nearby Norfolk Island to make masts and spars.

It might also be that the British wanted a new base for their trade with China. A settlement at Botany Bay would also be useful in case of war with the Dutch or the French who had interests in the region.

For all or any one of these reasons the British government in 1787 sent 736 convicts to Botany Bay. Over the next seventy years 160,000 convicts would be sent on that long voyage to an unknown land.

ALL OF EASTERN AUSTRALIA BECOMES A BRITISH POSSESSION

There was nothing Arthur Phillip did not know about the sea. He had spent most of his life in the British navy. He had served in a number of wars. But he had never founded a colony of convicts in an unknown land on the other side of the world.

There were more than a thousand people on board the eleven ships which left England on 13 May 1787. Seven hundred and thirty-six of them were convicts – 548 men and 188 women. The rest were members of the Royal Marines who were sent out to protect the colony from attack. A number of officials were also sent to help the Governor. Some of the officials and even a few of the convicts brought their wives with them. There were thirty-seven children.

On board the convicts were crammed into spaces between the decks just 137 cm high. They slept in double bunks 90 cm wide – just 45 cm for each convict. Lying down was almost as uncomfortable as standing up.

The ships were very slow. For months the convicts breathed the foul air of their quarters and felt the great swell of the sea. When the gales blew they must have all feared for their lives. Few of them had been to sea before. Fewer still had the faintest idea where Botany Bay was.

One convict of the first fleet escaped in a small boat when the ships reached Teneriffe in the Canary Islands. He was soon recaptured. Captain Phillip and his officials drank tea and ate ice cream at Teneriffe with the Spanish governor of the islands.

Near the equator ships entered the doldrums. Often they lay for days without a breath of wind to move them.

Between the decks the convicts lay stifling. 'The sufferings of the imprisoned wretches in the steaming and crowded hold were piteous to see,' said a man who travelled on a convict ship in 1797.

Some ships were worse than others but on every convict ship some convicts died as a result of disease and ill-treatment.

Further south the first fleet stopped at Rio de Janiero where they were welcomed by the Portuguese Viceroy and took on supplies of meat, vegetables, rice and rum.

It was 18 January 1788, eight months after leaving England, when the first fleet finally arrived in Botany Bay.

Below decks on a convict ship.

The beginning of a journey to the other side of the world: convicts being rowed out to transport ships bound for Sydney Cove.

About forty Aboriginal people gathered on the south shore making signs and shouting at the newcomers.

At three o'clock in the afternoon Phillip landed on the north shore. He made friends with the Aborigines there by offering them beads and mirrors. Another member of the party gave them wine.

But Botany Bay was a disappointment. Cook had reported seeing 'green meadows'. The first fleet saw only arid land and swamps. Phillip decided to explore the coast to the north.

Shortly before they left Botany Bay the British were startled by the arrival of two French ships. The French, under the command of Count de la Perouse, had been on a long voyage of discovery in the Pacific. The British made them welcome, but after they sailed away in March they were never seen again. They were wrecked in the New Hebrides.

North of Botany Bay Phillip entered Port Jackson. It was the 'finest harbour in the world' he said. When fresh water was found at Sydney Cove some of the officers and marines went ashore and raised the the Union Jack. They also fired off their guns and drank some porter. It was 26 January. This was to be the site of the new settlement.

The Aborigines had given the white men water at Botany Bay and carefully followed their voyage around to Port Jackson. The tribe at Sydney Cove now watched the ships disgorge their strange inhabitants.

The male convicts came ashore first. On 3 February a sermon was preached to them by the Reverend Johnson. No women were present at either the first raising of the flag or the sermon. They were not brought ashore until 6 February, eleven days after the first fleet's arrival.

When the Union Jack was raised those Aboriginal people who watched did not know that Captain Phillip had just declared that all their land – all of eastern Australia in fact – now belonged to Britain. (Norfolk Island also belonged to Britain now – Phillip had sent Lieutenant King to take possession.)

The Aboriginal people at Sydney Cove did not know that they had just become British subjects and from now on they would have to obey British law. They did not know that soon nearly all of them would be dead.

Six months after it was first raised, the Union Jack still flies in Sydney Cove. The settlement looks peaceful and orderly but the settlers were beginning to go hungry.

A MOST VALUABLE ACQUISITION

For thousands of years the Aboriginal people of Port Jackson had lived by fishing, hunting and gathering. They were self-sufficient. Arthur Phillip had been told to make the white settlement self-sufficient too. But within a year the whites were nearly starving.

Food was in such short supply Phillip warned the convicts and marines that anyone who stole the 'most trifling' article would be hanged. A dozen or more were hanged in the first year, from a tree between the male and female quarters. In these first years stealing a fowl or a piece of salt pork was enough to have a man or woman 'launched into the other world'.

At Rio de Janeiro the first fleet took on 'all such seeds and plants . . . as were thought likely to flourish on the coast of New South Wales, particularly coffee, indigo, cotton, and the cochineal fig'. At Cape Town they brought on board close to five hundred animals, including fat-tailed sheep, cattle, pigs and poultry. The sight reminded one officer of Noah's Ark.

But the first vegetables and grain planted did poorly in the Sydney soil. The cattle wandered off into the bush and were not found for years. All but ten of the sheep soon died.

Although they had guns the British were at first not very expert at hunting the wild animals, and they could not match the Aborigines' skill at fishing.

For Phillip the convicts and marines proved as difficult as the animals. The convicts were not skilled at farming. Many of them were too old or sick.

The marines were not keen to help build a settlement. They felt that their job was only to defend it. The commander, Major Ross, hated the place. He wrote to the British government saying there was no worse place to found a colony.

Three months after settlement and the governor has built a 'mansion' for himself, set up a farm and had a road made to it. Out in the bush parties of convicts are risking attack by Aborigines as they cut wood and quarry for stone and clay for buildings.

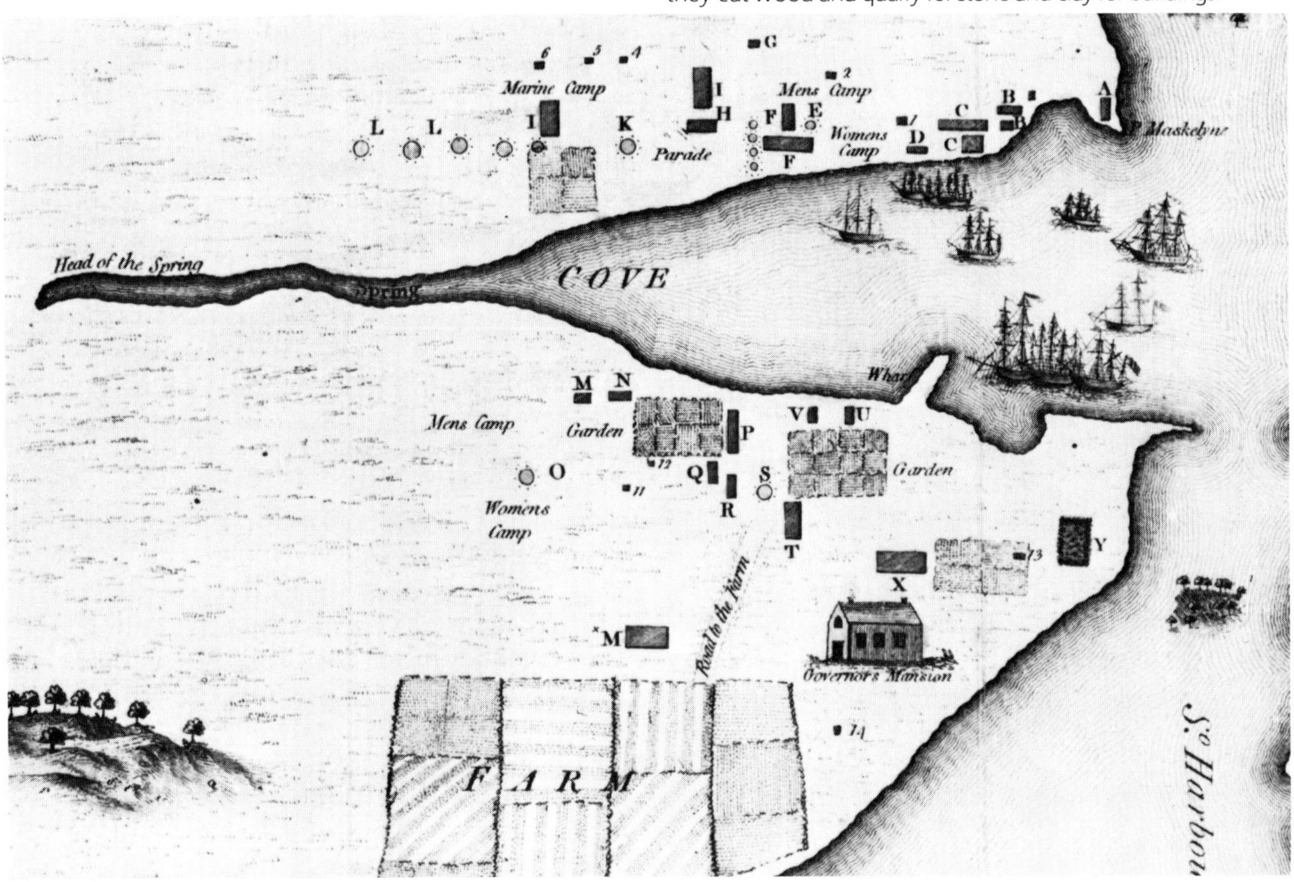

Five hundred lashes of the cat o' nine tails was not an uncommon punishment for stealing, escaping or refusing to work. But convicts also knew that their work was badly needed and they could bargain with their employers for time off.

But Phillip kept his faith in the venture. He was sure it would succeed if the British government would do more to encourage free people to come out from Britain. Phillip believed free emigrants would come if they were offered grants of land. The colony would prosper because they would work hard.

The convicts could be put to work for them. But, to people in England, America was a more attractive place for immigrants. It was easier to get there *and* easier to return home. Only thirteen free migrants came to New South Wales in the first five years.

By the end of 1789 the people at Port Jackson were beginning to think they had been abandoned. No supplies had arrived and one of the colony's two supply ships had sunk near Norfolk Island. Phillip sent their last ship, *Supply*, to Batavia (now called Djakarta, Indonesia) to get food and other essential goods. The little colony just had to wait.

They were saved by the arrival of the second fleet in June 1790. But the ships brought new problems.

It had been an awful voyage. Of just over one thousand convicts who had left England, 267 had died from diseases caused by shocking ill-treatment. In some cases men and women had died while chained together standing in waist-deep water in the hold. They died of scurvy, dysentery and fever because their living quarters were filthy and cramped and they were neither exercised nor properly fed.

On one ship, *Neptune*, one in every three convicts had died. Their bodies were thrown overboard. They were still dying when the ship reached Port Jackson. People on shore found bodies from the ships washing on to the rocks. Only forty-two convicts from the *Neptune* were able to drag themselves ashore. More than one hundred and twenty convicts from the second fleet died after landing.

It was a similar story with the third fleet which arrived the following year. But somehow the settlement began to establish itself. Some of the marines decided to stay.

They were given grants of land and assistance in farming it. Most of them did well on their farms at Parramatta and along the Hawkesbury River.

Some convicts – men and women – were also granted small plots when they had served their sentences. They were called emancipists – people who had been set free.

In October 1792, three and a half years after the first fleet had arrived, Phillip proudly reported that nearly 5000 bushells of maize had been harvested. There were 1700 acres under cultivation. Whalers and sealers had begun operating from the port. It was still a tiny settlement on the fringe of the continent, but it was beginning to look like it could last.

Phillip was sure it would. He returned to England in December 1792 convinced that New South Wales would one day be 'the most valuable acquisition that Great Britain ever made'.

OUTCASTS IN THEIR OWN LAND

Governor Phillip had been told by the British government to make friends with the Aboriginal people and to punish those who gave them any 'unnecessary interruption'. To take another people's land and food was not considered interruption.

When the British first arrived Aborigines were both amused and frightened by them. They were amused by the clothes the newcomers wore. They laughed at the men with clean shaven faces, because they thought they must be women.

They were frightened too, because they believed that these white people were spirits of the dead – that the visitors had once been like them and that they had now come back in white bodies. Sometimes they thought they recognized old friends and relations amongst them.

The Aboriginal tribes of Sydney Cove were also frightened by the awful punishments the whites handed out to the convicts. They had never seen people flogged before, or hanged, as convicts and marines were when they stole food.

When they realized the white people had come to stay the Aborigines became angry. They became angrier still when convicts stole their spears and fishing lines, and yet would not share their own weapons and implements. It took a long time to make a spear or a fishing rig. If it was stolen there was nothing to gather food with until another one had been made.

Soon the Aborigines were taking out their anger on unprotected whites. In May 1788 two convicts who had been cutting rushes by the harbour were found dead. Several others who wandered too far from the settlement were also killed.

Officers from the first fleet trying to be friendly with an Aboriginal woman who, understandably, doesn't trust them.

Bennelong

The main battle was about having enough to eat. When winter came in 1788 there were less fish in the harbour for the Aborigines to catch. The land from which they had always gathered food at this time of year had been taken over by the whites. The tribes around Port Jackson began to go hungry.

Worse was to come. Aborigines began to die from smallpox. A disease like this was unknown to them. The whites found bodies on the beaches, around the camps and in caves. Phillip realized that the disease must have come with the fleet. Soon it spread from Sydney Cove. One officer visited Broken Bay and found 'in many places our path was covered with skeletons'.

Phillip had been puzzled from the beginning by the Aboriginal people. He had wanted to be on friendly terms with them but they would not co-operate. Now he decided that the best way to get to know them was to capture some. Perhaps his prisoners would teach him their language and tell him what their people were thinking.

Two Aboriginal men called Colbee and Bennelong were caught and taken to Government House. Here they were tied up in a dark room guarded by convicts. Colbee and Bennelong were terrified. Eventually both of them escaped.

Bennelong later came back and became friendly with Phillip. When the Governor returned to England he took Bennelong with him, together with a boy named Yemmarrawanie. Phillip wanted the English to see what Australian Aboriginal people looked like. Few English saw Yemmarrawanie. He died not long after he arrived.

Bennelong was introduced to King George III. He stayed in England for nearly three years and grew more and more homesick. When he left in 1794 Bennelong was so ill it was thought he would probably die. Somehow he survived. When he got back to New South Wales he began to live some of the time with his tribe and some of it with the whites. Aborigines did not like the white man's habits which Bennelong had picked up. He wore strange clothes and spoke in a strange way. Bennelong began to drink heavily and fight.

Soon the whites did not like him either. They said he was ungrateful. They had done so much for him, they said, yet he insisted on going back to his people, or getting drunk. They could not see that all they had done was to make Bennelong look foolish to both whites and blacks.

By the time Bennelong died in 1813, Aboriginal tribal life had been severely disrupted. There weren't many Aborigines left at Sydney Cove. Those who were still alive lived miserably. They no longer had their land so that they had to get food from the white settlement. Many of them had diseases which had been brought by the whites. Many were addicted to the whites' alcohol.

The Aboriginal people had been masters of the land just a few years before. Now they were beggars.

Bungaree (or Bongaree) in the uniform given to him by Governor Macquarie. Bungaree went exploring the coast of Australia with Matthew Flinders in the ship **Norfolk** in 1799.

STARTING A NEW LIFE

Once free, convicts had an opportunity to make good in New South Wales. They could find work as labourers, get a small grant of land or start a business. Whether they stayed poor or made a fortune – and most of them stayed poor – former convicts were rarely allowed to forget their past.

Those who had not been convicts (the 'exclusives' as they were called) insisted that former convicts ('emancipists') were *always* in some way convicts and that they could never be 'unconditionally free'.

Samuel Terry was one emancipist who made a fortune. He had been a labourer in Manchester when he was found guilty of stealing four hundred pairs of stockings and transported to New South Wales for seven years. Terry arrived in Sydney in 1801.

When his sentence expired in 1807 he farmed for a while near the Hawkesbury River. In 1810 he moved to Sydney where he kept an inn. He married another former convict called Rosetta Marsh whose two previous husbands had died serving sentences.

Some people said Terry earned his money dishonestly. Governor Lachlan Macquarie swore that he was an honest man. However he did it, by 1820 Samuel Terry owned half of all the land held by former convicts.

In later years he established flour mills and breweries, erected great buildings and became a director of the Bank of New South Wales. He contributed money to the church, and he became active in politics arguing the case for emancipists.

Even at the end of his life there were some who would not accept Terry because of his convict background. But the man who had begun life in New South Wales cutting stone in a convict gang, and who had been flogged for neglect of duty, died one of the richest people in the colony.

James Ruse worked hard but died poor. He arrived as a convict on the first fleet. Governor Phillip admired his good behaviour and as a reward, soon after their arrival, gave him the use of sixteen

Convicts were used to do work now done by heavy machinery. This re-creation of a human plough was made for an Australian film, **For the Term of his Natural Life**. The actors look rather better fed and cleaner than the convicts would have done.

hectares of land, tools and seed to sow. Phillip hoped that doing this would encourage other convicts to behave.

Ruse was possibly the first person to farm successfully in Australia. He knew that the soil would be richer if the timber that he cleared was burnt and the ashes dug in. He paid attention to the soil and treated it with care.

By 1790 his little farm was producing enough food to feed himself, his wife Elizabeth, a child and two convict labourers. In 1791 Governor Phillip made him the owner of the land.

Although he had done well, James Ruse wanted to return to England. Before leaving he sold his land and took a job to make some extra money.

We don't know why, but he never sailed. Twice more over the years he tried farming but he was unable to make a success of it.

Most of his life he spent working for wages, but he always remembered that first achievement. When he died in 1837 a tombstone was erected on his grave and the words on it read

My Mother Reread Me Tenderly
With Me She Took Much Paines
And When I Arrived In This Coelney
I Sowd The Forst Grain and Now
With Me Hevenly Father I hope
For Ever to Remain.

A CHANCE FOR FREE MEN TO MAKE THEIR FORTUNES

At first Europeans made friends with the Aboriginal owners of the land by offering them trinkets they had never seen before.

In Aboriginal society no single person owned the land or made profits from the food it grew. Everyone received a share of the day's hunting and gathering and together they owned it and the land.

The British believed in private ownership of property and the right of individuals to sell food and other goods at a profit. But the British government was more concerned at first with punishment than profit in New South Wales.

In fact for a while it seemed that the British government was scarcely interested in the little settlement at all. Governor Phillip must have wondered if the British government had forgotten all about the place and the people it had sent there.

After Phillip returned to England the colony was governed by two military officers, Grose and Paterson.

Grose and Paterson allowed other officers to take over large amounts of land and they provided convicts to work for them. It soon became clear that the large landholders were going to have an important say in what sort of colony it would be.

These people soon ran the business of New South Wales. They bought up all the goods arriving on ships and all the food arriving in the colony and sold them at any prices they liked.

In the first few years there was no money which people could use in exchange for things they wanted, so they exchanged goods. People wanted rum. The officers of the New South Wales Corps bought all the rum and exchanged it for food and goods. The Marine Corps became known as the Rum Corps and

Some convicts could work for themselves at weekends.

the colony became known for drunkenness.

In bad seasons the small farmers of New South Wales got so heavily into debt they had to sell their land to the large landholders. The land and the wealth of the colony fell under control of a few people, just as it had in Britain.

When the new governor, John Hunter, arrived in 1795 he tried to help the small farmers. The governors who came after him, Phillip Gidley King and William Bligh, followed the same policy. They were acting on orders from the British government which still thought of New South Wales as a self-supporting penal colony rather than a profit-making place.

But the Rum Corps believed that New South Wales should offer the chance to free men to make their fortunes. What was good for them, they said, was good for the colony.

In 1797 one of the officers of the Corps, John Macarthur, imported some Spanish merino sheep. They thrived in the Australian environment. Soon their fleeces were being exported to Britain for use in the textile trade.

It was clear to Macarthur that the colony's future lay in the land. The men who owned it would make great fortunes and, he said, Britain would have a useful settlement, not just an expensive dumping ground for convicts.

But it was the convicts who built roads, bridges and houses. They cleared and ploughed the land on government farms. They did the same work for the landowners and looked after their flocks and herds.

Convict women did many of these tasks and others as well. They worked as household servants, raised their children and often those of the free settlers.

For the smallest offence – like pretending to be ill, disobeying an order, or being insolent to a master – convicts could be flogged. For a more serious offence, they might be hanged.

Many of the convicts were hard and brutal people. They were the 'dregs' of British society as people often said. But it was on their work that the future of New South Wales depended.

The first products to be exported from New South Wales came from whaling and sealing.

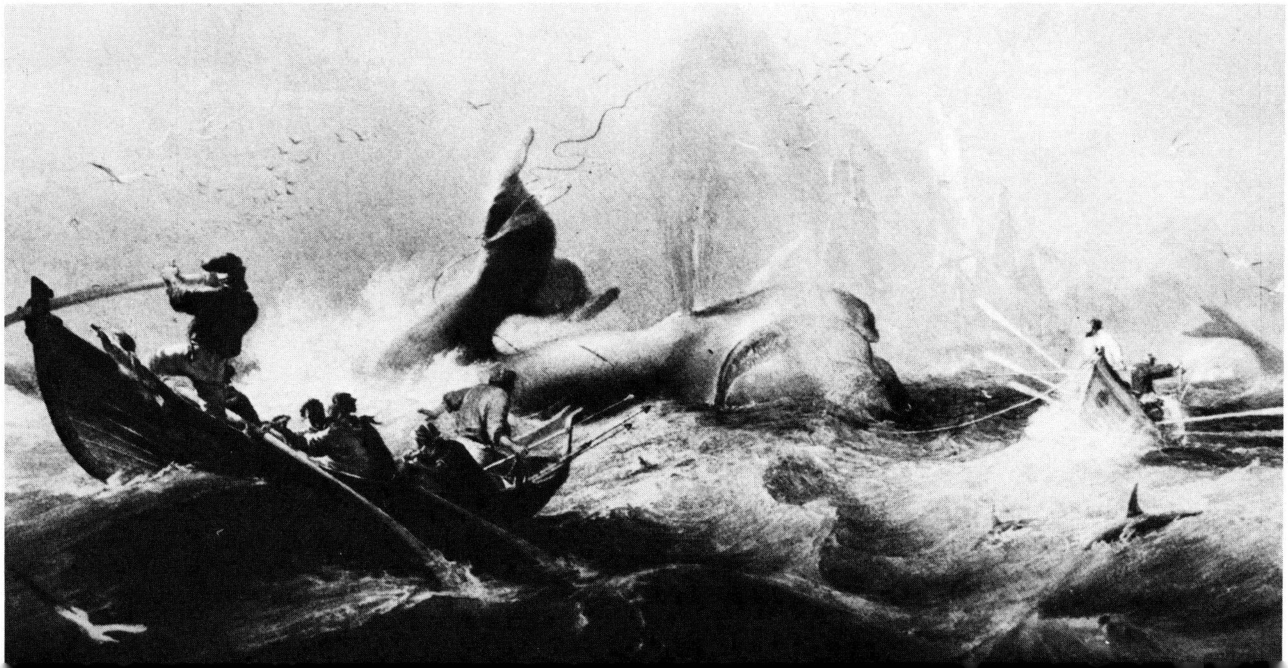

Rebellion

The battle cry of the convict rebels at Castle Hill was 'Death or Liberty'. For eight of them it was death and no one won his liberty. This is how the rebellion was portrayed in a 1970s television series, *Against the Wind*.

Convict men and women were not entirely at the mercy of their masters. The records show that they often refused to work even though it meant they might be flogged. Getting drunk, blaspheming and swearing, and being rude to their masters were other ways of thumbing their noses at authority.

Sometimes the convicts rebelled in more drastic ways. Although the penalty for escaping was death, from the very beginning of the settlement there were convicts who preferred to take their chances as outlaws in the bush. They became known as bushrangers. The first bushranger was a man known as Black Caesar, a negro convict who escaped soon after the first fleet arrived.

One night in March 1791 Mary Bryant, her husband William and their two children aged just one and three years, escaped with seven other convict men in the governor's open boat. They travelled nearly five thousand kilometres up the east coast of Australia, through Torres Strait and reached Timor.

Eventually Mary Bryant, four of the convict men and one of the children reached England. Mary was re-tried for her crime and, surprisingly, given a pardon.

Major George Johnston led the troops who put down the Irish rebels at Castle Hill. Later he rebelled himself, against Governor Bligh, was sent back to England and dismissed from the army. In 1813 he returned to settle in Australia.

Mary Bryant had more success than many of the convicts who simply escaped to the bush. The convicts found that they could not live off the land. They did not know the habits of the animals – where to find possums and bandicoots, how to catch fish and eels in the streams and swans' eggs in the marshes. They did not see the fruit on the bushes which Aboriginal women would have gathered.

In the early years many convicts died in the bush. Others gave themselves up and faced the consequences.

However, as settlement spread out bushrangers found they could live by raiding remote farm houses. In the 1820s men like Jack Donohue and his gang were so well protected by the hills between Goulburn and Bathurst it took a small military operation to bring them in.

Like so many bushrangers, Bold Jack Donohue was Irish, and like so many of them he was executed.

In 1804 an Irishman named William Johnston got three hundred convicts together and led them towards Parramatta and Sydney. Armed with swords and guns and pikes they swore they would win their freedom or die. The governor, who was already very suspicious of the Irish convicts, got word of the rebellion and sent out the soldiers to meet the convicts at Castle Hill. The rebels were defeated.

The leaders of the Castle Hill rebellion were hanged and the main followers were either flogged or sent to a special camp at Newcastle where they were forced to mine coal and attend the Church of England. The governor thought it might be because they were Catholics that they were so troublesome.

People are likely to rebel when their freedom is taken away or they feel that they have been unjustly treated. In 1808 it was the rich not the poor who felt their freedom threatened and turned on the governor. The governor was Captain William Bligh.

Bligh had arrived in Sydney in 1806. He was famous for two things – his terrible temper and a six thousand kilometre voyage in an open boat after the crew of his ship *Bounty* mutinied in the Pacific.

In New South Wales Bligh made enemies among the ambitious landowners and merchants. He attempted to stop the rum trade and the power of the New South Wales Corps. John Macarthur was furious, especially when Bligh threatened to take away his grant of land.

Macarthur's temper was as bad as Bligh's. He also had a lot of supporters among the rich men of the colony. He persuaded the acting-commandant of the Corps to arrest Bligh. For more than a year Bligh was held in Sydney while New South Wales was governed by the Corps.

It was not until 1809 when a new governor, Lachlan Macquarie, arrived that Bligh returned to England. The men who led the rebellion also went back to the old country – to face trial.

A cartoon from the time shows Bligh attempting to hide from the officers who have come to arrest him. It was a rumour the officers liked to spread.

GEORGE BASS

George Bass came to Australia in 1794 on the same ship as the new governor of New South Wales, John Hunter.

Bass was a ship's surgeon – a sawbones. There were no antibiotics or penicillin to cure infection then, so limbs were quickly amputated. There were no anaesthetics, only rum. George Bass and his patients needed strong stomachs.

Bass soon had a patient on his voyage to Australia. Bennelong was going home from England and he was very ill.

Matthew Flinders was also on the ship. He had grown up just a few miles from Bass's home in Lincolnshire. The two men became good friends.

Soon after arriving in New South Wales Bass and Flinders began exploring the coast to the south in a tiny open boat called the *Tom Thumb*. They had what all great explorers need – skill and strength, imagination, courage and good luck.

Matthew Flinders, Bass and his servant boy off the coast of New South Wales.

George Bass

In December 1797 Bass and crew of six sailed in a nine metre open boat through terrible seas around the southern tip of the Australian continent and on to discover that Van Diemen's Land was separated from the mainland by a narrow stretch of water. They named it Bass Strait.

On his way back Bass and his men found seven escaped convicts stranded and starving on a little island off Wilson's Promontory. The boat could only carry two more people so Bass took on board those who were most frail. The other five were put ashore on the mainland with as many provisions as Bass could spare, but they were never seen again.

The following year Bass and Flinders sailed right through Bass Strait and around Van Diemen's Land.

Flinders later became the first man to circumnavigate Australia.

Bass wanted to make his fortune trading in the south seas. In February 1803 he set sail from Sydney for South America. After calling at the north island of New Zealand he was never heard of again.

There is a story that he was captured by the Peruvian government who took him to be a pirate and made him a slave in their lead mines.

It is more likely that his ship sank in the Pacific. Whatever happened, George Bass' luck had run out.

1810-1829

1811 Thomas Davey, Governor of Van Diemen's Land.

1813 Blue Mountains crossed.
Bennelong dies.

1814 On Matthew Flinders' suggestion, 'New Holland' becomes 'Australia'.

1815 John Oxley explores Lachlan River.
Napoleon defeated at Waterloo.
William Sorell, Governor of Van Diemen's Land.

1817 John Oxley and George Evans discover Liverpool Plains, New South Wales.

1821 Thomas Brisbane, Governor of New South Wales.

1823 Oxley discovers Brisbane River.

1824 Hamilton Hume and William Hovell reach Port Phillip from Sydney.
British establish Fort Dundas (near Darwin).
Penal settlement established at Moreton Bay (later Brisbane).

1825 Ralph Darling, Governor of New South Wales.
George Arthur, Governor of Van Diemen's Land, which becomes a separate colony.

1827 Allan Cunninghame discovers Darling Downs.

1828 Brisbane founded.
Droughts in New South Wales.

1828-9 Charles Sturt travels the Murray River to its mouth in South Australia.

1829 George Stephenson's steam train, 'Rocket' travels at fifty-six kilometres per hour on Manchester-London railway line.

A convict on his way to work in an iron gang.

'HURRAH FOR OLD SYDNEY AND THE SKY OVER IT'

There were four times as many men as women on the first fleet and it was to be fifty years or more before the numbers evened out.

One of the women was Esther Abrahams. She was only seventeen when she was found guilty of stealing some lace from a shop in London and transported to New South Wales for seven years. Esther was pregnant when she committed the crime. When the transport ship, *Prince of Wales*, sailed in 1787 she carried with her a baby born in Newgate Prison.

Like nearly all the women transported to Australia Esther Abrahams was poor. Most convict women were household servants who had been convicted of theft. It is easy to imagine how tempting it was for a poor woman to steal from a rich household and how hard it would be to defend herself in the courts.

In many of the early writings about the colony the convict women were described as 'immoral', 'depraved', 'drunken and abandoned'. This was true of some of the women convicts, as it was of the men. But many of them were neither drunken nor particularly immoral.

Two very different images of convict life. The drawing of the time shows how people expected convicts and their friends to behave. The peaceful scene of convict women strolling through a white washed Sydney Town comes from the television series, **Against the Wind**.

Esther Abrahams

Because they came from the poorer classes, and were convicts after all, gentlemen as a rule did not consider taking convict women as wives. But they often took them as mistresses.

George Johnston, an officer in the Royal Marines, took Esther Abrahams for his mistress on the voyage out. Not long after the arrival of the fleet in Sydney Cove a child was baptised: 'Abrahams or Johnston, George, son of George Johnston, Captain Lieutenant of Marines and Esther Abrahams, convict'.

For the next twenty-five years Esther was George Johnston's mistress. They had several children. Johnston built a mansion on his estate at Annandale. When he was sent back to England for arresting Governor Bligh in 1808, Esther managed the estate until his return.

Esther Abrahams was luckier than most convict women. When they arrived in the colony women were assigned to a master. They were to work for him and, if he wished, be his mistress. A brutal master could make her life a misery.

But if a woman found a good master she might eventually think that transportation was the best thing that ever happened to her. When one Irish girl was sentenced to be shipped to the colony a second time, she cried out, 'Hurrah for old Sydney and the sky over it.'

Women were also put to work in 'female factories' which were built in both New South Wales and Van Diemen's Land. Here the women wove cloth which the colonies needed.

The factories also had punishment sections. At the Cascades factory in Van Diemen's Land prisoners who misbehaved were crowded into dark stinking cells. Punishments were designed to be both humiliating and painful. Offenders had their heads shaved, were confined alone in cells, put in stocks, and sometimes made to wear a heavy iron collar. As if these punishments were not bad enough a treadmill was built at Cascades. The treadmill was the most painful punishment of all.

The female factories were meant to isolate convict women from the men, but men frequently visited them to choose their wives. At the Parramatta factory every Monday morning the best behaved of the convict women were paraded before an audience of free unmarried men – usually emancipists. The men and women talked together and afterwards services were held for those who decided to get married. It was called marrying 'out of the factory'.

A number of convict men became wealthy and influential in Australia but convict women had few chances to succeed in business and no opportunity at all to play a part in politics. Such activities were not expected of them. Mary Reiby was an exception. She inherited her husband's merchant business in Sydney and ran it very successfully.

Esther Abrahams also led an exceptional life. She lived in comfort at Annandale, and, twenty-five years after she bore his first child, George Johnston married her at last.

BEYOND THE BLUE MOUNTAINS

The explorers celebrating their discovery. It took over two weeks to find a way through. When a road was cut the journey would take just a couple of days.

The white settlers at Sydney Cove had no way of knowing what lay on the other side of the mountains they could see to the west. Was it paradise? A great swamp? A desert? An inland sea? What sort of people lived there?

Some convicts were sure that if they crossed the mountains they would find China, and from there be able to find their way back to England. Several of them tried to find a way over and died in the effort.

The governors sent out a number of exploring parties to find a way. George Bass led one of them in 1797. He took great ropes to scale the cliffs and lower himself into the valleys. But even George Bass could not get through.

Until the mountains were crossed the settlement could not grow. The settlers needed more land to graze their sheep and cattle herds which became larger every year. In droughts they needed to push their animals into new pasture. When disease struck their flocks and herds they looked for somewhere else to take the healthy ones. But for more than twenty years the mountains stood in the way.

In 1813 William Lawson and Gregory Blaxland were desperate to find land for their sheep and cattle. They were joined by William Charles Wentworth, a young man who was to become one of the most famous men of his time.

William was the son of the surgeon, D'Arcy Wentworth and Catherine Crowley, a convict. D'Arcy had rescued her from the hold of the *Neptune*. She lived with him until her death in 1800. D'Arcy and Catherine had several children. William was the most ambitious. He became rich and an important politician in New South Wales. He was always loyal to the colony he had been born in.

Blaxland, Wentworth and Lawson decided that the best way to cross the mountains was to follow a ridge from Emu Island in the Nepean river.

They also agreed that it was essential to take great care in plotting their course. Lawson was a surveyor so this was his job. Their main aim was to stay on top of the ridges. They knew that they would exhaust themselves if they got into the valleys.

The Blue Mountains are not very tall but they are very rugged. When the first explorers tried to follow the valleys, they ran into cliffs fifty metres high. When they followed the ridges, they had no more success — the ridges ran out and they found themselves looking down precipices into the valleys.

The explorers took four men to help them, four horses and five dogs. The mountains were covered in thick low scrub. The men hacked their way through. When a ridge seemed to be running out one of them would climb a tall tree to find the route to more high ground.

The explorers knew that a wrong step might send them plunging through the cloud into a gorge. They were exhausted and sick when they finally got through. Wentworth took many years to recover from the ordeal. But they had found a marvellous expanse of grassland. It was enough to feed all the cattle and sheep in the colony.

Now the governor ordered a team of convicts to cut a road through. The western edge of the mountains was the hardest part. The descent from Mt York was almost vertical and so it was a steep, windy and treacherous road they had to build.

Carts could get down it only if huge logs were tied on behind to steady them. To get up ropes were tied to iron rings pinned into the rocks and bullock teams were dragged forward bit by bit.

Along this new road squatters, and explorers such as John Oxley, travelled out on to the plains of New South Wales. Once the Blue Mountains had been crossed nothing could hold back the spread of settlement.

A CITY TO BE PROUD OF

At the end of the first year in New South Wales a convict woman wrote home to say that no one who had not seen Sydney could imagine how awful the place was.

There were just two streets of 'the most miserable huts' with windows made of twigs. All the glass had been used on the houses of the governor and the officials. At the end of the streets there lay a burial ground which by July 1788 already had thirty-five graves.

The governor's new house was made of bricks and stone. 'We now make very good bricks and the stone is good,' wrote Governor Phillip. He planned to build a church with them soon.

The church was finished in 1793. Soon other solid buildings went up – two mills which saved the convicts from the job of grinding corn by hand, a windmill, a gaol and, in 1796, a theatre which was almost immediately closed down. In time the convicts got brick huts.

No one in the first twenty years knew much about building so the houses were simple and small. 'There is not such a thing in the colony as a set of stairs,' one man wrote. The roofs were made of wooden slabs and shingles or they were thatched with straw.

Gardens were planted from the start. Nearly every house had one and often an orchard as well. Fruit trees grew in the middle of town.

When the new governor, Lachlan Macquarie, arrived in 1809 Sydney was still a shambles. Macquarie wrote later:

> I found the colony barely emerging from a state of infantile imbecility, and suffering from various privations and disabilities; the country impenetrable beyond forty miles from Sydney; agriculture in a yet languishing state; commerce in its early dawn . . . the public buildings in a state of dilapidation and mouldering on decay; the few roads and bridges formerly constructed rendered almost impassable . . .

Macquarie Lighthouse built by Francis Greenway, the convict architect. The lighthouse was not just vital for shipping — it was a landmark for the people of Sydney and a sign of civilization.

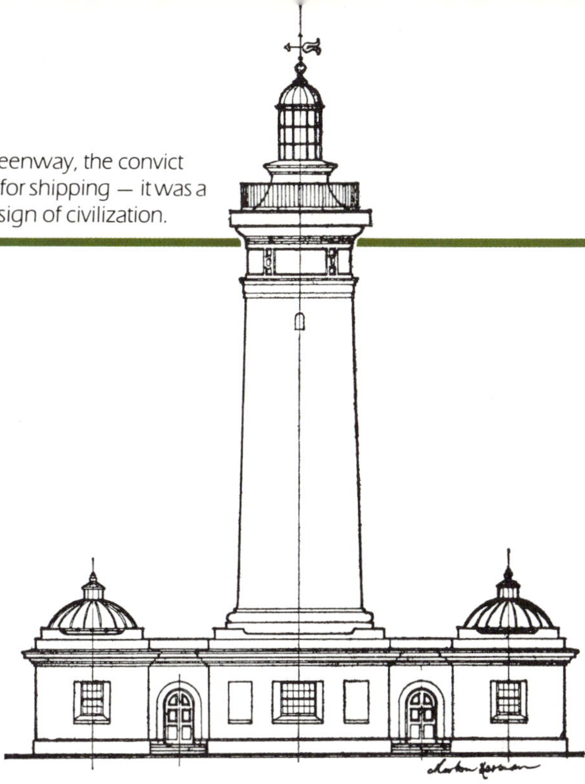

Macquarie was a great planner. He built new streets and widened old ones. He gave them names: George Street after the King of England, Pitt Street after the Prime Minister. Others were named after English dukes, Phillip, Hunter, King and Bligh after the governors of New South Wales. He named Macquarie Street after himself.

Macquarie had signs put up to show people the way about. He made them drive their animals and their carts and drays on the left-hand side of the road, as they did in England.

To keep drunks and rowdy convicts off the streets at night he built a barracks and a watch house and employed a police force. To keep dogs, pigs and goats off the streets he opened a pound for strays.

Macquarie wanted to build a city to be proud of. With the help of the convict architect Francis Greenway he erected fine buildings that would last.

The new buildings were more than they seemed. The hospital, the barracks and the lighthouse were landmarks. The people of Sydney found their way around by them. And when people arrived in Sydney for the first time they now saw more than a shanty town. They knew that Sydney was there to stay.

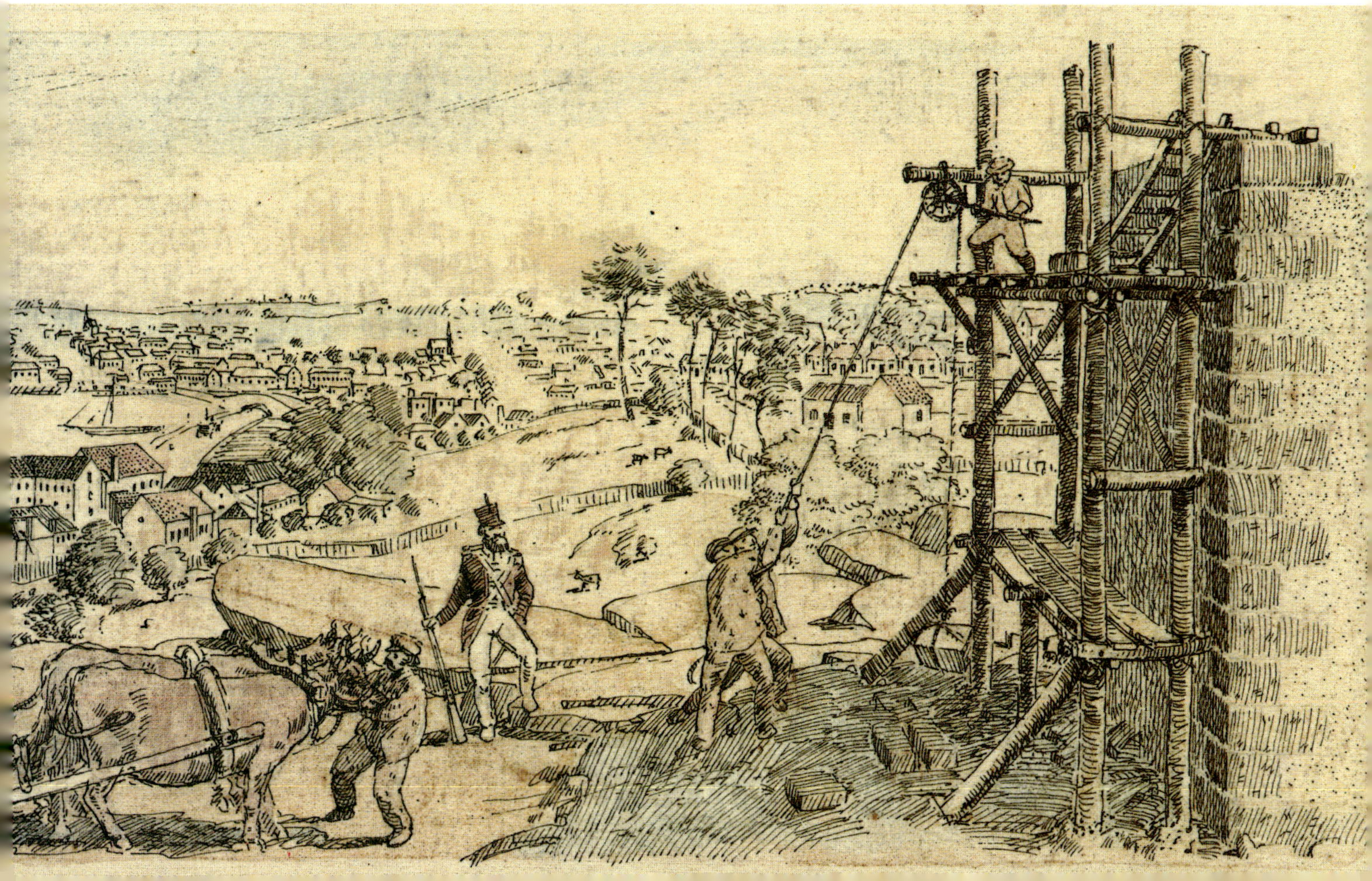

GOD AND NEW SOUTH WALES

Army officers, free settlers and their wives — people who had not been convicts — were called exclusives. They avoided mixing with convicts and emancipists — the rough classes. This is a picnic of exclusives.

The British at Sydney Cove thought it was wise to thank God as often as possible. It was a lonely and dangerous world. They wanted God to know that they were there and smile upon them.

A church service was held in the open air on the second Sunday after the first fleet arrived. The Church of England minister asked the convicts to think about what they could do for God in return for all that God had done for them.

The Church of England thought there were many things a person could do to please God. Obeying the ten commandments would be a good start. They should pray. They should lead honest lives. They should not drink too much, or swear. They should get married. They should obey their masters.

These were not easy rules for a convict to stick to. It was hard for people to get married when there were far more men than women. It was hard not to swear when life was terrible. It was hard not to drink if you were addicted to rum and rum was all you seemed to have to help you forget your troubles. It was hard to respect your master if your master was unjust. And who could thank God if there appeared to be nothing good in life.

It did not help the convicts' Christian feeling that their masters did not practise what they preached. To the convicts and the poor, the rich seemed to be more interested in becoming richer than they were in being good Christians.

Jesus said that the poor and meek would be blessed. But the leader of the church in New South Wales,

The Reverend Samuel Marsden

Samuel Marsden, was neither meek nor poor. In fact he was one of the richest men in the colony. He sentenced convicts to floggings. Once he had a woman flogged and dragged through the streets of Parramatta behind a horse and cart.

Samuel Marsden despised the Aborigines even though Jesus said that all people were the children of God. And Marsden fought constantly with his master, the governor, Lachlan Macquarie.

Governor Macquarie was a religious man. He built churches, insisted that Sunday was a day of rest not work or play, cut down the supply of liquor, and started schools so that young people could be taught Christianity and other useful things.

Macquarie believed that people would want to act decently if they were rewarded for it. He gave important positions to convicts who had worked hard and behaved well. Francis Greenway was made the official architect of the colony and two other former convicts, Simeon Lord and Andrew Thompson, were made magistrates. Macquarie even invited them to tea. The rich people of the colony hated him for this.

The church worked hard in New South Wales but without a great deal of success. The rich fought among themselves in their efforts to get richer. The poor continued to drink and fight.

Many of the poor were Irish Catholics whom the English generally disliked and feared. A Catholic priest was not appointed until the 1820s.

There was a lot of talk about God in New South Wales in these early years. There was a lot of talk about heaven and hell. For instance, when a person was hanged it was said that he 'plunged into eternity', or was 'launched into the next world', or went 'to meet his Maker', when the ladder was pulled from under him.

People spoke much of God's will and God's judgement – of being in the hands of God. However visitors often said that it seemed as if God had very little say in what went on at all.

People brought their religions with them — the Irish, Catholicism; the Scots, Presbyterianism. They may have felt the need for religion most when they were leaving home and on the dangerous sea voyage. A priest here blesses some Irish migrants about to leave.

VAN DIEMEN'S LAND WAS A WILD PLACE

Convicts attempting to escape from Port Arthur had to get across Eaglehawk Neck. Here the Governor and his wife inspect the security arrangements.

The British in New South Wales had always been suspicious of the French ships which periodically sailed into Australian waters. They suspected that the French might be planning to take a portion of the country for themselves.

When a fleet of French ships under the command of Nicolas Baudin stopped at Van Diemen's Land in 1802 Governor King decided it was time to act. He sent Lieutenant Bowen with forty-nine convicts to form a settlement on the Derwent River in the south of the island, and Lieutenant Colonel Paterson with 181 convicts to establish a post on the Tamar in the north.

In Britain the government was nervous. Britain was at war with France and did not want her enemy to establish bases in the Pacific. So Britain sent Lieutenant David Collins and two shiploads of convicts to establish a settlement on Bass Strait.

Collins first landed inside the heads of Port Phillip. He set up his camp where Sorrento now is. The land thereabouts did not impress him and he did not explore enough of the surrounding country to see what great potential it had for pastoral use. Nor did he find the Yarra River which later became the site of the city of Melbourne. Collins decided to leave for Van Diemen's Land.

When they set sail across Bass Strait they left behind a convict named William Buckley. Buckley had escaped. Thirty years later when Port Phillip was finally settled the new settlers found him, the 'Wild White Man', living with an Aboriginal tribe.

Collins' party settled at a place they called Hobart Town, at the foot of a mountain which was later named after Wellington, the conqueror of the French. Soon after their arrival the group which had settled a little further up the Derwent joined them.

Van Diemen's Land was a wild place in the early years of settlement. In Hobart Town the convicts mixed with whalers and sealers many of whom had been convicts themselves.

Convicts soon escaped into the bush and the hills surrounding the settlements became their strongholds. Van Diemen's Land was good country for bushrangers. They could plunder the settlers in

After a time the lash was used less at Port Arthur and solitary confinement more. It was just as cruel. Men and women were placed alone in these underground cells which were pitch black day and night. Convicts frequently went mad.

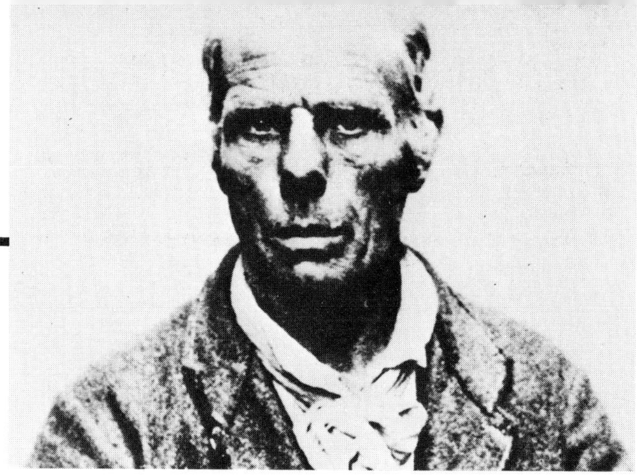

A man who had been transported as a teenager, photographed at Port Arthur forty years later.

the valleys and disappear quickly back into the hills.

Matthew Brady and Michael Howe ran their bushranging gangs like small armies. Howe was very cocky. He called himself the 'governor of the ranges' and the real governor the 'governor of the town'.

Bushranging nearly always ended in death for the bandits. Lawlessness had to be wiped out in new settlements. Brady and Howe and their gangs were tracked down and destroyed.

Convicts, however, sometimes preferred a short and dangerous life as bushrangers to the terrible gaols of Van Diemen's Land. The gaols at Port Arthur and Macquarie Harbour were built for 'incorrigible' convicts – those who had committed further crimes in Australia and who were thought to be beyond reform.

Port Arthur and Macquarie Harbour were famous for their cruelty. Floggings and long periods of solitary confinement in the 'black cells' were common punishments. So was the ultimate penalty, death. In one year, 1824, one hundred convicts were hanged in Van Diemen's Land.

The Aboriginal people of Van Diemen's Land were murdered and abused by free men and convicts alike. In return, they attacked the settlers who stole their hunting grounds. In the end Aboriginal society was destroyed.

Slowly order came to the colony. Farms and villages were established along the banks of the Derwent and, after the Aborigines had been beaten off, imposing houses were built by sheep and cattle farmers, in the rich countryside.

People in the colonies wanted their surrounding to look like home. They planted their farms and gardens with the common trees and shrubs of England. They built their houses along old familiar lines.

Most of the settlers in Van Diemen's Land were English – there were not many Scots and Irish among them – and Tasmania still looks more like England than most other places in Australia.

The Hobart house of George Augustus Robinson, missionary and later Protector of Aborigines. Two members of Tasmania's upper classes pass by. The lower classes hang about and yarn.

'PURE MERINOS'

Spanish merino ram.

If New South Wales and Van Diemen's Land were going to prosper they had to have something to sell. This meant growing a product which thrived in Australia and was needed in Britain and other parts of the world.

Britain needed wool, especially during the long war with France. Woollen clothes and blankets kept the army and navy warm.

The first sheep to come to Australia were intended to provide meat for the settlers, not wool to export. However John and Elizabeth Macarthur had a different view.

John Macarthur came as an officer of the New South Wales Corps in 1790. He was probably the most bad-tempered man in the colony in those early years. He fought a duel with the captain of the ship he sailed on even before he boarded it at Plymouth. A few years later he seriously wounded his commanding officer in another duel.

Elizabeth Macarthur was the first educated woman in the colony. She was loyal to John but she was also clever and strong in her own right. In the end she probably did more for New South Wales than her husband did.

In the 1790s John Macarthur imported merino sheep from the Cape of Good Hope and Bengal and some more from the royal flocks at Kew in London. On his land at Parramatta Macarthur bred the first Australian merinos.

Soon he had sheep growing large fleeces of the long fibre wool which British factories wanted. The sheep thrived in the Australian climate and on Australian grasses.

In 1802 Macarthur was sent back to England to stand trial for fighting that duel. He was already a very rich man. Governor King said sarcastically that if Macarthur came back it might as well be as governor because 'one half of the colony already belongs to him and it will not be long before he gets the other half'.

Macarthur took some of his merino wool with him. The English textile makers were impressed and so was the British government. Macarthur was given two thousand hectares of the best land in the colony.

Macarthur set himself up at Camden and the fortune of this famous family was soon made. When

John Macarthur.

Elizabeth Macarthur.

A still for making rum.

Governor Bligh arrived in 1806 John Macarthur was by far the most powerful man in the colony.

Bligh of course thought that the governor should hold sway on all matters. The two men became bitter enemies. In 1808 Macarthur organized the rebellion in which Bligh was overthrown.

For his part in the rebellion Macarthur had to go back to England. For nine years he was exiled from the colony. He fretted for his family. In his letters to Elizabeth he told her constantly of his love for them and how they were always in his prayers. It took six months for his letters to reach Sydney and six months for Elizabeth's replies to reach him in London.

Elizabeth managed Camden all this time. With a well-organized team of convicts more land was cleared for grazing and planting. Magnificent gardens and orchards were grown. Camden Park became the showpiece of the colony. And each year the ever-increasing flocks of sheep were washed and shorn and the fleeces packed on ships at Sydney Cove.

Elizabeth took care of it all and raised six children as well. The boys, John, William and James were sent to school in England. They came back to Australia to become great landowners and politicians themselves.

John Macarthur also came back eventually and began managing Camden Park again. He had grown quite cranky. But he was still convinced that the colony's future lay in merino sheep, and history proved him right.

Elizabeth Farm, the Macarthurs' property. The rich people of New South Wales — unless they had been convicts — were sometimes called 'Pure Merinos'. It meant that they were aristocrats in the colonies, although few of them would have been in Britain.

NO 'RICH AND ROMANTIC LAND'

Swan River settlers were led to believe that the place they were going to was rather like Paradise. This scene was painted during Captain Stirling's 1827 expedition.

In 1791 Captain George Vancouver discovered a beautiful harbour on the south-west coast of Australia. He called it King George III's Sound. The land was not like the barren north which Dampier had seen a century before. There was plenty of fresh water and good supplies of fish. Before he sailed Vancouver planted some pumpkin seeds.

No one gave much thought to the west coast of Australia until 1826 when Governor Darling set up a military outpost at the place Vancouver had discovered. Some French ships had been in the area and Darling feared that they might be planning to build a base there.

The following year he sent Captain James Stirling to the area. Stirling sailed eighty kilometres up the Swan River. It was a 'rich and romantic land' he saw. He decided that a new colony should be created.

The British government agreed that such a colony would be a good idea but they did not want to spend too much money. They did not want a convict colony. Free men and women would start it with their own money and their own labour.

It took courage to sail to this new land, however promising Stirling's descriptions were. The people who sailed on the first ships to Swan River did not know what sort of dangers they would have to face. For all they knew they might be met by hordes of cannibals.

The British government provided three ships. Captain Charles Fremantle sailed in the warship, *Challenger*. He went on ahead to take possession of the area in the name of the King.

Yagan. After he was killed the white settlers preserved his head by smoking it.

Behind came two smaller and slower ships, the *Parmelia* and *Sulphur*. The *Sulphur* had the men of the 63rd Regiment on board with their wives and children. There were 70,000 pounds of biscuits on board, 2000 gallons of beer and 10,000 bricks. The bricks soon proved too much for the *Sulphur* – they had to be unloaded at Portsmouth.

Captain Stirling had been made governor of the new colony and he sailed on the *Parmelia* with his wife. It seemed to be a good omen when she gave birth to a baby on the way. There were tragedies too, as there always were on such long voyages. In Table Bay at the Cape of Good Hope one woman watched as her husband and daughter drowned. She sailed on to Swan River with her other four children.

A much greater disaster nearly struck the expedition when the *Parmelia* reached the mouth of the Swan River. She ran aground on a sand bar and remained stuck there for days while heavy seas battered her. The *Parmelia* seemed certain to be lost and all the supplies with her. The women and children were taken off and put on a nearby island where they huddled in terror in the teeming rain. Miraculously the ship refloated itself. But it was not a good start.

Swan River was indeed beautiful. But Stirling had made the mistake of thinking that because the place looked beautiful it was also fertile. In fact the soil was very patchy and the best of it flooded in winter.

Many of the plants which grew there proved to be poisonous to stock. There was little good pasture. The forests were too dense for men and women to clear.

The government had decided to give people free grants of land if they got to Swan River before the end of 1830. So people poured into the colony. Twenty-five shiploads arrived in the first six months. They trekked inland looking for pastures. Many of them died.

A rich adventurer named Thomas Peel enticed four hundred people to emigrate. The government promised him half a million acres of good land if he got them to Swan River before 1 November 1829. Peel was late and received half a million acres of poor land instead. Peel was bankrupted.

In those first years the Swan River settlers had a terrible time. Trapped between the ocean and a barren inland, for the majority of settlers this was no 'rich and romantic land'. It was a desperate, lonely place.

To the Aboriginal people of Swan River the ships entering the Swan River looked like great-winged monsters. At first they took the whites to be spirits of their own dead, but their incompetence at living off the land soon made it clear that if they had once been Aboriginal people they had forgotten everything they knew.

Hungry whites were soon seizing the Aboriginal hunting grounds and keeping the Aboriginal people at bay with guns. The Aborigines tried to drive them out but they were shot down. Some Aboriginal men who stole food from white settlers suffered the fate of white convicts – they were flogged. One at least, a man named Yagan, was shot by a bounty hunter after he had killed a white man in defence of his land.

Hungry, resentful, and far from home.

LACHLAN MACQUARIE

Had he been born a generation or two earlier, Lachlan Macquarie might have been chief of his Scottish clan. He was born on the little island of Ulva off the Scottish coast in 1764. It was less than twenty years since the Scottish Highlanders had been defeated by the English at the Battle of Culloden.

But in Macquarie's day there was nothing much else for a Scottish Highlander to do but join the British army. Macquarie became a lieutenant and travelled all over the world. In 1809 he was appointed governor of New South Wales.

Macquarie wanted to bring civilization to New South Wales. He dreamt of a day when thousands of good Christian men and women would make an honest living off the land.

Macquarie tried to help the Aboriginal people of New South Wales by educating them and punishing white settlers who mistreated them. He tried to stop the drinking and gambling of whites and blacks alike.

Lachlan Macquarie.

The Governor's House at Rosehill. The wooden construction on the right is a set of stocks for punishing and humiliating convicts in public.

Lachlan Macquarie was a devout Christian. He never had any doubt that he was doing what God wanted him to do. He was always sure that he was right. People like Samuel Marsden and John Macarthur were not so sure.

They thought Macquarie had too much power, and that he spent too much money on his public buildings, roads and bridges. They also resented his friendships with former convicts and his efforts to create opportunities for others to reform and prosper. Macarthur, Marsden and several other rich men of New South Wales wanted a greater say in the colony's affairs.

Finally Macarthur and his friends convinced the British government that Macquarie should be brought home to England.

Macquarie left in 1822 and, as the *Sydney Gazette* said, Australia 'saw her benefactor for the last time'. Macquarie was the 'parent' and Sydney his 'child', the newspaper said.

Lachlan Macquarie was bitter. He died an unhappy man just two years after his recall from Sydney. His wife, Elizabeth, took his body back to the islands in Scotland where the Macquaries had lived and died through countless generations, and there he was buried.

1830-1849

1830 Attempt to round up all the Aborigines of Van Diemen's Land in 'Black Line' fails.

1831 Richard Bourke, Governor of New South Wales.

1831-5 Thomas Livingstone Mitchell explores in eastern Australia.

1834 Aborigines defeated at Battle of Pinjarra, Western Australia.
Henty brothers land at Portland, Victoria.

1835 Port Phillip settlement founded.
Halley's Comet appears.
Settlement of Tasmanian Aborigines on Flinders Island.

1836 South Australia founded: John Hindmarsh, Governor.

1837 Queen Victoria on throne of England.
Sir John Franklin, Governor of Van Diemen's Land.
George Gawler, Governor of South Australia.
First sheep overlanded from New South Wales to Adelaide, by Edward John Eyre.

1838 George Gipps, Governor of New South Wales.
Myall Creek massacre of Aborigines.
Caroline Chisholm arrives in New South Wales.

1839 Bicycle invented in Britain.

1840 Edward John Eyre survives attack by Aborigines to reach Western Australian coast from Adelaide.
Transportation of convicts to New South Wales ceases.

1841 First photograph known to have been taken in Australia, of Bridge and George Streets, Sydney.

1842 Queen Victoria in England makes her first journey by rail.

1843 John Ridley invents world's first mechanical wheat stripper, South Australia.

1844 Sturt fails to find an inland sea in central Australia.

1844-5 Ludwig Leichhardt reaches Port Essington, Northern Territory from Moreton Bay.

1845 Copper discovered at Burra, South Australia.

1846 Potato famine in Ireland.
Charles Fitzroy, Governor of New South Wales.

1847 Last forty-four Aborigines removed from Flinders Island.

1848 Ludwig Leichhardt sets out from Darling Downs to cross Australia. No trace of his party ever seen again.

1849 Amelia Bloomer shocks the world with a new comfortable outfit for women — very loose-fitting trousers.
Californian gold rush.
Transportation to Western Australia commences.

Louisa Clifton, an early settler in Western Australia.

MEAT THREE TIMES A DAY

By the 1830s the Australian colonies offered great opportunities to British people who were brave enough to pack up and sail to the other side of the world.

For those with a little money there was a chance to get land – something they had no hope of doing at home. There was even the chance to grow rich.

The colonies needed people with various skills who were willing to work hard. Builders, bricklayers, rooftilers, thatchers and carpenters were needed: blacksmiths, saddlers, coachbuilders, and wheelwrights, bootmakers, tailors and hatters.

The colonies also needed women. 'Female servants of all kinds are wanted by the thousands, especially if young,' the Sydney papers said. The men needed wives and female servants to cook and sew for them, to decorate their houses, milk the cows and have their children.

Caroline Chisholm, an Englishwoman who believed that she was doing God's work, organized a system under which thousands of young women were brought to the colonies. Caroline was convinced that women would help to bring order to Australia. They would civilize the men.

People came to the colonies because the colonies offered them more than Britain did. The British government encouraged emigration. Britain wanted to be rid of its poor.

People read in the British newspapers that they would soon find well-paid work in New South Wales or Van Diemen's Land.

But there were many things to discourage a person too. No one much likes to leave a home and family. The long and dangerous voyage frightened people. So little was known about Australia. It seemed a much better idea to go to America, if one was going to leave at all.

Male settlers in Australia wait to catch wives as they arrive from Britain. This cartoon was drawn in 1832.

The voyage to Australia was not always as frightening as this, but rarely was it pleasant and there was always danger close by. Quite a few ships were wrecked on the Australian coast, the migrants drowning within sight of the land they had sailed so far to settle in.

People began to emigrate to Australia more freely when they learnt more about it. They read in 'Emigrants Guides' that there was nothing to fear in Australia and that the opportunities were boundless for people who were willing to work. Meat, they were told, was so cheap and plentiful even an ordinary worker ate it three times a day.

It helped if people knew someone in Australia. Once one member of a family emigrated the others often followed, knowing that they would not have to face the new world alone.

To help people get to Australia the British government arranged to pay settlers a 'bounty' if they would pay the fares of emigrants. The settlers needed the labour. The British government needed to get rid of its surplus population.

In Ireland and the Highlands of Scotland there was no work for the people and a shortage of food. In the 1840s the potato crops were struck by a disease called 'blight'. A terrible famine set in. In Ireland thousands died from disease and starvation. The Celtic people of Scotland and Ireland had no choice but to leave.

The poor Irish and the Highland Scots generally spoke Gaelic rather than English. They knew even less about the Australian colonies than the English emigrants. Now they found themselves crammed on to ships bound for America or Australia. For most of them it was a terrifying experience.

There was misery as each day took the ship further from home. There was the fear of shipwreck and epidemic diseases which so frequently broke out on the emigrant ships.

For example, on one ship in 1852, fifty-three children died from an outbreak of measles. A passenger on the ship wrote home to his friend in the Highlands: 'Oh Sandy throwing out my two boys into the deep sea it will never go out of my heart'.

The colonies were full of homesick people. But even the man who lost his two boys at sea soon wrote home to tell his friends and relations that they should join him. He was earning more money than he had ever dreamt of. He ate well. He was looking after more sheep than any Highlander had seen in a lifetime.

There was nothing to fear in Australia, he said. 'The natives will hurt no person. I have to tell you that this country is the best country in the world.'

The cottage of a poor family in Islay, an island off the coast of the Scottish Highlands.

A SQUATTER ON THE MONARO

This squatter's first home is decorated with emu legs and a dingo's head on the wall. A lot of squatters had been soldiers which might explain the sword. This one was a gentleman: he read books, but with little else for company he kept the dog inside.

It was tempting for new emigrants to live in the town. There was usually work to be found. Town life was what most new emigrants had been used to in Britain. And there was less to fear in the town. There were no wild Aborigines. No strange animals. And it was never so lonely as life in the bush.

But for some people the country was the place to go. They did not want to be cooped up. They did not want to work for someone else. They knew that there was land to be had and with land they could lead free and independent lives. For people like this, land was the main reason for coming to the colony. They were known as squatters.

Squatters usually had come from a farming background. They needed enough money to buy themselves a flock of sheep or herd of cattle. A squatter also needed a horse, dogs, a team of bullocks and a dray and, if possible, some convict and Aboriginal servants. He needed supplies of food, guns and ammunition, blankets and a tent, axes, picks and shovels.

From Sydney a squatter could go north to New England, and beyond to the Darling Downs which had been explored in 1828. West lay the plains of the Lachlan and Darling Rivers, south, the Murrumbidgee and Murray Rivers.

By the late 1830s men were driving their stock even further south into northern and western Victoria. They followed the cart tracks of Major Thomas Mitchell, the explorer who had discovered the land in 1836.

When he found good, well-watered land, the squatter settled his flocks. He rode around and decided on his boundaries. By paying the government a small fee he could legally graze his animals on vast amounts of land known as 'runs'. A run might be twenty thousand hectares or more.

The squatter's flocks and herds increased. If droughts or diseases did not wipe out his stock he had a good chance of becoming a rich man. In time he

A most peculiar Australian creature.

would build a great house and find a wife to bear and raise his children.

There were usually a lot of children. Like poorer women, many squatters' wives died in childbirth. In many country cemeteries you will find a squatter buried alongside two wives – and often children who died in infancy.

Farquhar MacKenzie was a typical squatter. Like so many of them he came from Scotland. The Scots badly wanted to own land and helped each other get it.

Soon after he arrived MacKenzie was out on the Monaro high plains looking after another Scot's sheep. The sheep were MacKenzie's only companions, though sometimes wandering bushmen called into his little hut and yarned.

When he was alone Farquhar MacKenzie read the Bible. In his diary he wrote of how it sometimes worried him that he did not read the Bible more.

MacKenzie loved the world about him. He drew and described the strange animals he saw.

In summer the Monaro is hot. In winter it is terribly cold. The frosts sometimes hang from the trees all day. In spring MacKenzie saw the new lambs in his flock and he thought what a wonderful country it was. But for long periods he must have been lonely.

MacKenzie noticed that white settlers were changing the face of the land. The banks of rivers and lakes were broken down by the hard hooves of sheep and cattle. Sheep ate out the native grasses and bushes. The land eroded. Weeds appeared. The native animals and birds rapidly disappeared.

MacKenzie took his flocks to Port Phillip and soon found good land. He found a wife as well. He married the daugher of his business partner. Her name was Patty Murchison and with Farquhar MacKenzie she had ten children.

As squatters built more fences, fewer shepherds were needed.

THE GREATEST LANDOWNER IN THE WORLD

Three Aboriginal tribes lived by the shores of Port Phillip – the Wotowurung, the Wurundjeri and the Bunurong – and they lived well. There was plenty to eat: ducks, geese, eels, fish, kangaroos and many other kinds of game were there in plenty. There was rarely a shortage of vegetable food and ample fresh water from the streams.

In cold weather they cloaked themselves in possum skins. In summer they went almost naked.

One day in 1835 a group of about twenty-five Port Phillip women were out gathering food. All but one of them had a baby on her back. They carried buckets, baskets, tomahawks and bags. Some of the women had axes made from an old iron cartwheel. Perhaps it had been left behind in 1824 by the explorers, Hume and Hovell.

The tribes in the Port Phillip area would have known something about white men. They must have seen their ships. And William Buckley, the convict who escaped from Collins' settlement at Sorrento in 1803, had been living with them for years.

Now the women saw four more white men. They came towards them with seven Aboriginal men. The women must have been frightened but they sang and danced for the Aboriginal men. The leader of the newcomers, whose name was John Batman, gave the women beads and mirrors.

John Batman was a great white bushman. He had grown up in Sydney. His father was a convict. When he was just twenty years old John left home and went to Van Diemen's Land where he began farming.

Batman lived in a tent with his few animals nearby. One night a young woman called Eliza Callaghan staggered in. Eliza had escaped from prison for the fourth time. She had been fearfully treated in gaol. More than once she had been put in the stocks and she had been made to wear the iron collar.

Batman hid her. After several years John and Eliza married and John arranged with the government for Eliza to receive a pardon. They had six children.

Batman became a rich man in Van Diemen's Land. He was given more land as a reward for work he did for the government. He hunted bushrangers and rounded up Aborigines, some of whom he shot.

William Buckley, the convict who escaped and spent thirty years living with the Aborigines of Port Phillip.

But John Batman wanted land on the south coast of the mainland. In 1834 he heard that the Henty brothers, who had not been able to make a living in the Swan River colony, had settled at Portland. Batman decided to go and look for himself. That was how he came to meet the Aboriginal women of Port Phillip. By then he had seen enough. Port Phillip had land 'as good as land could be'.

John Batman had a plan. He would not simply take the land from the Aborigines. He would 'buy' it from them. He drew up a contract with their leaders. He would get nearly a quarter of a million hectares. The Aborigines would get nearly 100 pairs of blankets, 100 knives, 100 tomahawks, 50 suits of clothing, 50 looking glasses and 50 pairs of scissors. The contract was a fraud.

When John Batman reached Launceston again he rushed into his favourite hotel and shouted, 'I am the

What respectable women were wearing in the 1840s.

greatest landowner in the world.'

The owner of the hotel was John Fawkner. Like Batman he was the son of a convict. And like Batman he wanted land at Port Phillip. He sailed across Bass Strait and took up a large run on the Maribyrnong River. No one took much notice of Batman's contract.

Port Phillip grew. In 1836 the government sent down a superintendent, a regiment and a party of convicts. Overlanders came down with their cattle and sheep on to the plains of the western district and Gippsland. The wool and the meat they grew rolled into the ports of Melbourne and Geelong.

Gentlemen and ladies came to Port Phillip, as well as wild characters from Van Diemen's Land. The gentlemen set up clubs, raced their horses, went hunting, and fought duels with each other. The ladies liked to go boating on the Yarra River and take tea in the newly planted gardens.

Men like John Fawkner improved conditions in Melbourne. He started newspapers and encouraged people to be public spirited. Hotels, shops, banks, wharves and warehouses appeared in Melbourne. In the country the squatters started to build mansions. By 1851 Port Phillip was big enough to be made a separate colony.

The Aboriginal people of Port Phillip had been all but wiped out. Those who survived the white man's invasion of their land were put on to missions run by the churches. John Batman had gone too. He died just four years after he had declared himself the world's greatest landowner.

The post office at Port Phillip a few years after Batman landed. It took four months or more for letters to reach Britain where few could have imagined a scene like this.

THE MASSACRE AT MYALL CREEK

Some settlers thought the Australian Aborigines were barely human. That was what newspapers in nineteenth century Australia and Britain often said. It was believed they were the lowest race on Earth and bound to die out in the end.

Yet other Europeans decided that the Aboriginal people were the finest-looking human beings they had ever seen. If they worked with them, they noticed how quickly Aborigines learnt new skills, how easily they mastered the new language, and how much they could depend on them.

White people got their ideas from a lot of different places. A Christian might believe that all people were equal in the eyes of God. But some believed other things as well. Some Christians argued that the Bible said all people must plough the land and grow crops. The Aborigines did not seem to be doing that. So white settlers argued that they had no right to the land.

Each Aboriginal tribe believed that spirits lived in their land. To be driven away from it not only cut them off from their supply of food, it cut them off from the spiritual life they had always had.

The Aborigines of Myall Creek are led away to be slaughtered — as an artist pictured it.

When the white people came Aborigines had a choice. They could fight them and try to keep their land. Or they could work for the whites and live off the handouts they were given.

If they lived off the whites' handouts, things usually went wrong. They were not used to living in one place or wearing heavy European clothes and blankets. A constant diet of flour and sugar weakened their resistance to illness. They died from European diseases. The European drug, alcohol, killed them too.

If they decided to stay in their own country and fight, Aboriginal people were frequently hunted down and shot. The white settlers valued their sheep and cattle more highly. If sheep and cattle were killed or stolen the blacks were made to pay with their lives.

In some places white men decided that the best way to settle the country was to kill every Aboriginal inhabitant.

At Myall Creek in New South Wales in 1838 a group of white men decided on this course. They rounded up twenty-eight Aboriginal men, women and children, roped them together and killed them with swords and guns. Then they burnt the bodies.

The story of the massacre spread to Sydney and the governor, Sir George Gipps, heard of it. The

Aboriginal tribes had no 'chiefs' or 'kings'. White settlers thought they should, and presented brass breast-plates to certain Aborigines.

Aboriginal people were British subjects under his care. It was his duty to punish the murderers. He tracked the men down and had them arrested.

At the trial the murderers said that they did not know it was a crime to kill Aborigines. They said most white people believed that the blacks could be shot like animals. But Gipps was determined to teach the settlers that killing any person, black or white, was murder. The murderers of Myall Creek were hanged.

But the killings went on. The only difference was that now the whites kept it secret. There were stories of Aboriginal groups being given poisoned flour and meat. They were driven into waterholes and shot, cornered on cliffs and forced into the sea. The whites recruited other Aborigines to a Native Police force which was used to track down and capture or kill Aboriginal people.

Those who were not destroyed in the war with the settlers were eventually brought into missions in an attempt to convert them to Christianity. Often Aboriginal children were taken from their parents to be raised and educated by whites. The whites thought it was the only way to save them.

It did not seem to matter much whether a white settler thought the Aborigines good or bad. So long as they stood between him and success he would destroy them. Take Henry Meyrick for example. A squatter himself, Meyrick wrote in the 1840s that he was sickened by what other squatters were doing to the Aborigines. It was one of the darkest pages in human history he said. But the same Henry Meyrick said he had no doubt that if he caught an Aboriginal stealing one of his sheep he would shoot him down like a dog.

Aborigines could not win in a pitched battle like this against European guns and horses. They were more successful when they made surprise attacks on isolated white settlers, or on their sheep and cattle.

A LARGE AND RESPECTABLE COUNTRY TOWN

The towns of inland Australia grew to meet the needs of people who travelled the roads or worked on the runs. Towns often began as no more than inns – roadside stops for drovers and shearers, gathering places for stockmen and shepherds.

Towns grew when people realized that there was money to be made from supplying things people in the district needed. The town became a storehouse for the district and the place for the police station and court.

The first white men explored the Goulburn plains in 1818, but it was another decade before the place was settled. A road was made by convicts who spent their days and nights shackled together in an iron gang. They were building a road to their own gaol, for that was the first building erected at Goulburn.

In 1836 a missionary called James Backhouse came to the little settlement on the Wollondilly River. He saw 'a courthouse of slabs, covered with bark, a lock-up house, a few huts occupied by the mounted police and constables, a cottage of roughly cut timber, and a small inn.'

Mr Backhouse was not very impressed. Goulburn was a brutal and immoral town, he said.

There was a gibbet for hanging people and triangles for flogging them in Goulburn. 'Black Francis' was the most hated man in the district. It was his job to ride from farm to farm with the local magistrate and flog any convicts who had misbehaved. Some convicts ambushed 'Black Francis' one day, and killed him.

There were bushrangers in the hills for several years. Jack Donohue – 'Bold Jack Donohue' – was one of them. Most bushrangers were escaped convicts. It took a regiment of mounted police to defeat them. The last bushranger was a man named Whitton. He was sentenced to death in a Sydney court and taken down to Goulburn in a cart. The hangman travelled with him.

No one knows how many Aboriginal people were

living in the Goulburn area. In 1834 a traveller noticed that they had old pock marks on their faces. This probably meant that many had died in an epidemic which spread through the inland tribes soon after the first settlement at Sydney Cove.

No doubt others were killed by whites in the struggle for the land. But disease probably killed more, especially an epidemic of influenza in 1846. Missionaries arrived and tried to save them, but there were only a couple of dozen Aborigines left in Goulburn by 1850.

Droughts came and many settlers moved on to new pastures. Floods washed away soil and stock and cut the settlers off for weeks. The price of meat and wool fell – so the settlers killed their stock, boiled them up in huge vats, and sold the fat to English soapmakers.

Despite the hardships, the people of Goulburn built a large and respectable town. Caroline Chisholm helped more than anybody else.

An old settler remembered meeting her once at five o'clock in the morning on the Goulburn Road.

> Mrs Chisholm herself, wrapped in a loose cloak, was seated on the top of a dray, laden with casks and bales of goods, provisions for a settler at Goulburn. Beside her and around her were seated twelve or fourteen young girls. Alongside the dray walked about thirty others . . .

Mrs Chisholm was taking the girls to good families in the district.

New industries started in Goulburn. By 1843 there were four churches. Overlanders came through with their sheep and cattle and spent their money in the pubs and shops.

Even the Governor and his wife made a splendid visit in 1842. The gentlemen of the town rode out to meet them – the magistrates, the ministers and the squatters. The gentlemen escorted the couple back to town and introduced them to their wives.

That afternoon the ladies and gentlemen of Goulburn had a lavish lunch with their visitors and no doubt congratulated themselves on their fine country town.

SOUTH AUSTRALIA WOULD BE BETTER

In 1826 people in New South Wales were wondering if it would ever rain again. The land in many places turned to dust. Governor Darling decided to encourage exploration deeper inland, in the hope that good land and water would be found.

The settlement at Port Jackson was nearly forty years old but the interior of Australia was still a mystery. No one knew where the rivers ran – to the coast or to some inland sea?

In 1828 Darling sent Captain Charles Sturt out into the western plains of New South Wales to try to find the answer. On his first expedition Sturt came across a large river flowing south which he named the Darling. But he returned without discovering where the Darling went, and the land he travelled through had been dry and parched by drought.

In November the following year Sturt and a party of fourteen travelled down the Murrumbidgee to its junction with the Murray. Sturt did not know that this great river was the same one crossed by Hume and Hovell on the way to Port Phillip in 1824.

Sturt's party had a whaleboat. By day they rowed downstream and camped at night on the river banks. On 23 January they came to the junction of the Murray and the Darling – so one riddle had been solved.

It is unlikely that any white men had ever been in this country before. The numerous groups of Aborigines along the banks of the Murray had almost certainly never seen white faces. But the white men's diseases, smallpox and syphilis, had reached them. Sturt noticed the effects on many of the Aborigines.

Three months after they had left Sydney, Sturt's party rowed into a beautiful lake which they named Alexandrina. Across a headland they could see waves breaking. They had reached the mouth of the Murray. The mystery of the rivers had been solved.

Sturt and his men were short of food and tired. It took an almost superhuman effort to row sixteen hundred kilometres back against the current. They were ill, exhausted and half-starved when they finally reached safety fifty-six days later.

The land at the mouth of the Murray had been a disappointment. It was a sandy waste, and there was little prospect of establishing a great harbour there. But to the west of the Murray Sturt saw hills and inviting country.

In England Sturt's observations were read by Edward Gibbon Wakefield who had long been

Aboriginal people watch as Captain Charles Sturt discovers that the Darling River flows into the Murray.

Finding water was always a problem in inland Australia. Not all overlanders were as skilled as these.

interested in starting a colony along completely new lines. Apart from Sturt's report nothing else was known about southern Australia except what could be learnt from the writings of Matthew Flinders and Nicolas Baudin who had charted the coast thirty years before. But Wakefield and his friends thought they knew enough to plan a model colony.

The founders of South Australia were dissatisfied with society in England which they said was undemocratic, cruel and unjust. The other colonies in Australia, they believed, were either corrupted by the convict system or had been badly planned. South Australia would be better.

The founders had in mind an orderly, religious-minded colony where hard-working farmers would earn a good living for their families and their children would receive a proper education. There would be no convicts in South Australia.

But without convicts who would do the work? Those people who could not afford to buy land, said Wakefield. In South Australia land would be sold, not given away. Poorer people would have to work for wages until they had earnt enough to buy their own farms.

The first migrants arrived in 1836, and in the next three or four years thousands more arrived. Colonel Light, the government surveyor, laid out the town at the foot of the Mt Lofty Ranges, and it was named Adelaide, after the Queen.

The colony was not at all orderly in these early years. Rather it was a shambles. The land was poor and the new migrants struggled to feed themselves. They began to move inland looking for places to farm.

While the founders of South Australia wanted to build a free and just society, they also wanted to make money. Some of them bought up land and sold it to new immigrants at a great profit. Life was very hard for those early settlers. For a while it seemed as if the whole colony would fail.

Mining saved South Australia from collapse. In 1845 copper was discovered at Burra Burra and within five years £750,000 worth was extracted. Cattle overlanded from New South Wales were used to haul the copper ore to port. In the valleys to the north of Adelaide German migrants planted vines and made wine. Good land in the south was opened up for wheat and sheep.

South Australia was never the perfect place Wakefield hoped it would be. The men who established it were too greedy for that. But it continued to grow. A beautiful city was laid out. It became the leading agricultural colony – the granary of Australia. And because there had been no convicts in the early days, the people of South Australia went on believing that they were just a little bit better than those from the other colonies.

TASMANIANS AT WAR

A few weeks after the first white people settled in Van Diemen's Land a group of Tasmanian Aborigines was fired on and several were killed. It was a taste of things to come. The white man who gave the order to fire said he thought the Aborigines were going to attack. Other observers of the incident said they had come in peace.

In the early years of the settlements at Hobart and Launceston, supplies were so short that the governors allowed the convicts to roam in the bush looking for food. They were instructed not to kill or mistreat the Aboriginal peoples. However killing and mistreatment were common from the start.

Stories came back to the settlement about convicts killing Aboriginal men and stealing Aboriginal women. The Tasmanian Aborigines fought back.

By the time Governor Arthur arrived in Van Diemen's Land, free people had begun to migrate there. They came in search of land on which to run their sheep. But in the 1820s it was not safe to farm in much of the colony. Some isolated farm houses had iron screens that could be pulled over the windows in time of attack. Murderous bushrangers roamed the hills – and murderous Aborigines.

The battle between the Aboriginal Tasmanians and the whites was over the good land in Tasmania's interior. It belonged to the Aboriginal people. The Europeans needed it to graze sheep. The Aborigines needed it to survive. It grew the vegetable food they gathered and fed the game they hunted.

Governor Arthur offered five pounds for every Aboriginal adult captured and three pounds for every child. White bushmen went out to round them up. Some were caught and some who resisted were killed.

The Europeans became more and more determined to rid themselves of the Aboriginal threat. Governor Arthur also wanted a solution, but without further bloodshed. The Aboriginal people had been killed, captured and afflicted with European diseases. There had been about three thousand Aborigines in Tasmania at the time the Europeans arrived. Thirty years later there were only about four hundred left.

For the white settlers, and the governor who was supposed to protect them, the remaining four hundred Aborigines were a grave problem. They continued to attack the settlers, raiding their homesteads and killing their stock.

White settlers under siege from Aborigines during the war over the land.

The missionary George Augustus Robinson, with the young Trugannini on his left, encouraging Tasmanian Aborigines to leave their homelands and come to Flinders Island.

Arthur tried a new tactic. Hundreds of armed men were recruited to drive the Aboriginal people into a corner of Van Diemen's Land. The men lined up and marched through the island.

The operation became known as the Black Line. It cost £30,000 – the men had to be paid and supplied with food, clothing and guns. But at the end of it all only one Aborigine – a boy – had been caught. All the rest had slipped through the Line.

A missionary, George Augustus Robinson, then offered to round up the blacks. With Aboriginal assistance he walked all over the island persuading the Tasmanian people still living in the bush to come with him. Robinson planned to take them to Flinders Island in Bass Strait. There he would teach them how to farm and to pray to God.

On Flinders Island the Tasmanian Aborigines were treated like children. They longed for their own country. Some of them left. A great many died. Robinson could not understand what was going wrong. The settlement was eventually abandoned. Only a graveyard and a chapel remained.

Trugannini was said to be the last of the Tasmanian Aborigines. As a young girl she had been captured by sawyers and brutally treated. Her mother, her sister and the young man to whom she was to be married were all killed by white men.

Trugannini and her husband, Wooraddy, helped Robinson round up their people and for a while they lived on Flinders Island. But Trugannini, who had once thought that Robinson's plan was the best hope for her people, changed her mind. She criticized Robinson and left Flinders Island. In Port Phillip she joined other Aborigines in raids on settlers huts.

Trugannini died in 1876. She had seen her people almost completely wiped out. As she was said to be the last of the Tasmanian Aborigines, some white people wanted to preserve what they could of her body.

Trugannini knew what had been the fate of the bodies of other Aboriginal people. Scientists had taken the bones, even the skin. Before she died she pleaded that her body be left in peace. But her skeleton was hung up in the Tasmanian museum.

Australians have been told that Trugannini was the last of her race. But descendants of Aboriginal Tasmanians still live in Tasmania and on Cape Barren Island, near Flinders Island, in Bass Strait.

CAROLINE CHISHOLM

Caroline Chisholm was born in England in 1808. When she was twenty-two she married a Scotsman, a captain in the British army. Captain Chisholm was a Catholic and Caroline became a Catholic too.

The couple agreed that their marriage would not stop Caroline doing the good works she planned to do. Caroline wanted to serve God.

In 1838 the Chisholms came to New South Wales. Many of the poor migrants then flocking into Sydney were young women who had neither a job nor a home to go to in the colony. Caroline was anxious to find good homes for them.

Caroline Chisholm

Caroline became convinced that Australia and England would both benefit from a sensible and humane emigration scheme. In Australia there was still a far greater number of men than women. In many country areas, particulary, there were virtually no women.

In England the plight of destitute young women was a major social problem. Caroline Chisholm decided that by carefully supervising the emigration of young English women and good hard-working English families both societies would be improved.

Colonial gentleman looking for wives and servants among newly arrived female migrants.

Caroline believed that the best influences on colonial life were marriage and families. She hoped to see the inland of Australia made productive by the work of Christian families.

Caroline Chisholm persuaded the governor of New South Wales to set up a home for female migrants in Sydney as a half-way house for newly arrived young women. She worked in New South Wales for several years, spending a good deal of her time riding about the countryside on her white horse, Captain. The other Captain in her life, Captain Chisholm, had gone to fight in India.

Caroline's work for the migrants became famous. She went back to England to encourage more people – poor people – to emigrate to Australia. She did much to have conditions on the migrant ships improved.

Men wrote poems about Caroline. Her portrait was painted. A migrant ship was named *Caroline Chisholm*. Caroline Chisholm was famous. She and her husband remained poor all their lives. Neither was much interested in money except what they raised to help others.

In 1854 the Chisholms returned to Australia and stayed there, mainly in Victoria, for twelve more years. They both died in England in 1877.

1850-1869

1850 Port Phillip, Van Diemen's Land, Western Australia and South Australia become separate colonies. Port Phillip to be called Victoria.

1851 Gold discovered at Bathurst, New South Wales in May and in August at Ballarat, Victoria. Rushes begin.
Black Thursday bushfires devastate Victoria.

1852 Gundagai, New South Wales, swept away in a flood — seventy-seven die.

1853 Queen Victoria uses chloroform as an anaesthetic for the birth of her seventh child. In future it will be used generally for surgery.
Transportation to Van Diemen's Land ends.

1854 First steam train runs in Australia.
Britain at war with Russia. War scare in Australia, volunteer armies formed.
Eureka Stockade.
Van Diemen's Land to elect parliament. From now on called Tasmania.

1855 New South Wales, Victoria, South Australia and Tasmania to elect parliaments. Women not to vote.

1856 Queensland to be a separate colony.
Workers in building industry win eight hour day.

1858 First Australian Rules Football match played.
A.C. Gregory explores northern Australia.

1859 Thomas Austin of Geelong imports twenty-four rabbits to Australia. Plague begins.
Queensland to elect parliament. Women not to vote.
Charles Jardine Don first workingman elected to parliament in Victoria.
In England, Charles Darwin publishes **On the Origin of Species** showing that life on earth is much older than previously believed.

1861-5 Civil war in America.

1861 First Selection Acts in New South Wales attempting to put small farmers on the land.
English cricket team visits Australia.
Burke and Wills die at Cooper Creek.
Chinese attacked at Lambing Flat, New South Wales.
T. S. Mort in New South Wales builds first machine refrigerator.

1862 John McDouall Stuart reaches Arafura Sea, Northern Territory and returns to Adelaide. Expedition provides route for overland telegraph.

1863 First South Pacific Islanders brought to Queensland sugarcane fields.
John Sutherland and other squatters move sheep and cattle into northern Australia.

1865 Joseph Lister in England carries out germ free surgery using carbolic acid as an antiseptic.
Carpet sweeper invented.

1866 Swedish scientist, Alfred Noble invents dynamite.

1867 Gold rush to Gympie, Queensland.

1869 Suez Canal opened: will dramatically reduce sailing time from Europe to Australia.
Another expedition searching in the desert for Leichhardt.

Tar boy, employed to dab tar on sheep accidentally cut by shearers' blades.

GOLD FEVER

A clergyman who had been out preaching to the people on the sheep runs once showed the governor of New South Wales some gold he had found. 'Put it away,' said the governor, 'or we shall all have our throats cut.' This was about 1840.

New South Wales was still a penal colony. The governors wanted to keep order, particularly amongst the convicts. They imagined crime and chaos if there was a gold rush. So whenever reports of gold came in – and there were plenty of them – the governors hushed them up.

Despite the protests of squatters who wanted cheap workers, convicts were no longer sent out to New South Wales after the 1840s. Meanwhile, the settlers of Western Australia were so desperate for labour they begged the British government to send them convicts. So the convict system began in the Swan River colony as it was ending in New South Wales.

Opponents of the convict system claimed that it was brutal and degrading. They eventually convinced the British government that so long as convicts continued to arrive the colony would remain a 'moral dunghill', and large numbers of free people in Britain would be unwilling to migrate.

By the end of the 1840s the government had decided that a gold rush was worth the risk. Any problems would be outweighed by the wealth gold would bring to Britain and her colonies. A reward was offered for the discovery of gold in 'payable' quantities.

Edmund Hargraves had just come back from the goldfields of California. There he had learnt where to look for gold and how to mine it in various ways.

Near Bathurst Hargraves panned a few specks of gold from a creek and took the sample back to Sydney to show the governor. It was hardly sufficient to be considered 'payable', but Hargraves convinced enough people to start a rush, and collected the £10,000 reward.

People seemed to lose their senses. Thousands dropped whatever they were doing and trudged off to

the diggings to get rich. In the towns, men abandoned their jobs and businesses – and often wives and children. Sailors deserted their ships. On the sheep runs, shepherds and stockmen deserted their masters.

A few months after the New South Wales rush began, Port Phillip became the separate colony of Victoria. Thousands of people from Port Phillip had packed up and gone to the New South Wales fields at first. But the rush north soon halted when gold was discovered at Buninyong, Ballarat, Bendigo and Mt Alexander in Victoria.

Appalled,the governor of Victoria wrote off to London about what had happened in the new colony.

> Within the last three weeks the towns of Melbourne and Geelong . . . have been in appearance almost emptied of their male inhabitants . . . Cottages are deserted, houses to let, business is at a standstill, and even schools are closed.

People came to the colonies from all over the world. They came from Britain, America, Germany, Poland, Italy and China. There were rich and poor. There were many among them who had never done a day's hard work in their lives.

The aim was to get to a new field as quickly as possible, and stake a claim. The new diggers bought food, blankets, tents, guns, pots and pans and picks and shovels and began the long walk to the fields.

In summer the new roads were dustbowls. In winter horses and bullocks and people sank deep into the mud and the bush rang with the cracking of whips and the shouts and curses of men. The skeletons of animals lay on the roads whitening in the sun.

Gold was like a lottery – the chance for a poor man to become rich. With luck anyone could do it. Or so it seemed.

AT THE DIGGINGS

When a digger found a likely-looking site he bought himself a legal claim to it, and started work.

On new fields it was usually possible to get surface gold. A few extremely lucky diggers found large nuggets close to or even on the surface and made a small fortune from them. But the great majority had to work much harder than this.

Panning and cradling were the two main ways of getting surface or alluvial gold. The aim was to wash away the earth and gravel and leave the gold, a much heavier substance, in the bottom of the pan or wooden cradle. Panning was a one-man job. Cradling took two to four.

Gold also lay in seams under the ground. To get at it a shaft was dug and lined with timber. Then a winch was installed to raise the dirt. While one miner went down and dug, another stayed on top and wound up bucketfuls of earth.

Working in deep shafts required strength and patience. It also needed courage because the work could be very dangerous. Miners were often seriously injured. People who were new to the life suffered all sorts of aches and pains and blisters until they got fit.

The diggers lived in tents and huts and slept on the rocky ground. Soon the goldfields were almost stripped of trees. The wood was used to line the sides of shafts, to make cradles, huts and furniture, and for cooking and for warmth on cold nights.

At times it was impossible to keep dry. Tents and huts leaked and the shafts filled with water. Illnesses such as pneumonia were very common on the goldfields because diggers might work and sleep in wet clothes for days on end.

The miners did not know much about hygiene. Little care was taken to see that streams were kept clean for drinking water. Once they became polluted, the gold fields were hit by epidemics of typhoid. Goldfield cemeteries today contain many graves of typhoid victims.

A street in Gulgong, a gold town in New South Wales.

A pan and a cradle for washing.

At first life on the goldfields was thought to be too hard for women. But more and more women arrived as time went on. They worked with their husbands, and raised families in the tiny shacks with makeshift furniture. Some ran pubs and stores for the diggers.

Gold could usually be sold to buyers on the fields. Some men carefully saved their earnings in the hope that one day they would have enough to buy a house or land. Or they wanted to return to their families overseas with their fortunes made.

Others spent their money in the pubs and sly grog

Quartz-crushing machines like this one were introduced when alluvial gold ran out. Diggers who could not afford a crusher used hammers.

shops on the fields, or went to the city from time to time and splashed it all on booze and fancy clothes.

Clergymen came to the goldfields and preached to the diggers in the open air. Storekeepers, blacksmiths, tinsmiths, doctors, chemists all made good livings. There was usually much more money to be made from selling goods to the diggers, pulling out their rotten teeth, setting broken limbs, and making ointments for their aching backs, than there was from digging for gold.

Large permanent towns grew out of some of the rich fields. Other places grew quickly and then, when the gold ran out, faded away into ghost towns.

There are deserted places in the Australian bush where once ten thousand or more people lived in tents and huts. No buildings remain. But the signs of their high hopes and hard work are there in the half-filled shafts and mounds of gravel and dirt.

THE EUREKA STOCKADE

During the first few years of the gold rush every digger had to pay a license fee of thirty shillings a month. This was more than many diggers would earn in a month. The government hoped that a large fee would encourage people to stay in their jobs.

But people went to the fields just the same. Thousands more arrived every month from overseas. Those diggers who found a lot of gold did not mind the fee too much. But others objected to the monthly visits of soldiers and mounted police who collected the money – often at the point of a bayonet.

The miners came to hate the license hunters who were known as 'Traps'. Word that they were coming was passed through the fields. When miners without licenses heard the cry 'Trap!' they hid themselves.

But it was not easy to escape the license hunts. In Victoria in 1854 the governor had more than one thousand troops visiting the fields twice a week.

There were ten thousand men digging at Ballarat in 1854. Gold was becoming harder to find. Many of the diggers were desperately poor.

There were men at Ballarat who said that they had come to Australia because they thought they would find more freedom here than in their own countries. Instead, they said, the colony was run by tyrants. Why should they pay a license fee when they had no say in the government? Some of the miners spoke of having a revolution like America had had.

Meetings of thousands of diggers were organized. There were people from Ireland, England, Germany, Italy and America. The diggers declared that they wanted the license fee abolished and the right to vote at elections. They wanted democracy.

At a meeting on Bakery Hill near Ballarat in 1854, ten thousand miners met under a new flag. The men who raised it believed that it should be Australia's flag. 'There is no flag in Europe, or in the civilized world half so beautiful,' one said.

Under the flag the men burnt their licenses to show the governor that from now on they would defy the law. But the Governor, Sir Charles Hotham, was determined to defeat the miners. On the morning after the licenses were burnt, mounted soldiers charged a gathering of diggers injuring several.

'There is no flag half so beautiful.'

That afternoon the diggers met again on Bakery Hill. Peter Lalor, an Irishman, wrote later:

> I looked around me; I saw brave and honest men, who had come thousands of miles to labour for independence. The grievances under which we had long suffered, and the brutal attack of that day, flashed across my mind; and with the burning feelings of an injured man, I mounted the stump and proclaimed 'Liberty'.

The stockade was reconstructed for the telemovie **Eureka Stockade**. To make their stockade as much like the real one as possible the film-makers read accounts written by people who were there in 1854.

Peter Lalor, the miners' leader.

With Lalor as their leader the men armed themselves with guns and pikes, as the convicts had done at Castle Hill fifty years earlier. They marched to the Eureka field and built a stockade. They swore to defend the stockade against any attack.

There were only about 150 men at the stockade at dawn on Sunday, 4 December 1854. A lot of them were asleep when about three hundred soldiers charged. Ten minutes later about thirty miners and six soldiers lay dead or dying. The soldiers rounded up the surviving diggers who had not fled and marched them off to gaol. And they tore down the Southern Cross.

Peter Lalor was wounded in the battle but managed to escape. That night he hid in the house of a priest and his wounded arm was amputated.

The miners at Eureka had lost the battle but most people in Victoria were on their side. The newspapers condemned the soldiers' brutality and said the governor should not have ordered the attack. The miners who had been arrested and charged with high treason were found not guilty. Outside the courts crowds gathered and cheered when the verdicts were announced.

A new government was elected in 1855. The license fee was abolished. In future miners would pay just one pound a year for a 'miner's right' – the right to dig for gold and the right to vote.

FOREIGN DEVILS

Fishing on the shores of Port Phillip Bay.

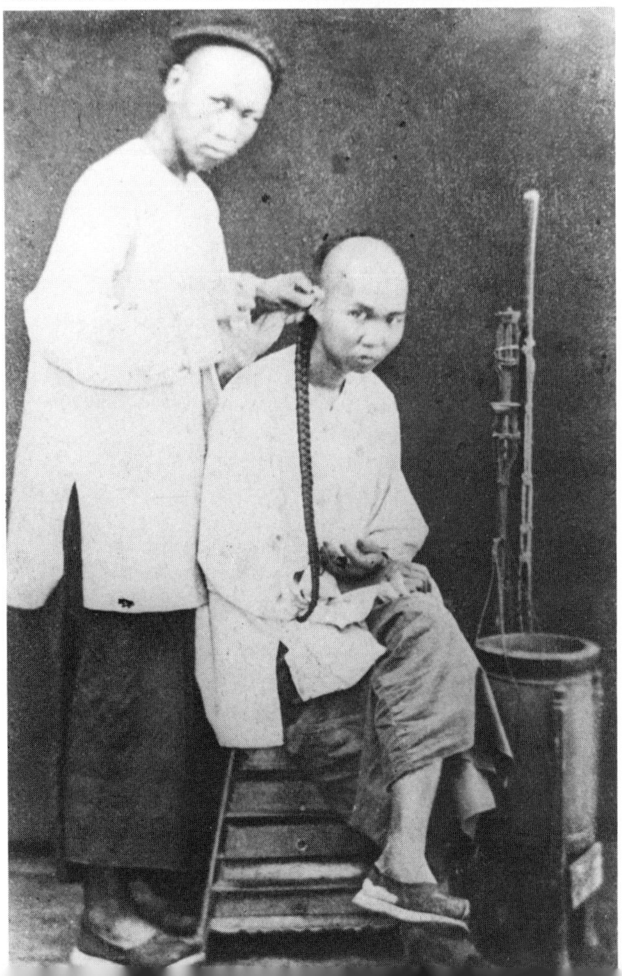

There were about two thousand Chinese people in Australia when the gold rush started. They had been brought out by squatters to work on their runs as shepherds and labourers. Others worked as cooks and household servants.

Thousands more Chinese came when news of the gold discoveries reached them. On the south coast of China people talked about Australia as *Hsin Chin Shan*, meaning the 'new gold mountain'.

A lot of Chinese who sailed for Australia never saw the goldfields. Conditions on the ships from the Chinese ports were as bad as any convict ship. Hundreds died on the voyage. White settlers in the colonies were faintly amused by the Chinese migrants. They joked about the pigtails they wore. The Chinese all seemed to dress in the same blue jumpers and trousers, shoes made of silk with wooden soles, and wide brimmed straw hats. Their belongings were carried in baskets at either end of a long pole which they supported on their shoulders.

The hats were good for keeping off the hot Australian sun. And a Chinese man could travel faster on foot

A Chinese barber shop.

with everything he needed in his baskets than most Europeans could with their wagons and drays.

The Chinese worked very hard on the goldfields. They worked together in teams. As a rule they did not sink deep shafts. They worked over the surface soil and gravel for alluvial gold. Often they found profitable amounts of gold in the gravel heaps and streams which European miners had abandoned.

The Chinese tried to live in Australia as they had at home. In the cities and the goldfield towns they built little temples called joss houses. Inside there was an altar and wooden statues of their gods. The air was always full with the smell of incense. The Chinese came to the joss houses with presents of food and wine for their gods, and to have their fortunes told on fortune cards. A very large Chinese camp was established at Guildford in Victoria. At one time there were more than five thousand Chinese there, all of them working over an abandoned mine which the European miners had given up. There was a joss house, a fan tan parlour, Chinese cobblers and tailors, Chinese doctors, Chinese book and art shops.

At first the Europeans did not mind the Chinese coming. But as the gold ran out they started to resent them – particularly as they seemed to be able to find gold where Europeans could not. The Europeans began to say that the colonies of Australia should only be open to other Europeans.

The Chinese harmed no one but now they were described as a threat to British civilization in Australia. It was said that they were opium smokers. A lot of Chinese did smoke opium, but it caused much less havoc than the alcohol Europeans drank. They were portrayed as dirty and disease-ridden. Newspapers had pictures of Chinese men looking like hideous fiends. Readers were told that they made a habit of stealing European women. Most people believed what they were told.

In Victoria a special tax was put on the Chinese. They were made to pay a fee when they arrived in the hope that this would stop them coming. But the Chinese dodged the tax. They landed in Robe, in South Australia, where there was no tax. Then they walked to the Victorian goldfields.

In some places the Europeans attacked the Chinese and beat them viciously. The tents of the Chinese were pulled down and burnt. Some Chinese were killed. The worst attack was at Lambing Flat in New South Wales in 1861.

The Chinese were generally law-abiding, hard working and sober. Like many Europeans who came to Australia in the goldrush, they hoped to make enough money to be able to return home and keep their families in comfort. But when times got hard on the goldfields people looked for someone to blame. The Chinese were singled out.

Hatred for the Chinese became a way of thinking in Australia. Eventually all the colonies passed laws to keep them out.

A Joss House.

The hatred European diggers came to feel for the Chinese turned to murder at Lambing Flat, New South Wales.

BURKE AND WILLS AND THE DIG TREE

The heroes depart — with supplies for two years.

Still no one knew what lay in the centre of Australia. Charles Sturt had gone deep into the desert north of Adelaide in 1844. He and his men dragged a boat with them. They hoped to find an inland sea, but all they found was desert. And the desert drove them back to Adelaide, exhausted.

Four years after Sturt, a German, Ludwig Leichhardt set out from western Queensland to cross the continent to Perth. He took herds of bullocks and sheep to eat on the way. But Leichhardt and his party vanished without a trace.

In 1860 Victoria and South Australia decided to send separate expeditions across the continent from south to north. The governor of Victoria called it 'a glorious race'.

The South Australian expedition was led by a Scotsman called John McDouall Stuart. An Irish policeman, Robert O'Hara Burke was the leader of the Victorian expedition. His second-in-command was to be twenty-six year old, William John Wills.

Great crowds gathered to farewell Burke and Wills when they left Melbourne on 20 August 1860. The party was very well-equipped. Enough food for two years had been packed on horse-drawn wagons and the backs of camels. Revolvers, rifles and shotguns, eighty pairs of boots and thirty cabbage tree hats were taken. There were gallons of lime juice for the men and rum for the camels, fishing lines and six tonnes of firewood, packets of seeds to plant. They also took 120 mirrors and a kilogram of beads to give the Aborigines they were sure to meet.

The expedition moved very slowly. By the time they reached Menindee, Burke had grown impatient. He decided to divide the party.

He, Wills, John King and Charley Gray pushed on to Cooper Creek with six camels, a horse and provisions for three months. The rest of the party, led by William Wright was to follow as soon as possible, with the additional supplies.

From a base at Cooper Creek Burke's party set out for the Gulf of Carpentaria. It could not have been a better season. Heavy rains had fallen and the desert was in bloom.

As they travelled further north, 'the country improved at every step . . . everything was green and luxuriant,' Wills said in his diary.

But they reached the Gulf in the wet season. The camels became bogged in the mud and the swamps. It was almost unbearably hot. When they finally saw the sea, on 11 February 1861, they had already eaten two thirds of their rations. And the men and the animals were desperately tired.

William Brahe had been left at Cooper Creek with some other men. Wright was to join him from Menindee and wait for Burke and Wills to return. After four months neither Wright, nor Burke and Wills, had arrived. Brahe and his men were running out of food.

Convinced that Burke and Wills were not going to return, Brahe set off for Menindee. It was a hard decision to make. Brahe was well aware how disastrous it would be if the explorers did survive only to find the Cooper Creek camp deserted. To be on the safe side he buried some food under a tree. He also buried a note telling Burke where he had gone. Into the tree's trunk he cut the word DIG.

Three of the explorers did survive the journey back from the Gulf. Gray died from hunger and exhaustion on the way. The others struggled into the camp at Cooper Creek just a few hours after Brahe had left.

What were they to do? They did not have the strength to catch up with Brahe, Burke thought. And they would never make it to Menindee without help. Burke decided to head for a settlement at Mt Hopeless 150 miles down the creek. It was a fatal decision.

Before leaving the camp Burke wrote a note saying where they were going and what time they had left. But he buried it under the tree marked DIG which did not make it obvious that they had been there.

On the way back to Menindee Brahe met Wright, who was at last on his way to Cooper Creek. The men returned to the camp. Just a few miles down the Creek, Burke, Wills and King were camping, half starved.

If Brahe had found Burke's note he could have saved them. But he saw no sign of Burke's return. All he saw was the DIG sign he himself had cut on the tree. So Brahe and Wright went back to Menindee.

A little way down from the camp at Cooper Creek Burke and Wills died from starvation and exhaustion. Only King survived. Unlike Burke who drove away Aborigines when they came with food, King went to live with them. The Aborigines were still looking after him when a rescue party arrived months after Burke and Wills had died.

The bones of Burke and Wills were brought back to Melbourne, the colony mourned the deaths of their brave heroes. In Adelaide they celebrated. John McDouall Stuart got through to the northern coast and returned half dead, but triumphant.

A. W. Howitt is shown the explorers' remains by King, the only survivor. The bodies were taken back to Melbourne for a lavish funeral.

AN 'AMUSEMENT OF MADMEN'

In winter in Sydney working men played the English game, rugby. In Melbourne a football game similar to one played in Ireland was invented to keep cricketers fit during winter. The game became known as Australian Rules Football.

The first game of Aussie Rules was played in 1858 between Scotch College and Melbourne Grammar School. There were forty players on each side. The first side to kick two goals was to be the winner. But when, after three days play neither side had managed to do this, the match was abandoned.

Football soon became the most popular game in Melbourne. Working men and women who were lucky enough to have Saturday afternoon off from work went along to barrack for their local team.

Melbourne and Carlton were the first two teams to play regularly. Melbourne were known as the 'Fuschias' and Carlton as the 'Blues'. They were great rivals and fighting amongst players and spectators was very common. The working class people of Carlton thought the 'Fuschias' were snobs. Both sides often thought that the umpire was a crook.

A visitor from overseas who went to see a match between the two sides came away thinking Australian Rules Football was the 'amusement of madmen'. 'Towards the end of the game one man fainted; several must be lame for weeks, and every man must be bleeding or scarred,' he reported. 'The crowd', he wrote, 'howled and shrieked and applauded' all this brutality. When the Melbourne players left the ground they were stoned by a group of Carlton larrikins. It was a 'disgrace to our civilization', the visitor said.

Cricket is a much gentler game. English immigrants thought it the best of all. So it was a great honour when in 1861 a cricket team came out from England. They were cheered as they rode from the Melbourne docks in a fine coach.

As soon as the English players had recovered from their voyage they played a Victorian side.

A new grandstand was built for the occasion. Tents and marquees were put up around the ground. One man brought a ladder which he hired out to people who wanted a good view of the match from trees.

Victoria fielded twenty-two players against England's eleven. But England still won. The

A gentle game.

The Flying Pieman performed great feats in the colonies. Once he beat the coach from Brisbane to Ipswich. On another occasion he wheeled a barrow 1½ km, took 50 flying leaps, picked up 50 stones 50 metres apart, ran backwards for 800 metres and carried a live goat for 2½ km, all in 12 minutes — or so it was said.

Australian Rules Football.

Melbourne newspapers said the Victorians would never beat the English until they learnt to stop the ball in the field.

Then the English played an Aboriginal team and beat them as well. After the cricket game the Aboriginal players gave a demonstration of their athletic abilities. One man ran one hundred yards backwards in only fourteen seconds.

A year or so later an Aboriginal team toured England and won as many matches as they lost. Between matches they gave exhibitions of boomerang throwing. One of them showed his skills with a shield. He invited the English team to throw as many cricket balls as they liked at him.

Horse racing was almost as popular as cricket and football. In every new settlement it was not long before squatters and stockmen organized a race meeting. The whole community took part. It was the day for a picnic, and the chance to have a bet.

In the colonies people gambled on just about anything. Betting is a simple way to get excited. Two bored people could bet on two ants crawling up a gum tree. In the cities and towns and shearing camps men gathered to gamble on two-up. Two pennies were all they needed.

Australians liked to bet on politics, boxing matches, football, cricket, cards, quoits, running and jumping, cow, camel and piggy-back races, who could shear the most sheep in a day, who could shoot the most kangaroos, who could drink the most beer or rum.

They also enjoyed picnics. The bush was never far away. City people liked to go to the country or the beach with their families, friends and workmates. Country people liked to take their lunch down to a shady gully. There were flies and ants and occasionally snakes, but it was good to be out in the open air.

Dancing an afternoon away in the bush.

A DREAM OF A SMALL FARM

The view from a squatter's homestead. His sheep grazed on the land as far as the eye could see.

When the gold rushes ended countless diggers who had failed to make their fortune on the fields demanded land. They imagined that with a small farm they would be able to make a secure living and raise healthy families. Being a farmer, they thought, meant being free – free of a boss, free of the city, free of the threat of unemployment.

All the good land in the colonies was held by squatters who had it on lease from the government. They were determined to keep it. They claimed the land should be theirs because they had taken the risks when they first settled it. They had worked hard at making the land productive and had grown to understand and love it. They would not let it go without a fight.

However, the majority of people in the colonies believed that the land should be opened up to those who wanted to be farmers. In the cities, business people who resented the power of the squatters, or believed that it was foolish and unjust to have so much of the country in the hands of so few people, supported the cry to 'unlock the lands'. Many politicians argued that people on small farms would be law-abiding and happy with things as they were. The churches also liked the idea – one clergyman said farmers were always 'nearer to God'.

Eventually the colonial governments passed acts which were intended to make it easy for people with little money to acquire small farms. Any man or woman who wanted a farm was free to go out into the country and select a small block. Payment of a deposit gave the selector the right to farm the land. The balance was to be paid within a few years.

The acts were largely a failure. The squatters had a variety of tricks to keep the best land. They used members of their families or employed people to buy up the good parts of their runs. They bribed politicians and land agents to sell the land to them.

In parts of South Australia, the Darling Downs in Queensland, northern Victoria and the Wimmera, many selectors eventually established prosperous farms. In these areas, the squatters largely lost the battle. But more often the Selection Acts only meant that the squatters became the owners of the great estates they had formerly leased.

When a selector did get a block of land he had to work terribly hard to survive. His selection had to be cleared. In some areas the farms were covered with dense scrub, in others mighty eucalypt forests had to be cut down. If there was no other water supply, dams had to be dug. The farms needed fences to keep cows in and kangaroos out. The land had to be ploughed. A house had to be built. It was all backbreaking, heartbreaking work.

It could take months to clear just an acre or two of ground and sow it with grass seed or maize. Then birds might take all the seed, or frost destroy the crop. Droughts drove many selectors off their farms. Sometimes they discovered that the land they had

Inside a bush hut.

selected was infertile and nothing would grow.

A single accident could mean the end of a selector's hopes. An injury to his horse, for instance, left him nothing with which to haul logs, pull out stumps, drag the iron scoop to make a dam or the plough to cultivate the land. There was rarely enough money to replace an animal.

An injury or illness in the family was equally serious. Much of the work was dangerous and accidents were common. Doctors were usually miles away, so many injuries and illnesses went untreated. As a result, simple injuries sometimes became crippling ones and illnesses like pneumonia and whooping cough were frequently fatal.

An illness in the family meant the loss of a worker. Everyone worked on a selection. Children helped milk the cows, gather firewood, chase pests away from crops and look after the farm animals. Both girls and boys did this sort of farm work. In addition girls had to learn to cook and sew and keep house.

Women were usually responsible for looking after the dairy and the pigs and poultry. It took several hours to milk the cows each night and morning. The family drank some of the milk, the pigs and calves drank the rest.

It was common for a selector's wife to have up to ten or twelve children. When no doctor was available women helped each other in childbirth. Selection families could only keep going by helping each other.

In ramshackle huts with dirt floors the selectors raised their families. Though many were forced to give up, in some places selectors managed to hang on and later generations benefited from their hard work. In Gippsland, Victoria, the Darling Downs in Queensland and other places farmers now live prosperously on land cleared by families of selectors more than a century ago.

The house is built, but it will be years before this farm in Tasmania will be producing enough for the family to live comfortably. Just as likely they will fail to make a living and return to the towns.

RAFFAELLO CARBONI

Raffaello Carboni was a soldier, a scholar and an Italian patriot. Born in 1820, like many young Italians of his day he resented the rule of France and Austria over much of his country. In the battle against the French at Rome in 1849 Carboni was wounded three times.

Raffaello left Italy and toured Europe for three years. In London in 1852 he read in the newspapers about the gold discoveries in Australia. He decided to try his luck.

On arrival in Melbourne Carboni went immediately to Ballarat and managed to make a living on the alluvial fields there until his gear was stolen. He left the goldfields and took a job as a shepherd for a while, then lived briefly with an Aboriginal tribe.

But Carboni could not resist the gold fever for long and returned to Ballarat where the miner's campaign against the licence fee had just begun.

The troops who collected the licence fees so brutally reminded Carboni of the Austrian and French troops in his own country. He decided to join the miners' struggle.

Raffaello Carboni.

Breakfast on the goldfields.

Peter Lalor appointed him organizer of the non-English speaking miners at the Eureka Stockade. Although Carboni was not there when the soldiers attacked he was charged with high treason. Like the others he was acquitted.

In 1855 he wrote a book about the Eureka Stockade and sold it to the diggers on the fields. It was a colourful and passionate account, and the only first-hand history we have of Australia's brief civil war.

The year after publication of *The Eureka Stockade*, Carboni returned to Italy. He wrote operas and plays, but sadly no one much liked his style and his works were never performed.

Raffaello Carboni died in Rome in 1875. Although largely unknown in his native land, as a result of his book, he is well-remembered in Australia.

1870-1889

1870-71 War between France and Prussia (Germany).

1872 Gold rush to Charters Towers, Queensland; rush to Palmer River the following year.
Ernest Giles treks from Alice Springs to West Australian coast and back again the next year.
Australia joined to London by telegraph cable.

1873 W.C. Gosse first white man to see Uluru (Ayers Rock).
Aborigines attack telegraph station at Barrow Creek, central Australia.
NSW Marriage Act allows women to keep control of their own money after they marry.

1874 John Forrest, later Premier of Western Australia, explores from Geraldton to Alice Springs.

1876 Bell invents telephone in America.
Ernest Giles' last expedition confirms central Australia is desert.
Truganinni dies.
Robert Bowyer Smith invents stump-jump plough in South Australia enabling cultivation of thousands of hectares of scrubland.

1877 Queen Victoria declared Empress of India.

1878 Electric street lighting in London.

1879 Frozen meat from Australia sold in London.

1880 First test cricket match played in England.
World Exhibition Melbourne.
Ned Kelly hanged.
A German, Karl Benz, drives the first petrol driven car.

1883 Julia Bella Guerin of University of Melbourne, first woman to graduate from an Australian university.
Sydney-Melbourne rail line opened.
Two thousand tailoresses strike for better conditions in Melbourne.

1884 Charles Rasp discovers silver at Broken Hill.
Women's Suffrage Movement formed, demanding right to vote.

1885 William Lane arrives in Australia.
Silver-lead mine opened at Zeehan, Tasmania.

1886 Spence forms Amalgamated Shearers Union. Twenty thousand shearers from Australia and New Zealand join in the next four years.
Gold and silver discovered at Mt Lyell, Tasmania.
Gold discovered in Kimberleys Western Australia, Mt Morgan, Queensland.

1888 Scotsman, J. B. Dunlop invents inflatable tyre.
Kodak 'box' family camera invented in America.
Louisa Lawson starts a newspaper called **The Dawn** which demands equal rights for women.
Brisbane-Sydney rail line opened.

1889 Trade Unions of Australia and New Zealand meet.

A young woman photographed in a Melbourne studio in about 1870. She came from an Aboriginal mission station.

A SUPPLY OF CHEAP LABOUR

The landowners of Australia well knew that the less they paid their workers the more they made for themselves. They needed a reliable supply of able-bodied people to work on their properties. At various times they employed convicts, Aborigines, Indians and Chinese, and paid them next to nothing.

In the 1840s, Benjamin Boyd, a squatter with huge runs in New South Wales, brought in South Sea Islanders and put them to work as shepherds. Unfortunately both for the Islanders and for Boyd, they hated the work. Aborigines attacked them and some were killed. Others died from illness. Many of them wandered away from Boyd's runs and tried to find their way home.

Pacific islanders on their way to a Queensland plantation. The man in the white jacket on the right is probably the 'blackbirder' — the man who recruited them.

Pacific Island women labour in the cane fields.

In 1863 the owner of a Queensland cotton plantation sent a ship to the Solomon Islands. The ship's captain told the Islanders and missionaries there that his master, the plantation owner, would pay ten shillings a month to any Islander willing to come to Queensland and work for him. He assured them that they would be given ample food, a place to live and, at the end of six months, they would be returned safely home.

The ship returned with sixty-seven Islanders on board. Europeans called them Kanakas.

Towards the end of the 1860s white men moved in to north Queensland and began growing sugar cane. It was to become one of Australia's biggest industries.

Immediately the cane growers began to recruit Kanakas to work in the fields and sugar mills. Ships toured the islands of the south Pacific enticing prospective labourers aboard from places like Vanuatu, the Gilbert Islands, the Solomon Islands and New Guinea.

The Islanders who went to Queensland generally

South Sea Island labourers and their white masters.

wanted to go. But they were often deceived by stories of how good life would be there. Sometimes Kanakas were simply kidnapped.

Thousands of them came to Queensland. The cane growers said it was the only way their industry could survive because they could not afford to pay the wages Europeans demanded. They also claimed that even if they could have afforded to pay them, white men and women were not physically capable of working in tropical climates.

The use of the Kanakas in north Queensland had many critics who argued that their treatment was inhuman, and compared them with African slaves in the cotton plantations of America.

The Queensland plantation owners replied that the Kanakas were better off working and receiving wages than they were at home, where there was no work and no money.

But the photographs of the Islanders do not show happy people. The work was monotonous and hard and the hours were long. The plantation owners built them flimsy and unsanitary huts. The Islanders were cut off from their families and their homelands and there was no way they could return until their contracts had expired. Many of them fell ill and died.

White society in Queensland never accepted the Islanders, except as useful workers. They were never regarded as equals. Like the Chinese they were frequently mistreated and abused.

When the Islanders did go home they often found their villages deserted. Many of their people had fallen ill with diseases brought by the white men.

The sugar industry flourished. The plantation owners became rich and respectable men. But it was all at a great cost to the Islanders.

Eventually the Queensland government put a stop to the Kanaka trade. The government was influenced by those people who said that in a democracy all people should be free – and the Kanakas were not free.

There were others who opposed the use of Kanaka labour on different grounds. They said that no black people should be allowed into Australia on any condition. They demanded a 'white Australia'.

DEALING WITH DISEASE

People migrated to Australia because they thought that they would be better off. But sometimes they were worse off than they had been at home. For instance, in Sydney in 1875 one child out of every ten died from disease. That was a worse death rate than any city in Britain.

These days we never hear of diseases like whooping cough, diphtheria, polio and scarlet fever. Last century – and even until the middle of this one – there were no vaccines to prevent them, and no sure way to cure them. Measles, influenza, dysentery and pneumonia were fatal diseases too. They often came in epidemics and there was very little communities could do to help themselves.

All sorts of cures were sold for illness. Concoctions with names like Weston's Wizard Oil, and Dr Koch's Blood Purifier, were of no use to anyone except the crooks who sold them. Some 'quack' doctors advertised electrical treatments. They claimed that electrical shocks could cure just about everything from backache to mental illness. Electric corsets and electric belts were for sale. People bought them and all sorts of other phoney cures because they had tried everything else.

There was not much doctors could do for major diseases. To relieve pain opium was widely used, even for small children. There were many popular family remedies and tonics. Sometimes they helped, but they were unlikely to cure anything serious.

Hospital was the last place a sick or injured person would want to go. Most of the hospitals were filthy because it was not until the last years of the century that doctors and nurses began to understand that germs carry disease.

A policeman chats to women from The Rocks in Sydney around 1900. The girl stops skipping to stare at the camera.

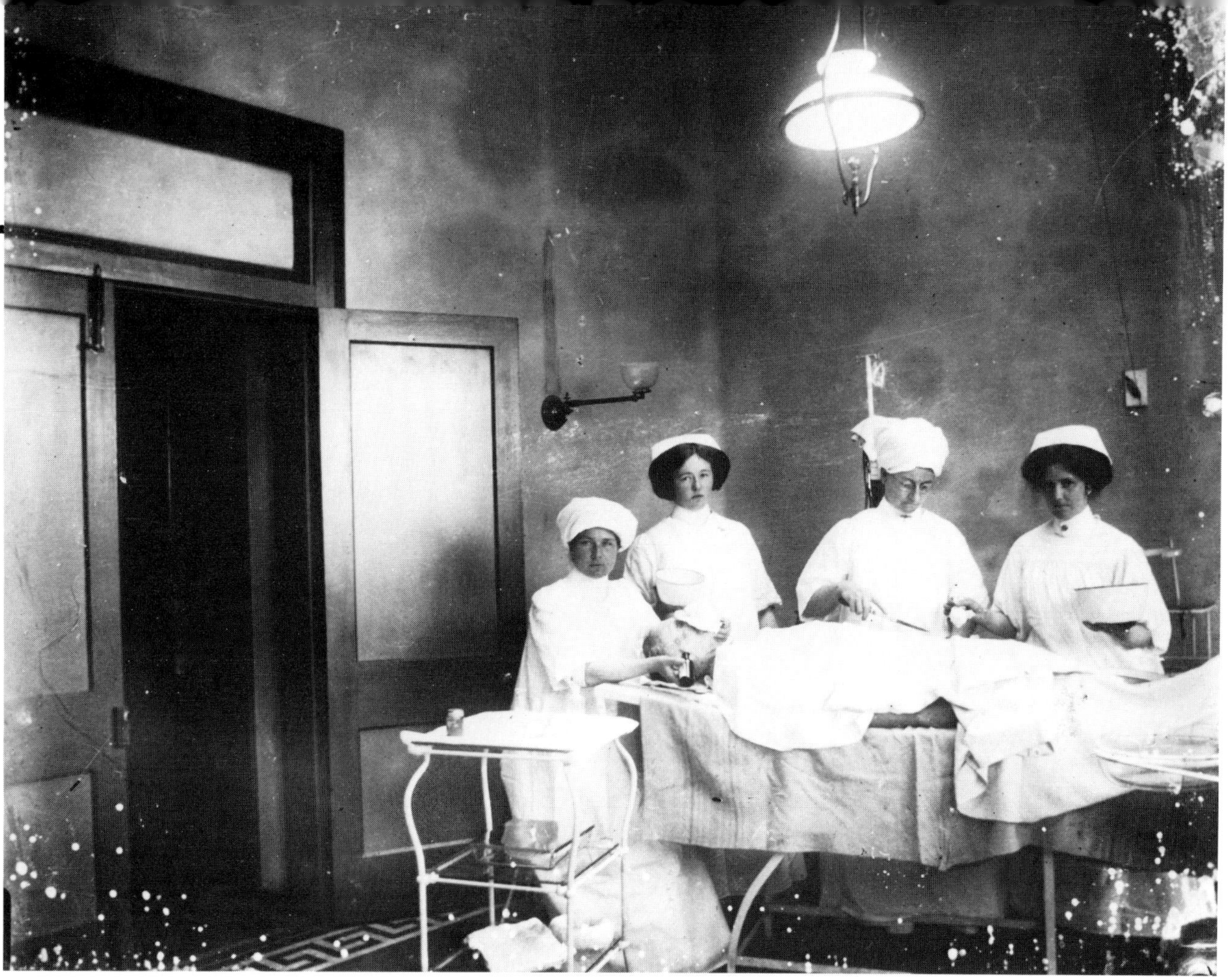

An operating theatre in Gundagai, New South Wales. The nurses are wearing neither gloves nor masks, so the chance of infection is high. At the patient's head a nurse holds a bottle of ether — the anaesthetic.

Sick people got new diseases in hospital. Because they did not know much about setting bones or stopping infection doctors did not think twice about cutting off limbs. Then, if the patients were lucky enough to survive the surgery, they were quite likely to get another infection and die anyway.

There was no chance of the people's health improving until the causes of disease were removed. Disease was most common in the poor areas of the city. In tiny crowded rotting houses with no sewerage or drainage, and often with no water supply, people were bound to get sick.

Diet was a cause of illness too. The basic diet for a poor family was bread, meat and potatoes, along with flour, tea, sugar and milk. Green vegetables were not eaten much and children often suffered from a lack of vitamins. As a result they got such diseases as scurvy and rickets. The milk supply was another problem. Milk was not pasteurized and often carried germs.

Towards the end of the century there was a lot of talk about what a wonderful place Australia was, and what an even better place it was going to be. But while some people were busy congratulating themselves on Australian achievements, many others were leading miserable lives and struggling to stay alive.

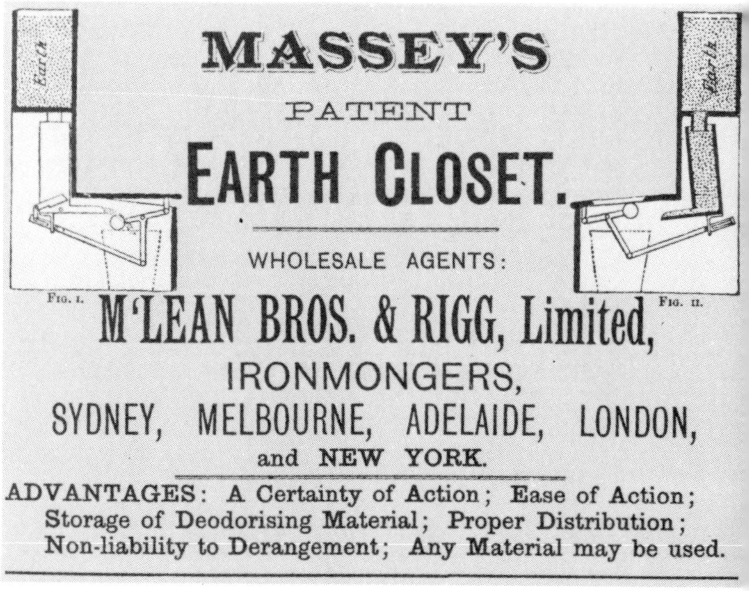

When the user stood up, earth sprinkled in the pan. A good idea perhaps, but the nightman now had to carry away the earth as well.

OPENING UP THE NORTH

The empty interior.

The expedition of Burke and Wills was not a total failure. The reports that came back of the good land they had seen in the north encouraged settlers to drive their cattle and sheep there.

Settling in the north meant braving a hard and unpredictable land and climate. There were times when the country was dry and parched and settlers' stock starved to death beside empty water holes. At other times the country flooded and rivers ran miles wide. But just as often the country bloomed and sheep and cattle thrived. The north was hard but fortunes were to be made there.

One of the first men to set up a station in the newly discovered country was John Sutherland. He bought eight thousand sheep from a station near Rockhampton in 1863 and commenced to drive them inland.

After a few weeks he stopped, sheared his sheep and waited for the ewes to lamb. The wool was carted two hundred kilometres to Port MacKay and sold.

Now the sheep were driven north-west, past the outlying stations and on to the Leichhardt River. Little was known about the country beyond the river. An explorer named A.C. Gregory had been in the area in 1858. He found the rivers dry and the country arid. John McKinlay had been there in a good season while looking for Burke and Wills.

Sutherland knew that the land held promise if only he could find a reliable water supply. He pushed on sixty kilometres past the Leichhardt River. They travelled through grass so long and tough they had to march the bullock teams ahead, with logs tied between them to roll down a path for the sheep.

All night and through the next day they travelled. At dusk they reached a waterhole, but there was only mud in it, and the men had to drive their thirsty sheep away.

Civilization on its way through the outback. A pianola bound for a station homestead on one of the camels imported to provide desert transport. Camel drivers from Afghanistan were imported too — and this camel is decorated with Afghan beads.

The men were exhausted and planned to camp for the night. The sheep, however, could smell water. In the middle of the night they stampeded down the creek bed. The men followed them in the dark.

Ahead they saw campfires blazing. It was an Aboriginal camp. Sutherland described what happened:

> On rushed the sheep through the fires, blacks and all other impediments, to quench their thirst . . . To be roused out of their sleep at midnight by some eight thousand sheep rushing madly and tumbling over them was something demoniacal to the natives who never saw or heard of jumbuks before. Of course the whole tribe took up their beds and ran quick smart.

When he saw the lake his sheep had discovered he established a station there. Later he realized that he was the first man to graze sheep in what is now the Northern Territory.

By the end of the 1860s the whole of the north from Darwin to Rockhampton was taken up by cattle and sheep. The settlers measured their stations not by the acre but by the square mile. Alexandria Station was more than 11,000 square miles. Victoria River Downs more than 5,000. In 1880, 20,000 cattle were overlanded in a single trip to stations on the Daly River in the Northern Territory.

Huge runs were needed for cattle because vegetation was sparse and the cattle had to graze far and wide. Vast runs also meant that big profits could be made – in good seasons at least.

The Aboriginal people of the north fought hard to keep their land. The tribe which had been frightened by the onrush of Sutherland's sheep came back within a few weeks and attacked the white men. In other parts of the north there were massacres of white settlers. Aboriginals also captured whole flocks of sheep, and herds of cattle.

The whites hunted the blacks without mercy. There were some fearful slaughters. The settlers of the north were hard and often brutal men. The explorer McKinlay saw them at Bowen on his way home in 1861. 'They looked quite fierce,' he said, 'with their long knives stuck in their belts, and revolvers at their sides.'

It was a war between blacks and whites in the north of Australia. Eventually the whites won.

Surviving Aborigines were sent to missions where they were taught to be Christians. Others worked on the cattle stations. Aboriginal men became superb stockmen. White settlers knew how valuable they were to their stations. They could not do without their labour. But they rarely paid them more than their rations of flour, tea and tobacco.

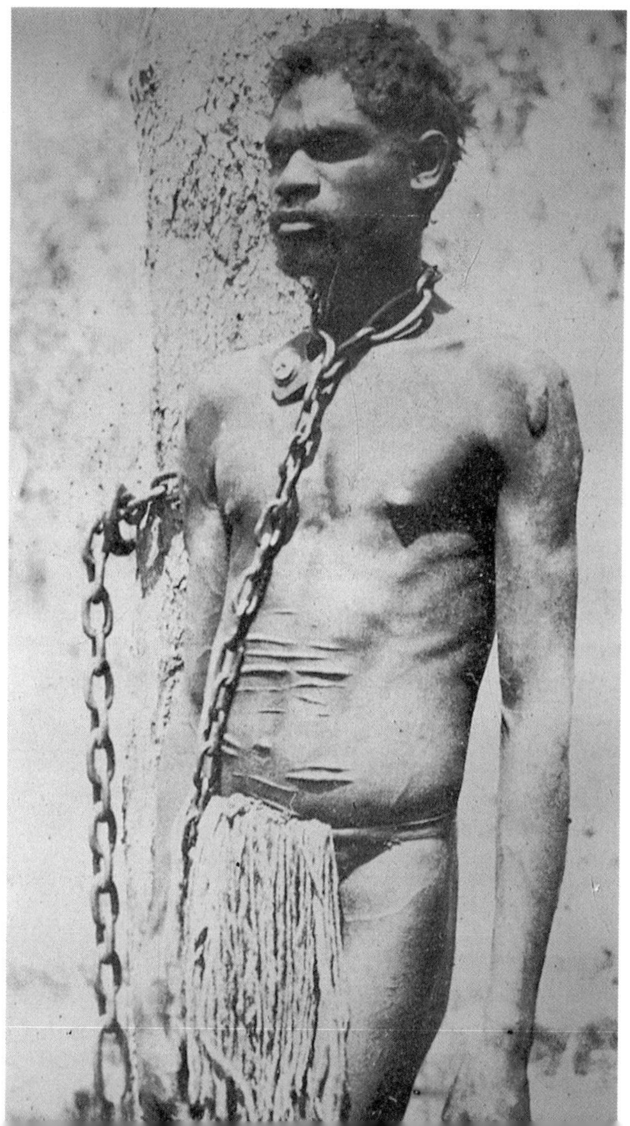

This man was accused of murdering a white. He waits to be taken to town for trial.

A MINING TOWN

In the region where, in 1844, Charles Sturt the explorer had hoped to find an inland sea, Broken Hill now stands. Sturt had found in the desert a range of ancient mountains which he named Stanley's Barrier Range. He noticed that there was iron ore in the mountains, 'and perhaps other metals', he said.

In 1884 a poor boundary rider named Charles Rasp pegged out a claim on a hump-backed ridge in the Barrier Range known as the Broken Hill. Rasp and seven other station workers had ridden over the hill many times. They were convinced that the Broken Hill was all tin.

It was better than that. They found silver. Rasp and his friends needed money to mine it and some rich pastoralists were keen to take part. They put up the money and formed a company called the Broken Hill Proprietary Company Limited – BHP. The BHP Company found they owned the biggest silver, lead and zinc deposits in the world.

Broken Hill was soon connected by rail to Adelaide and new smelters at Port Pirie, from where the ore was exported around the world. Goods were sent back by rail for the town's rapidly increasing population. By 1891 there were twenty thousand people living there.

For the miners, life was very hard. There were few more dangerous and unhealthy jobs. In the early years the ore was dug out with picks and crowbars. Miners were often injured in falls. Sometimes they were killed. In deep mines gas built up and there was always the risk of an explosion.

The miners used candles to find their way around. They carried a couple of spares in their pockets. But after a while many got so used to working underground they seemed to be able to see in the dark.

Around 1900, pneumatic drills were brought into the mines. The drills made it easier to get the ore out, but they also made a fine dust which the miners inhaled. After many years in the mines men often got a disease in their lungs called pneumoconiosis – known as Widow's Disease.

But even though there were great risks, the men of Broken Hill usually wanted to go down the mines. The money was good – better than any job above the ground.

A boy could start in the mines gathering up rubbish in a cart pulled by a draught horse. Mining was hard on horses too.

In the first years at Broken Hill the mine owners did

Underground at Broken Hill.

not seem to care what happened to the miners or their families. They did very little to make mining safer.

Miners who complained about the conditions they worked in were sacked. The company gave nothing to the wives and children of men who were killed in accidents. In the early 1890s, when the company's profits declined along with the price of silver, the miners' wages were cut.

Nor did the company do much for the town of Broken Hill. The mines put deadly chemicals into the air.

Primitive housing, a lack of clean drinking water and a permanent plague of flies led to outbreaks of diseases, especially typhoid. Broken Hill had the highest death rate of any town in Australia.

This was an awful place to live. Mining and grazing stripped all the vegetation away and, with nothing to hold the soil together, dust storms rolled into the town. On days like this it was probably better to be in the mines than above the ground.

BHP became the biggest of all Australian companies. From silver and lead mining at Broken Hill, the company began mining iron ore from the huge Iron Knob deposit, and smelting it at nearby Whyalla on the Spencer Gulf. Later the ore was shipped to the New South Wales coal towns of Newcastle and Port Kembla and smelted there.

During the Great War of 1914-18, BHP moved into the very profitable business of steelmaking.

These days BHP also produces oil from the sea in Bass Strait, and off the North West Shelf in Western Australia. The company employs about sixty thousand people all over Australia.

Broken Hill has grown to a city of more than thirty thousand. The people live comfortably in good houses and on wages that the early miners never dreamt of. But the memory of those terrible early days is still strong there.

At the turn of the century Broken Hill was visited by Herbert Hoover, later President of the United States. He said it was the most depressing town he had ever seen.

THE NED KELLY STORY

Ned Kelly at sixteen. He was already in trouble with the police — and ten years later he was dead.

Ned Kelly's father was an Irish ex-convict who had been sent to Tasmania for stealing two pigs. Ned's mother, Ellen Quinn, was also Irish – the daughter of free settlers who rented farmland just outside the new town of Melbourne. Ned was born one of eight children in 1855.

As an ex-convict, Ned's father was under police scrutiny and eventually he was jailed. He died soon after.

Ellen Quinn decided then to take up a small selection – a poor farm at Greta, near Benalla in north-eastern Victoria. There she struggled to raise the family.

Ned left school when he was eleven and went to work on nearby farms. He became an expert horseman, a crack shot with a rifle, and a good boxer. Ned and his friends dressed in flash clothes and gave a lot of cheek to the wealthier landowners in the district who accused them of stealing cattle and horses. The law was on the side of the squatters, so the Kellys were often in trouble with the police.

One day in 1878 when a police constable called Fitzpatrick went to the farm at Greta, fighting started and a shot was fired. It is not clear how it happened but Constable Fitzpatrick suffered a slight wound and, as a result, Ellen Kelly went to gaol for three years.

When he heard of his mother's arrest Ned came home. He and his brother Dan were also wanted by the police, although Ned had been hundreds of miles away on the day of the fight at Greta. With horses, guns and supplies they took to the bush and were soon joined by their mates Joe Byrne and Steve Hart. The four soon became known as the Kelly Gang.

From their hide-out in the ranges the gang began holding up coaches, plundering homesteads and descending on towns to rob banks. Once they captured Jerilderie, a town in New South Wales, for two days.

Some people in the district gave the gang food and shelter, and, either out of sympathy or fear, hid them from the police. Without this help they could not have lasted long.

In October 1878 four police were searching the Wombat Ranges in Victoria when the Kelly Gang ambushed them at Stringybark Creek. Three of the policemen were shot dead.

Ned claimed that it was a fair fight and that the gang had killed in self-defence. But now they were wanted for murder. They could be shot on sight. A reward of £16,000 was offered for their capture.

The police began arresting the Kelly Gang's supporters in the district. With their supplies now running low the men grew desperate.

Aaron Sherrit had been a friend of the Kellys but he passed on information about them to the police. On 26 June 1880 Joe Byrne rode up to Sherrit's door, called him outside and shot him dead.

Determined to wipe out the gang, the Victorian government despatched a special train load of police to the north-east.

The gang planned to attack the train at Glenrowan. Early that morning they herded the townspeople into the hotel. The gang and their prisoners waited, and waited, but the train did not come.

A party started. The outlaws and their captives drank and danced. Foolishly, Ned allowed the school teacher, Thomas Curnow, to leave. But instead of going home, Curnow ran along the railway line to

warn the train.

When night fell the four outlaws put on the armour they had made from scrap iron.

In bright moonlight the police surrounded the hotel and attacked. There was a terrible confusion of gun fire. Soon Joe Byrne was dead and Ned Kelly wounded.

Ned slipped away from the hotel during the night. Then as the first thin light of the sun came up, he returned, walking slowly in his heavy armour through the morning mist. The police poured bullets at him. But still he advanced, all the time firing his big revolver. Finally, hit twice in the leg, he staggered and fell. Ned Kelly was captured.

The rest was over quickly. The police set the prisoners free and burnt the Glenrowan Hotel to the ground. The bodies of the other three gang members were found in the ashes.

Ned Kelly was taken by train to Melbourne to stand trial for the murder of the policemen at Stringybark Creek. He was found guilty. On 11 November 1880, at the age of twenty-five, he was hanged in the Melbourne jail. His last words were 'Such is life'.

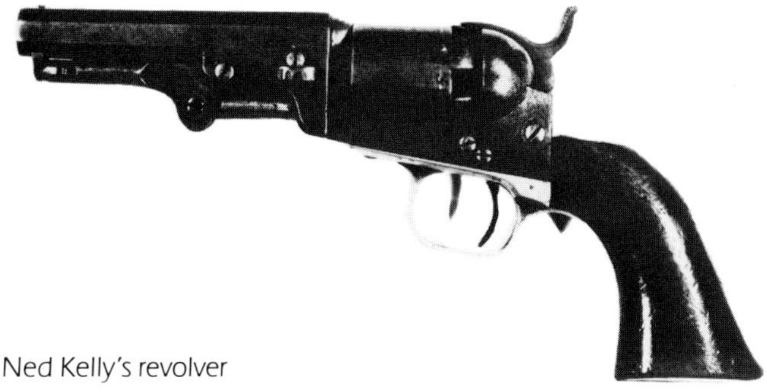

Ned Kelly's revolver

Ned Kelly about to die. Thousands of people outside the jail wanted him to live. Hanging Ned made him even more of a hero.

A JEWEL IN BRITAIN'S CROWN

In just forty-five years Melbourne had grown from a wilderness to a city that was famous throughout the British Empire. There were 280,000 people living in Melbourne in 1880. It was a thriving port, and parts of Melbourne looked almost as grand as the great European cities.

One writer said that Melbourne was as great as Athens in the days of ancient Greece. It was the 'Queen of the South', some said. 'One of the marvels of modern times', said another.

In 1878 the Victorian government decided to hold an international exhibition – like the magnificent exhibitions held in London and Paris. The government wanted to show the world what a marvellous city Melbourne was, and demonstrate that Victorian products matched the best from abroad.

A huge building was erected near the centre of the city. Into the port of Melbourne came samples of goods produced by companies from all over the world. On 1 October 1880 the Great Exhibition was opened. The day was declared a public holiday and thousands of people listened to the brass bands and the long speeches.

Inside the building there were 32,000 exhibits from about thirty countries and the six Australian colonies. Victoria was given pride of place among the colonies of course, and Britain among the countries.

Everything, from steam engines to flower arrangements, was there. From India came chutneys, curry powders, jute, woolsacks and coir ropes. From Mauritius came snuff and vanilla. Jamaica sent its finest rum. There were pianos, ham sausages, paintings and pasta from Italy, clocks and musical boxes from Switzerland, tapestries, perfumes and wine from France, and all sorts of machinery from Germany and the United States. Belgium sent a sample of a tramline.

Britain sent samples of just about everything you could imagine – as well as some quite unimaginable

The Melbourne Exhibition Building.

things. There were weighing machines for hospitals and lunatic asylums, earthenware lavatories and urinals, workboots, corsets, gunpowder, tinned meat, powdered soups and fishhooks, cutlery from Sheffield and pottery from Stoke-on-Trent, amputating equipment and artificial legs and eyes. Sir William Armstrong won a gold medal for his exhibition of 'warlike material'.

All the colonies sent examples of their produce – wool and wheat, potatoes and pumpkins, sugar and hops. Engineering companies sent ploughs and harrows, newly designed engines, fancy ironwork and furniture.

The best exhibits won gold medals. There were also silver medals, certificates and honourable mentions. Winning companies could display their medals on their labels and advertisements, as proof that their product was the best in the world.

The exhibition was an advertisement for Melbourne. It drew the world's attention to a great new city, a new jewel in Britain's crown.

It seemed as if Melbourne's progress would never end. But only ten years later the bubble would burst. Trade and industry would come to a standstill, and thousands of people would leave Melbourne for the country and the other colonies.

A lot would go to Sydney and probably as many to the new boom towns in the west, Kalgoorlie and Coolgardie, where gold had just been found.

GETTING THERE

When people started growing wheat in the Victorian Mallee or on the plains of Western Australia, or cutting cedar in the sub-tropical forests of Queensland, or making wine in the river valleys of South Australia and New South Wales, they needed a means of bringing in their supplies and news of the outside world, and taking out their produce and mail.

For years bullock teams did most of the work. The first roads inland were often bullock tracks. On a good track a team of bullocks could pull a fifteen tonne load about twenty-five kilometres in a day.

The roads were often almost non-existent. Bullock teams were used to haul timber out of wild forest country, and to bring supplies across mountains into new grazing land. The bullockies worked alongside their teams, cursing and cracking their long whips to urge them on.

Horses were always in great demand. They were used both as working animals and, for those who could afford them, as a private means of transport. For some years hardy Australian-bred horses supplied the British Army in India.

During the gold rush an American named Cobb started to run a horse-drawn coach service from the wharves of Melbourne to the centre of the city. Cobb knew he would do great business carrying passengers and mail from the ships. Soon Cobb and Co. had coach runs all over the colonies.

Australia's river systems were used intensively to transport goods by paddle steamers. Along the rivers in rich agricultural and pastoral areas there were large inland ports.

When people wanted to get from Sydney to Brisbane or Melbourne, or any of the ports in between, they often went on one of the many passenger ships which plied the coast. Ships – especially the new steamers – were faster and much more comfortable than the horse-drawn coaches which travelled corrugated roads and stopped each night at remote and rough bush inns.

The first steam train in Australia ran from Melbourne to Port Melbourne in 1854. By 1864 a rail line had been built through Bendigo to the Murray

The telegraph cable reaches Tasmania in 1869.

Knickers for ladies to wear while riding bicycles.

River port of Echuca. Trains connected Sydney to Goulburn and other major towns in New South Wales. Soon every country community wanted a train service.

Mining companies used rails and horse-drawn trucks in the most remote places. Later they brought in steam engines. Governments built lines from the mines to distant ports. Building the rail links provided work for a lot of people in the last half of the nineteenth century.

The lines were built by teams of surveyors, engineers and labourers. They spent months on the job in the bush. Cuttings had to be dug, timber cleared, bridges built, sleepers cut from the trees, and the line laid.

Nearly all trains got there.

The arrival of the first train along a new line was a day of great celebration in a country town or siding. The train was something of a miracle. It meant an end to isolation. Produce could be got to city markets fast. The goods that people wanted from the city were readily available.

Australia itself was now much less cut off from the rest of the world. Where it had once taken six months for mail to reach Australia from Britain, by the 1870s it took about forty-five days. Steamships made the difference.

News came with the ships. When a ship arrived in an Australian port newsmen were the first aboard to hear the latest 'intelligence from overseas'. Within a few hours people were reading about it in the papers.

For many years telegraph cables had been stretching out from Europe to the rest of the world. By the late 1860s people in San Francisco could receive messages from London within minutes.

In the next few years the telegraph line crept steadily closer across the world to the coast of north Australia. At the same time a line was stretched on thousands of poles from Adelaide to Darwin. There, in 1872, it met the London cable, and the first messages were tapped through from one end of the British Empire to the other.

The overland telegraph service was kept going by operators in lonely stone huts spread along the desert line. As each message came in – a report on the health of Queen Victoria for instance, or the latest price of wool on the London markets – the operators relayed it down the line.

Occasionally Aborigines cut the cable and used it for making fish hooks. And the porcelain insulators, they discovered, could be fashioned into spear tips. Dutifully the operators rode out and repaired the damage. The link with the mother country had to be maintained.

Brisbane once had trams.

JAMES AND GRACE FORSYTH

Two successful selectors.

James Forsyth was born on the east coast of Scotland. James' parents worked on a large estate. His mother possibly worked in the owner's mansion, or in his fields, as well as in the cottage in which she and her family lived.

For their work they were paid a small yearly wage and had the use of the cottage and its garden free of charge. The family could grow enough in the garden to feed themselves. They were poor but they lived rather better than the poor people of the cities, or the poor of Ireland.

James Forsyth came from a sober, hard-working Christian family. As most Scots do, his parents attended the Presbyterian Church. They had other Scottish traditions as well.

They knew Scottish rhymes and songs, used Scottish words and spoke with a Scottish accent that people from other parts of Britain could barely understand. They were loyal to the Queen of England and hostile towards Ireland and the Catholic Church.

James Forsyth emigrated with his family when he was a small boy in the 1850s. His mother and baby sister died on the voyage from Glasgow to Melbourne.

The family did not come to Melbourne to look for gold, or because they were going hungry. They came because they had heard they might be able to get their own land. In Scotland this would never have been possible.

James Forsyth grew up with his father working on a farm. When the Victorian government passed the Selection Acts in the 1860s James Forsyth took a horse and dray into the great forests of Gippsland and selected a block of land.

A hut was built and the land was slowly cleared of the huge mountain ash and blue gum trees, blackwoods and wattles, tree ferns and creepers. Vegetables thrived in the new soil. The land was sown with European grasses for dairy cows to graze on.

Around 1875 James married Grace Nairn, the daughter of another Scots family who had left Scotland to come to Melbourne in the 1850s. Most information about Grace's forebears has been lost but James and Grace had a lot in common in their pasts. They built a house on James' selection and raised three children, Albert, Herbert and Mary.

They were the first generation of white people in the region. They had seen the land as wilderness and turned it into farmland.

This couple were not wealthy when they decided to have their picture taken, on a visit to Melbourne in about 1910. But through hard work they had made a living from the land. And the land was theirs. The children were farming it by then. Their great-grandchild farms it now.

They no longer thought of themselves as Scots. They had forgotten a lot of the Scottish customs and words, and lost their Scottish accents. They thought of themselves as Australians.

1890-1909

1890 Depression — many thousands unemployed in colonies. Strikes at Broken Hill and in the pastoral and shipping industries. Western Australia elects a parliament. John Forrest, Premier.

1891 American Jessie Ackerman, begins the first public lecture tours by a woman in Australia, on questions affecting women's lives.

1892 Strike at Broken Hill.
Gold discovered at Coolgardie, Western Australia.

1893 William Lane and his followers depart for 'New Australia', Paraguay.
Devastating storms and floods in Queensland.
Gold discovered at Kalgoorlie — richest field ever discovered in Australia. Rush starts.

1894 Shearers' strike.
Women win right to vote in South Australia.

1895 Invention of the motion picture camera by Frenchman, Lumiére.
Terrible seven year drought in eastern Australia begins.

1896 Death of Henry Parkes.

1898 Pierre and Marie Curie, French scientists, discover first radioactive elements, radium and polonium.

1899 Federation of the states agreed to by majority of Australians.
Australian troops land in South Africa.
Women win right to vote in Western Australia.

1900 The Commonwealth of Australia formed.

1901 Queen Victoria dies, succeeded by Edward VII.
Opening of the Australian parliament.
Edmund Barton, Prime Minister.
Population of Australia, not including Aborigines: 3,773,248. Males 1,977,649; females 1,795,599. Aboriginal population estimated at 150,000.
Marconi sends first wireless message from Europe to America.
My Brilliant Career by Miles Franklin published.

1902 Drought in eastern Australian breaks. Drought and rabbit plague have halved the sheep and cattle population of Australia in past ten years.
Australia linked to America by telegraph cable from Southport, Queensland.
Explosion at Kembla Hills kills ninety-five miners.
Australia begins governing South-west New Guinea.
Women win right to vote in New South Wales parliament.
Sydney law graduate, Ada Evans, becomes the first woman in Australia to be called to the Bar.

1903 Alfred Deakin, Prime Minister.
Women vote for the Australian parliament, and three women stand for election.
Women win right to vote in Tasmania.

1904 John Christian Watson, Prime Minister.

1905 Alfred Deakin, Prime Minister.
Queen Victoria's birthday made a public holiday called Empire Day.
Women win right to vote in Queensland.

1908 Old age pensions paid by Commonwealth government.
United States naval fleet visits Australia.
Women win right to vote in Victoria.

1909 United Clerks Union reports that women are rapidly replacing men in office jobs on about one quarter of the pay.

Mary Hume at Bardon, Brisbane in 1897.

THE GREAT STRIKES

'Scabs' on their way to a wool shed. They are protected from angry shearers by armed troopers.

The colonies had grown rapidly in the 1880s, particularly the cities. Mine owners and pastoralists made big profits. Money poured in from rich British businessmen. There was money available to build houses, factories, roads and railways.

A lot of ordinary people now found they could earn good wages or start their own small businesses. Some now had the chance to buy a block of land and build their own homes. On the fringes of the cities new suburbs grew.

No one is really certain why – but in 1890 all this changed. The money stopped flowing. Prices for Australian exports fell. Wages were reduced. Shops and factories closed down. Banks closed down and many people lost their savings. Thousands lost their jobs. Many people no longer had the price of a meal.

At the same time a great struggle took place between the owners of the mines and sheepruns, and the people they employed.

Trade unions of workers had existed in Australia since before the gold rush. New, much bigger unions were created in the 1870s and 1880s. They were formed to protect the interests of workers – their rights to safe and healthy working conditions, a secure job, reasonable hours and a reasonable wage.

When employers refused to grant these conditions the unions' only weapon was to withdraw their labour – to go on strike.

By 1890 the workers in Australia's largest industries were unionized. The shearers, the miners, the wharf labourers and seamen all had unions.

The employers, particularly at a time when their profits were falling, saw the unions as a threat. When the depression set in they decided to crush them.

The employers insisted that they could employ

'Scab' labourers attacked at Broken Hill.

whoever they liked. Naturally they liked people who were not in the unions. This they called 'freedom of contract'.

The unions insisted that if the employers were allowed to do this the wages and conditions of all workers would be threatened. There would be no chance of a reasonable wage or of forcing an employer to improve conditions on the job. The employer alone would decide what workers got. The unions demanded that only union members be employed. They called this the principle of the 'closed shop'.

The strikes began on the ships which plied the Australian coasts. They soon spread to the shearing sheds on the great sheep stations, the coal and silver mines, and to the wharves.

Unfortunately for the strikers, the employers found it easy to replace them. There were thousands of unemployed people desperate for work. These hired labourers were known as 'scabs', or 'blacklegs'. Fights broke out between 'scabs' and unionists. Mounted police were called in to break them up.

Soldiers and police were used on the side of the employers and their 'scabs'. Before a big meeting of striking workers in Melbourne volunteer troops were commanded to 'fire low and lay them out'.

In Queensland soldiers and police rode from woolshed to woolshed to protect the 'scab' shearers. At Broken Hill where miners were on strike against cuts in their wages, hired labourers were brought in by train and hundreds of police travelled with them.

At Barcaldine in Queensland striking shearers armed themselves. They raised the Southern Cross, the flag of the diggers at Eureka, and said they would fight to the end.

In other parts of Queensland and New South Wales shearers fought back against employers by setting fire to woolsheds and crops. One night a group of striking shearers swarmed on to the paddle steamer, *Rodney*, which was taking a load of 'blackleg' labour up the Darling to a station. The strikers threw the 'blacklegs' into the river and set fire to the boat.

Soldiers and police hunted the culprits with orders to 'shoot on sight any person about to commit a crime, or who carried arms, or was suspected of carrying arms'. They were told 'Firing is to be effective. Pick on the leaders.'

Fortunately the orders were not carried out, but seventy-eight men were arrested and many were given long gaol sentences.

It was the same at Barcaldine, Broken Hill and everywhere else that the unions put up a fight. The union leaders were arrested and gaoled and the unions' funds were confiscated.

The Great Strikes ended in total defeat for the unions which just a few years before had seemed so strong. But at least one lesson had been learned.

It was clear that trade unions were not enough. Their defeat convinced them that they must have people in parliament committed to protecting and improving conditions for working people. In the next few years labour parties were formed in all the colonies.

Wealthy men dressed like wealthy men. Here they admire a new sheep shearing machine — soon to replace hand shears.

LIFE ON THE COLLINGWOOD FLAT

In the Australian cities of last century, rich people built their houses on hills or by the sea. They liked to have pleasant views, cool breezes and be well clear of the poor who lived on the flats.

The Collingwood flat, by the Yarra River in Melbourne, was always a place for the poor. New migrants, especially people from Ireland and Scotland, went there when they first arrived. So did a lot of poverty-stricken women and children – women whose husbands had left them, and widows. Ever since the gold rush there had been more women than men in Collingwood.

The people built their houses of the cheapest materials – timber from packing cases, canvas and hessian. The floors were usually earth.

Collingwood's business people built on the same side of the river but up the hill. Their sewage and rubbish washed down into the streets and houses on the flats. Blood and waste meat from the butchers on the slope came down as well. After heavy rain the people on the flat trudged around in filthy water up to their knees.

At times like this the Collingwood flat stank. People spoke of 'unhealthy vapour' in the air. But it was not the smell which carried disease. It was the open drains and cesspits, the filthy water lying around, overcrowding, and lack of clean drinking water.

Typhoid, diphtheria and pneumonia were common. A free medical dispensary was set up in 1869. The Methodist Mission also did its best to help. But many died, especially children. Being poor they were buried several to a grave, and usually without any religious rites, in the Melbourne Cemetery.

Industry came to Collingwood in the 1870s and with it came more pollution. Tanneries washed sheepskins and hides in the Yarra, soaked them in soap and soda, then rinsed them back in the river. The Yarra became a giant industrial drain and garbage tip.

Brickmakers, brewers and bootmakers were established. There were plenty of workers handy.

Stinking soap and candle factories boiled down the fat and entrails of animals into tallow. Textile factories employed Collingwood's female population.

The people on the hills were disgusted. They worried that they might catch some of the diseases which thrived down there. In the 1870s efforts were made to clean up the area.

Cesspits were filled in and garbage carried away. People were encouraged to install earth closets which were like modern lavatories but they used earth instead of water. Factory owners were encouraged not to pollute the Yarra.

Owners of land on the flat began to pull down the old houses and build new ones. They built them small and in terraces. This meant the owners could squeeze more people on to their property and get more rent. For the residents it meant less room inside and less land for keeping chooks and growing vegetables.

The typical new house on the Collingwood flat was five metres wide at the most, and had two to four small dark rooms. It was usually built of wood, but sometimes of brick. It was still likely to have an earth floor. Those people lucky enough to have boards nailed potato bags to them for a carpet.

Most houses had verandahs on to the street. On hot summer nights everyone sat on their verandahs to keep cool. At either end of the house a bucket of cow or horse manure might be burning. The smell drifted through the house to drive the mosquitoes away.

Lighting was by candle or oil lamp. Water came from a tap outside. Women washed their clothes by boiling them in a copper or an old kerosene tin.

The people of the flat gathered firewood from the banks of the Yarra and in the parks of Kew. It was a regular Sunday excursion. But 'Collingwood coke', scraps of leather collected from the boot factories, was thought to be the best fuel. It also gave Collingwood houses a smell of their own.

BUSH SCHOOLS

Henry Lawson, the Australian poet, went to several New South Wales bush schools in the 1870s. When he was older he remembered one of them like this:

> It was built of bark and poles, and the roof was full of holes
> And each leak in rainy weather made a pool;
> And the walls were mainly cracks lined with calico and sacks,
> There was little need for windows in the school.
>
> Then we rode to school and back by the rugged gully-track,
> On the old grey horse that carried three or four;
> And he looked so very wise that he lit the Master's eyes
> Every time he put his head in at the door.
>
> And we learnt the world in scraps from some ancient dingy maps
> Long discarded by the public-schools in town;
> And as nearly every book dated back to Captain Cook
> Our geography was somewhat upside-down.

The governments of the Australian colonies decided that it was their duty to ensure that all children learned to read and write and understand something of the world in which they lived.

State schools were set up wherever there were a few children. The children rode in from the surrounding farms. More often they walked, sometimes many kilometres a day. For many children it took great effort just to get to school. To encourage them to come, the Education Departments gave out special certificates at the end of each year to children who had managed not to miss a day.

Most of the bush schools had just one teacher, usually a man. If the man was married, it was often his wife's job to teach the girls at the school sewing and dressmaking. If someone in the district had a good voice and knew how to read music he or she might be asked to come to the school each week to teach music and singing.

Children learnt their subjects by rote – repeating things the teacher said over and over again until they knew them by heart.

They were instructed in good manners, correct speech, neat dress and cleanliness. They were also taught discipline, obedience and respect for their elders. Boys were expected to lift their hats to ladies.

A bush school at Gulgong, New South Wales, 1870s.

Ten pupils and three horses on their way to school.

Girls were expected to be quiet and ladylike. Both boys and girls were taught to speak only when they were spoken to, and to sit up straight.

There was always a right way and a wrong way to do things. Everyone had to learn the right way. Writing with your left hand, for instance, was wrong. Left-handed children were forced to write with their right hand.

Towards the end of the century many more schools were built. Industry needed more people with trade skills, so in the cities technical schools were started, as well as new high schools.

For some girls there were schools of domestic economy. They learnt how to be good housekeepers – or teachers of these skills.

Boys and girls learnt how important it was to be brave and patriotic. Boys were told that they must always be ready to fight for their country.

The people who set up the schools talked about giving every child a good education. But the time was still a long way off when all children would stay at school after the age of fourteen.

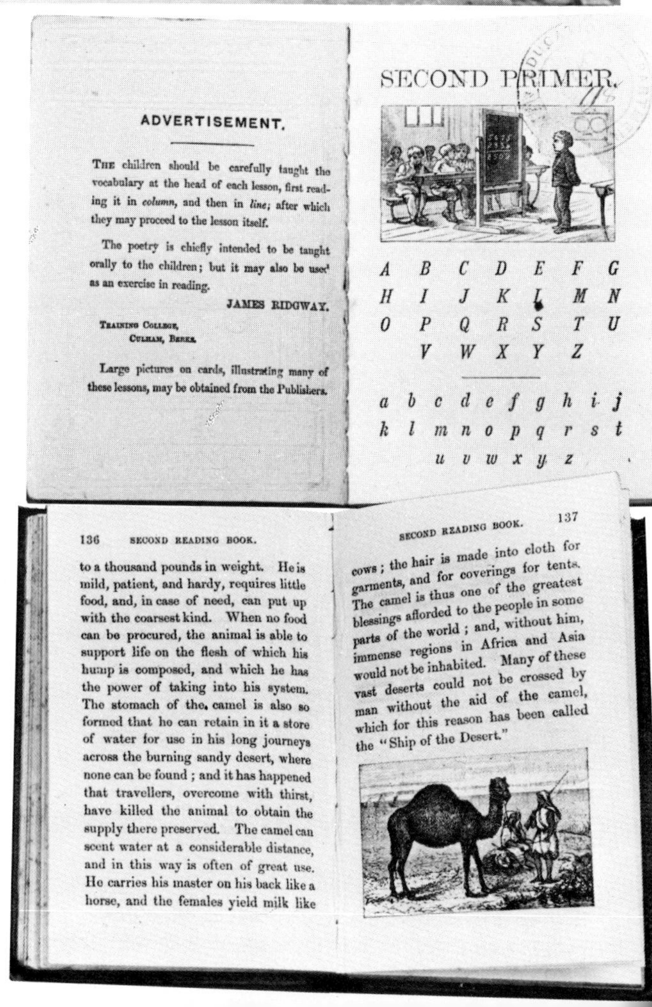

ADVERTISEMENT.

The children should be carefully taught the vocabulary at the head of each lesson, first reading it in *column*, and then in *line*; after which they may proceed to the lesson itself.

The poetry is chiefly intended to be taught orally to the children; but it may also be used as an exercise in reading.

JAMES RIDGWAY.

Training College, Culham, Berks.

Large pictures on cards, illustrating many of these lessons, may be obtained from the Publishers.

SECOND PRIMER.

A B C D E F G
H I J K L M N
O P Q R S T U
V W X Y Z

a b c d e f g h i j
k l m n o p q r s t
u v w x y z

136 SECOND READING BOOK.

to a thousand pounds in weight. He is mild, patient, and hardy, requires little food, and, in case of need, can put up with the coarsest kind. When no food can be procured, the animal is able to support life on the flesh of which his hump is composed, and which he has the power of taking into his system. The stomach of the camel is also so formed that he can retain in it a store of water for use in his long journeys across the burning sandy desert, where none can be found; and it has happened that travellers, overcome with thirst, have killed the animal to obtain the supply there preserved. The camel can scent water at a considerable distance, and in this way is often of great use. He carries his master on his back like a horse, and the females yield milk like

SECOND READING BOOK. 137

cows; the hair is made into cloth for garments, and for coverings for tents. The camel is thus one of the greatest blessings afforded to the people in some parts of the world; and, without him, immense regions in Africa and Asia would not be inhabited. Many of these vast deserts could not be crossed by man without the aid of the camel, which for this reason has been called the "Ship of the Desert."

School primers taught children reading, writing and arithmetic. School readers taught them tales of British and Australian heroic deeds.

TEXTILE WORKERS AND SWEATSHOPS

In Australia, as in Britain, it was a common belief that women should not take jobs. Their place was thought to be in the home, raising families.

But many thousands of women did work. In New South Wales in 1891, forty per cent of women aged between fifteen and twenty-four had jobs. Most of them worked as servants, but an increasing number were working in factories.

The most common factory work for women was in the clothing and textile industry. Sewing and weaving had always been seen as women's work. Few other jobs in factories were thought to be suitable for women. Clothing and textile manufacturers took them on and paid them less than half what they would have paid men.

In the factories women either sat on hard stools or packing cases or stood – for five or six hours without a break. Until steam and electric power was introduced the women had to operate treadles. It was not long before they began to suffer from arthritis, varicose veins, backache, failing eyesight and a number of other illnesses. But the most frequent complaint must have been exhaustion.

Many young women who had worked in the textile industry found that they were unable to have children. The long hours of standing and sitting in uncomfortable positions had done permanent harm.

A work-worn woman and her daughters, early 1900s.

The factories were also badly ventilated. In summer they were stifling. Often there was only one dirty toilet for all the employees – men, women and children.

In 1890 a newspaper sent journalists around to look at how textile workers lived and worked. This is what they found at one place where buttonholes were made.

> It is a small apartment, indescribably dirty and malodorous, located in the back yard of a wretched looking house, having a stable on one side and an outhouse on the other. Within this unhealthy place the man employs four or five women and his own wife and family. They have but little space to move about; they work from eight o'clock in the morning until eight o'clock at night, taking their meals on the spot.
>
> No one who worked at this place made more than fifteen shillings a week.

These workrooms were called sweatshops – meaning places where people were worked very hard by the owner for very little pay. There were hundreds of them in Australian cities. Often women were paid so poorly they had to bring work home with them.

A woman might have to get up before sunrise, do the housework and feed the children, and be at the factory by 7 a.m.

Here she worked for ten or twelve hours, returning in the evening to feed the children. Her day was still not over. For three or four hours before going to bed she sewed buttonholes or made trousers and shirts by candle or lamplight. At the end of the week she might have about twenty-five shillings for all this work.

If a women worker had children she had to rely on friends or family to look after them while she was at the factory, or leave the children to look after themselves. There were no child-care centres.

Like other workers, if she was injured or dismissed there was no pension and no dole to help her through. Workers had to depend on the charity of well-off people, the churches, and the Salvation Army.

Women went out to work for the same reason as men – they needed to earn a living. And like men they felt it was their right to work. Male workers were not so sure. Many of them feared that women might get

Melbourne Cup Day became a public holiday in Melbourne. For these upper class people on their way to see the race, life was always pretty much a holiday.

their jobs. Most of them thought that women should stay at home. As a result the trade union movement, which was run by men, took little or no interest in women workers.

Children worked in factories because their parents could not afford to keep them at school. There were thousands of children working in factories, even though the law said that they should be at school.

Sometimes children were not paid at all. Textile factory owners did not have to pay their apprentices, who were often sacked when they had finished their apprenticeships, and new ones were taken on.

Children worked the same long hours as adults. The work wore them out. For example, in 1882, a doctor reported the case of a girl who had been brought to him by her mother. She was 'a little worn-out looking thing', he said. 'She had been in a factory twelve or eighteen months already, and she is only thirteen now. She is like a little old woman, pale and shrivelled, and suffers from palpitations of the heart.'

Women making men's hats in the days when no man went outside without one.

NEW WAYS OF SEEING THE PLACE

Late in the nineteenth century many Australians still thought of England as home. It was not just because they had memories of it, or because they had friends and relations there to remind them; they believed that England was the most civilized country in the world. They wanted to be English.

English gardens were planted around Australian houses. Hawthorn hedges lined the paddocks. The streams were bordered by weeping willows. English animals, birds and fish were introduced. Some of them ran wild.

A plague of rabbits swarmed across the countryside, starving out the cattle and sheep and eroding the soil. Farmers killed millions of them with dogs, traps, ferrets, guns, poison and by herding them into yards and beating them to death with sticks.

For a long while a great many Australian settlers thought of their country as second rate. It was too young, they believed, to be as civilized as England. Some people were ashamed of its origins as a convict settlement, and were bothered by the thought that they might have convict ancestors.

Believing that Australia was too vulgar, rich Australians often sent their children to English schools. It was common for the rich and those who admired them to speak with upper class English accents, which was meant to show that they were more sophisticated than other Australians.

Well dressed families having a picnic at Hanging Rock in 1875. Despite the gum trees and the brilliant light, the scene looks very English.

Australians found it difficult to describe the country they lived in. They made it seem like England. It was rare for a writer to tell a story which accurately portrayed Australian life. It was much the same with painters. They painted Australian scenes which looked more like Britain or Europe.

Towards the end of the nineteenth century the writers and painters of Australia began to see things differently. Painters like Tom Roberts, Arthur Streeton and Frederick McCubbin went out into the bush. Their pictures caught the brilliant light of the Australian countryside, the huge skies and the heat and glare of the bush.

These painters had grown to love the Australian landscape. They were also proud of what Australian settlers had done in their struggle to make a living from the land. They painted shearers, stockmen and swaggies. Their paintings were scenes from life in which Australians recognized themselves.

Writers also began to tell tales about ordinary Australians. Like the new painters the short story writer and poet, Henry Lawson, believed that true Australians lived in the bush. City people were much the same anywhere in the world, Lawson thought. Only the bushman was unique.

Most of Lawson's own life was spent in the city, but most of his characters were men and women who had battled for a living in the country. They spoke with Australian voices, used Australian words and had an Australian sense of humour.

A.B.'Banjo'Paterson wrote poems and stories about Australian stockmen – brave adventurous men like 'The Man from Snowy River' and 'Clancy of the Overflow'. It was Paterson who wrote the words to 'Waltzing Matilda'.

Most of the important Australian writers of the 1890s published their work in a magazine called the *Bulletin*, which became known as the 'Bushman's Bible'. Among them were Joseph Furphy who, under the pen name of Tom Collins, wrote a book called *Such Is Life*, Barcroft Boake, Bernard O'Dowd, Miles Franklin, Mary Gilmore and Barbara Baynton. Baynton's view of life in the bush was quite different to Lawson's and Paterson's. In her stories the women were heroic while many of the men were cruel, unreliable or weak.

By the turn of the century these writers were very popular in Australia. They had expressed a national spirit which few people noticed twenty years before.

When Tom Roberts first exhibited his Australian landscape paintings in 1889 the critics thought they were awful. In 1900, however, it was Roberts who was invited to paint the opening of the first Commonwealth parliament.

Arthur Streeton's subject here is typically and proudly Australian – a pioneer selector resting from his labour in the heat and harsh light of the Australian landscape.

A WHITE AUSTRALIA

Australians at the end of the nineteenth century wanted to keep out of their country anyone who was not British.

The Chinese were especially disliked. During and after the gold rushes laws had been passed by the colonial governments which made it difficult for them to enter Australia. Between 1881 and 1888 only six thousand Chinese arrived, compared with 400,000 British migrants.

When the colonies federated into one nation in 1901 a law was quickly passed to prevent Chinese migration altogether. The same law applied to all other non-white people as well. This was known as the White Australia Policy.

Although there were quite large settlements of Germans and Italians in the colonies, the vast majority of people had either come from Britain, or their parents or grandparents had. They believed that Australia should be, as far as possible, populated by people like themselves. It should be British.

Australians were convinced that white people were better than all others, and that British people were the best of the whites. English people even believed that they were superior to the Irish.

"OUTSIDE, SIR! OUTSIDE!"

By the late nineteenth century most Australians believed that the Chinese were evil and a threat to their country.

Chinese fruit and vegetable seller.

By the end of the nineteenth century the British Empire had grown to be the biggest the world had ever known. India, Burma, Ceylon, Malaya, Singapore, Borneo, the West Indies, a huge part of Africa, parts of the Middle East, as well as Australia, Canada and New Zealand all belonged to the Empire. When they looked at a map of the world, British people just could not help thinking that they must be better than all others.

This was one reason why Australians wanted to keep out the Chinese and all other non-white people. They thought they would 'contaminate' their society: that if they married white Australians the children would not have all those good British qualities.

Like the people of many other countries Australians were racists. They hated or deeply feared people who looked different and had different ways of doing things.

Australian workers were frightened that Chinese would take their jobs. Squatters, plantation owners and shipowners had occasionally introduced Asian

Chinese children posing for the camera.

workers because they were cheaper to employ. Australians feared that if this was allowed to happen on a large scale they would have to accept the same low wages or go without jobs altogether. When Chinese were employed as seamen and shearers in the 1890s there were riots and strikes.

In fact most Chinese people living in Australia worked for themselves, as market gardeners or travelling salesmen. Many worked in factories owned by other Chinese.

Quong Tart grew up with Scottish mining families on the goldfields at Araluen, NSW. He moved to Sydney and prospered in business. Quong Tart married a European and earned wide respect for his efforts to foster a better understanding between Europeans and Chinese.

A lot of Australians believed that so long as there was more than one race in Australia there would be trouble. People of different races never could get on together, they said. The Aboriginal people no longer much concerned white Australians because they were convinced that they would soon die out. To allow any new race in would be madness, they said.

Australians were very much aware of being so close to Asia and so far away from Britain – which they called 'the mother country'. They wanted to be protected from all those Asians to the north who they imagined were keen to flood into Australia.

When the first Australian parliament met in 1901, all the members were in favour of keeping Australia white. Alfred Deakin, a Victorian politician who was soon to become Prime Minister, said the main reason for the colonies agreeing to become one nation was to make the White Australia Policy an Australian law. All Australians, Deakin said, wanted to be 'one people and remain one people without the admixture of other races'.

The White Australia Policy was to be like a fence around Australia's shores.

1900

Aus[illegible] first Prime Minister as seen by a cartoonist.

For more than a decade many politicians and businessmen had been trying to convince the governments and the people of the six Australian colonies that federation would be a good thing. They believed that Australia needed a single national government to make decisions for all Australians. The colonies would become states within the Australian nation.

The two most important people in the federation movement were Henry Parkes and Alfred Deakin. Parkes came to Australia in the late 1830s. For many years he ran his own newspaper, *The Empire*, in Sydney. He was always a poor businessman and frequently ran out of money.

But Parkes was a great politician. In 1899 in the little town of Tenterfield, New South Wales, he declared that the colonies should federate. By then he was an old man. Everyone knew him by his long beard and mane of white hair. He did not live to see the colonies federate. But for his early efforts Parkes became known as the 'father of federation'.

Alfred Deakin came from Victoria. He was a highly intelligent man and a great speaker. He became the second Prime Minister of Australia. Edmund Barton was the first.

One reason why Australians were keen to have a national government was their fear of invasion by Germany or some other rival of Britain's. Australians began to feel that they could not go on relying on Britain to defend them. A single government was needed to plan the best way to defend the country's coastline. Above all, they believed that Australia needed its own navy.

The people who wanted federation also said that the taxes put on goods passing between the colonies should be stopped. These taxes – tariffs – meant that everybody had to pay more for goods coming from other colonies. Federate the colonies, it was said, and food and many other items would be cheaper.

Australians were also growing to believe that they had a lot in common whichever colony they came from. They liked the idea of Australia being one country with one government.

In 1899 the people of Australia voted in favour of federation.

Elections were held for the parliament of the Commonwealth of Australia. The Duke of York sailed out from England to declare on 1 January 1901 that the new nation had come into being. He opened parliament at the Exhibition Buildings in Melbourne on 9 May 1901.

Everywhere the new flag was flown. But the national anthem was the same as Britain's. Australia was going to keep its loyal ties to Britain.

While Australia prepared for nationhood, bubonic plague broke out in Sydney's inner suburbs. These men were employed to kill the rats which carried the disease.

The Opening of the first Federal Parliament, 1901. The artist was the Australian Tom Roberts. The painting is owned by the British Crown and is lent to Australia.

WILLIAM LANE

In Australia a few people were rich, many lived comfortably, and a lot remained poor. Those who did the hardest and dirtiest work were among the poorest in the colonies.

William Lane wanted the work and wealth to be shared equally. He had come to the colonies from England in 1885, believing that in these young communities a fairer society could be built. It would be a paradise for workers – but only white workers.

Lane lived in Brisbane, where he began spreading his views through newspapers for working people called the *Boomerang* and the *Worker*.

In the 1890s there was great poverty in Australia. Thousands of workers were unemployed. Lane wrote that Australia must be drastically changed. He supported the trade unions and the unemployed in their struggles against employers who had sacked workers or cut their wages.

But when the struggles were over, the rich were as powerful as ever, and the trade unions were thoroughly defeated.

Lane could no longer see any chance of things improving in Australia. It was time to go somewhere and start an entirely new society, based on entirely different ideas.

William Lane

People would not compete with each other, they would co-operate. Nobody would own the land or the things that grew on it. The land would belong to everyone and its products would be shared. No one would work for wages – and no one would live off the labour of another.

In 1893 Lane and his family sailed to Paraguay with 220 others who shared his hopes for a good society. They settled on land which they called New Australia.

New Australia was different from old Australia but not much better. The settlers found it very hard work just growing enough food for themselves. Some of them left for an easier life in the cities.

There were arguments about Lane's leadership at the settlement. Some were expelled by Lane because they would not live by the rules he had laid down.

Eventually New Australia was abandoned. Lane started a new settlement at another place in Paraguay. This one he called Cosme.

But Cosme ran into the same problems as New Australia. Lane left for New Zealand bitter about his failures and no longer believing that people could build a perfect society.

Australians in Paraguay — at Cosme.

1910-1929

1910 Edward VII dies.
Andrew Fisher, Prime Minister.
Australia's own money replaces British gold, silver and copper coins.

1911 George V crowned King of England.
Roald Amundsen, Norwegian explorer, reaches South Pole.
Douglas Mawson, Australian scientist and explorer, departs Hobart for Antarctica, on the first of several exploring expeditions.

1912 **S.S. Titanic** sinks in the Atlantic — fifteen hundred people drown.

1913 War in the Balkan states of Europe.
Site of Canberra declared open, 1913.

1914 1 August: Germany declares war on Russia and France and invades Belgium. 4 August: Britain declares war on Germany.
War throughout Europe and the Middle East.
Britain, France and Russia versus Germany, Austria, Hungary and Turkey.

1915 Australian troops land at Gallipoli, Turkey, 25 April.
William Hughes, Prime Minister.

1916 Australian troops arrive in France.
In Dublin, Irish rebel against English rule — defeated.
Australians say 'no' in a referendum on conscription of men into army for service overseas.

1917 Communist revolution in Russia.
Russia makes peace with Germany.
First train crosses Nullarbor Plain to Perth.

1918 Germany surrenders. War ends. Twelve million dead. Twenty-one million wounded. Sixty thousand Australians dead.
First wireless messages exchanged between England and Australia.

1919 World-wide influenza epidemic kills at least ten million people. Many thousands of Australians die.
Ross Smith flies from England to Australia.
Country Party formed on behalf of Australian farmers.
Daisy Bates sets up camp with Aborigines at Ooldea, South Australia.

1920 Communist Party of Australia formed.

1921 Edith Cowan in Western Australia becomes first woman elected to an Australian parliament.

1922 Mussolini siezes power in Italy.

1923 Stanley Melbourne Bruce, Prime Minister.
Vegemite invented in Melbourne by Fred Walker.
First radio stations open in Australia at Sydney.

1925 First television images transmitted by a Scot, J. L. Baird.

1927 Australian Council of Trade Unions formed.

1928 First talking films in Australia.
Massacre of Aborigines at Coniston, Western Australia.

1929 Labor Government elected, James Scullin Prime Minister.
Great Depression begins.
Donald Bradman makes world record cricket score of 452.

Brothers, not rich but spruced up for a night out in the twenties. Both had fought in the trenches in France.

AN EDWARDIAN FAMILY

On 20 January 1901 Queen Victoria died and throughout the British Empire people mourned. She had been Queen since 1837. It was hard to imagine what the world would be like without her.

Victoria had been a homely queen – 'a good woman, a good wife and a good mother', a Sydney newspaper said. She had 'made the life of the English home what it is' – and the Australian home what it was, as well.

The 'respectable' homes of Australia expected the the woman to be a good wife, mother and housekeeper. The man should be a sober and reliable bread-winner. The children were to be seen and not heard.

In such households the husband had a steady job – a bank teller, for instance, an accountant or company clerk, or his own small business. He had at least one good suit, possibly two, a good hat, and maybe a silver watch and chain to attach to his waistcoat.

The wife had at least one good hat and a best dress which most probably she had made. Each child had at least one good outfit – their Sunday best. The family went to church.

Australian suburbs grew to house these respectable families. They were not rich enough to build mansions – or to have servants – but they liked to live in dignity out of sight of the poorer suburbs.

The houses were solid brick or weatherboard in streets lined with pin-oaks and plane trees. They had six to eight rooms. Unlike a factory worker's house, there were separate bedrooms for parents and children. The beds were neatly made each day.

The rooms were rather dark. There were lace and velvet curtains, velvet cushions, mats and rugs on the floorboards. A piano stood in one corner.

Pictures hung on the walls – a painting or even a photograph of grandparents, a scene in the English or Scottish countryside, and a portrait of King Edward or Queen Victoria. The more English a home was, the more 'respectable' the family.

There were ornaments too – made of porcelain and

brass. Somewhere in the room, perhaps on the piano, rested the large velvet-covered family Bible.

The family kept warm in front of a wood fire. Meals were cooked on a wood-burning stove, kept black and shining by the woman of the house. The wood was delivered by a woodman with a horse and cart.

A man came to the door selling meat. Another sold fish. The man who sold rabbits was called the 'rabbitoh'. A Chinese market gardener came by with vegetables. Milk came in a horse drawn cart. The nightman came to take away the can from the lavatory out the back.

These families saved money. They made clothes and prepared food for themselves in the old ways. There were home-made jams, pickles, chutneys, sauces, and preserved fruit and vegetables in the pantry. Vegetables grew in the backyards. On Sundays, when relatives dropped in, there were cakes and scones. There was meat in the meat safe, to keep it safe from flies. Nothing was wasted.

In the evening the streets were lit by a lamplighter. Inside by the kerosene lamp or candlelight, the children played the games their parents had played. They were simple games of cardboard, paper, matchboxes, string, beads, bits of cloth and playing cards. They had no radio or gramophone. They went to bed early and got up early.

Children were taught not to swear, to say their prayers, to speak only when they were spoken to. They were never to behave like the rough children of poor families. They were kept very clean. Girls were taught to brush their long hair a hundred strokes night and morning. Nits were a big disgrace.

The people who lived in these comfortable suburban houses did not like the idea of change. They were loyal to Britain and King Edward. When war came in 1914 the father, if he was not too old, or the sons, went off to fight. Mothers and daughters knitted socks for the soldiers. Everyone did their duty.

EMPIRE AND 1914

This sixteen year old put his age up for the army recruiting officer so that he could go to the war. His elder brother was already there. Both survived.

Early in the twentieth century Britain was still home for many people in Australia, even for some who had been born and raised here.

At school, children were taught that to be part of the British Empire was a privilege and a blessing, that to be British was to be noble and brave, and that loyalty to the Mother Country must never waver. Adults learnt much the same lessons from newspapers and books.

By 1910 or thereabouts a war between Britain and Germany seemed very likely. The British government told the Australian government that if war broke out in Europe Australia would be expected to send troops.

Australia began training its own soldiers. All boys from the ages of twelve to twenty-five were to be given military training. They had to put on a uniform and spend some of their weekends learning how to be soldiers.

Some refused to obey the new law which they said should not be tolerated in a free country. Thousands were taken before the courts, and many went to jail. But most boys put up with it, and even enjoyed gaining the skills of warfare.

Posters encouraged Australian men to go to the war. The mother looks accusingly at all those who have stayed home while her husband risks his life for his country.

For several years the nations of Europe had been preparing for war. On one side was Germany, Austria, Hungary and Turkey. On the other side was France, Russia, Italy and Britain. All of them had empires to call on, as well as their own people.

Both sides built more and more weapons and warships. Weapons were becoming much more sophisticated – the factories of Europe churned out huge guns and an unlimited supply of shells for them, rapid firing rifles and machine guns. Europeans had never been so well-equipped to kill each other.

But the people who ruled Europe were not as clever as the men who made the weapons. The rulers were mainly men whose ways of thinking had not caught up with the world. They imagined the war being won in great cavalry charges as wars sometimes had before. They thought it would all be over quickly.

Germany had a Kaiser who believed that war was glorious and that Germany must become the mightiest nation on earth. Britain was ruled by men who also believed war was glorious and who were determined that Britain should remain the mightiest on earth. Russia had a Tsar who believed that he had been appointed by God. The Tsar, the Kaiser and the King of England were cousins.

The war started in August 1914. The new Australian Prime Minister, Andrew Fisher, announced that Australia would fight for Britain to 'the last man and the last shilling'. Someone else writing in the *Australian Worker* said 'God help Australia! God help England! God help Germany! God help us!'.

For the great majority of Australians the war was a chance to show their love of England and prove themselves to the rest of the world.

War was the best place for a man to prove himself – and the best place for a nation. An excited poet wrote

> A nation is never a nation
> Worthy of pride or place
> Till the mothers have sent their firstborn
> To look death on the field in the face.

Young men rushed to join the army. It was like a great adventure. Some hurried because they feared the war would end before they got there.

From the troopships the Australian soldiers wrote home to families and girlfriends. Some said that it would have been unmanly not to go. Had they not joined up they could never have lived with their consciences – they could have never looked a girl in the face, they said.

Many Australian women encouraged men to go. Men who stayed home often received white feathers from women. A white feather was a way of saying 'Coward'.

Others joined simply because their mates had. A good many reckoned a soldier's pay was better than the wages they were getting. For a lot it was a simple choice between the army and unemployment.

Australian soldiers departing by ship for Europe.

A NATION AT WAR

The Australian soldiers went first to Egypt. They were grouped with soldiers from New Zealand to form the Anzacs – the Australian and New Zealand Army Corps.

The first few months were pretty good. In between training exercises in the desert the men enjoyed the streets of Cairo. Then they sailed to a place few Australians had ever heard of, Gallipoli in Turkey.

Very early on the morning of 25 April 1915 the boats carrying the Anzacs crept quietly towards the beaches of Gallipoli. The Turkish soldiers on shore heard them coming and opened fire. One Anzac recalled later what happened:

> Some of our men crouched in the crowded boat, some sat up without a worry in the world, some laughed and joked. We jumped into water up to our waists. On the beach we had to fix bayonets and charge. There was much swearing and cheering. Clean over a machine gun we went. Men were dropping all around me. It was mad, wild, thrilling. I felt as if I was going on some exciting chase or something.

By the time the sun came up the Anzacs were across the beach and digging trenches to protect them from the Turkish guns. The fighting continued all that day – and the next day, for weeks and months. Further up the beach British and French troops, and men from all over their empires in Africa and Asia, were also fighting and dying.

On 6 August the Anzacs launched a major attack at a place called Lone Pine. It was a bright sunny day. The Turks were only one hundred metres away when the Anzacs jumped from their trenches and raced

After a battle at Passchendaele in Belgium, 1917. At times the mud was so deep fighting was impossible.

forward, firing and screaming. There was a terrible struggle. In the first few days of the battle at Lone Pine four thousand Anzacs were killed.

The war was no longer a great adventure. 'There is nothing heroic or glorious in it', one solider wrote:

> The loss of life is awful. Rivers of blood – the trenches are red with the life blood of my friends. Today a man was shot dead in front of me. He was only a lad, a little fellow with snowy hair. He was walking down the path in front of me when he suddenly flung up his hands, and turned around. He stared at me for one second. Then he fell at my feet. In seconds his hair was scarlet, his clean white singlet all red.

At the end of the year, when the winter snows had started, it was decided that victory was impossible. The Anzacs were removed from Gallipoli. One of them wrote a letter home:

> The Turks have beaten us. Tonight is our last night here. It hurts to have to leave. I am sick of it and need a rest but to chuck the whole thing in – well, it makes me want to cry. And the Australians did not fail. We did everything possible. We feel it all very much. It is wrong to go and leave our dead friends here in their lonely graves.

The Anzacs now joined the fighting in France and Palestine.

Fighting had been raging in France for two years. The two sides faced each other from lines of trenches that stretched hundreds of kilometres across Europe. This was the Western Front.

More soldiers from Australia joined the fighting in France. The Anzacs had become famous for their courage at Gallipoli, and the troops on the Western Front were proud of their record. They believed that they had 'shown the world'.

Thousands of Australians were to die on the battlefields of France and Belgium.

The governments of Europe and their generals could not work out how to win the war. Through four long years soldiers fought their hopeless battles.

The trenches were often waist-deep in mud. In one bad winter many soldiers froze to death. They lived among the rotting flesh of men and animals. They made pointless charges into barbed wire and storms of shell, machine gun and rifle fire. It was slaughter. The survivors then retreated to the trenches, and waited for the next order to charge.

Both sides used poison gas – men were dying from the effects of it years later. They tunnelled under each other's lines to plant explosive then crawled back and watched as hundreds of men were buried alive in an instant. They dropped bombs on each other from aeroplanes. There had never been a war like it.

On 11 November 1918 Germany and her allies surrendered. About twelve million people were dead. Sixty thousand of them were Australian – sixty thousand out of a population of only four and a half million.

The Anzacs came back to a heroes' welcome. Most of them were proud of their achievements but few of them now thought that war was a great adventure.

Men from Australia and New Zealand fight a losing battle on the ridges at Gallipoli — and create a legend of heroism.

MIRACULOUS PROGRESS

The war was still a terrible memory in the 1920s. Sixty thousand young men had not come back. There were cripples on the streets – former soldiers – to remind people what the battlefields had been like.

There was a great pride in the achievements of the Anzacs, but also horror at the human losses. People wondered what it had all been for and looked for ways to forget an unhappy world.

Sport helped. Cricket, tennis and football matches drew big crowds of spectators, as they always had. In 1926 Australia lost the Ashes to England – Don Bradman the Boy from Bowral, had not yet arrived on the cricket scene.

When Australia won three gold medals at the Paris Olympics in 1924 the people at home marvelled at how such a new country could produce so many great athletes. Men like the swimmer, 'Boy' Charlton took on the best in the world and beat them – time after time. Some Australians wondered if a superior race of humans had developed under the Australian sun.

It was a great time for breaking records – in aeroplanes, motor cars and on bicycles. One man rode his bike from Sydney to Perth in just twenty-six days. Then two men made the journey by car in only six days. This was miraculous progress.

But not many people could afford a motor car. They went to work on foot, or by train, tram or bike.

They went to visit friends, on picnics to the beach and sometimes to the theatre the same ways.

For well-off people in the cities there was an occasional opera or ballet to see. Dame Nellie Melba, long regarded as the world's greatest soprano, came home to Melbourne to finish her career. People loved her as much as they loved 'Boy' Charlton.

The most popular entertainment of all was probably dancing. Every community had at least one building which could be used for dancing. In the country, people rode into town, came by horse and buggy, to fox-trot the night away in a council or church hall. The men danced in special shoes called dancing

Jazz grew out of the music of black American slaves. In the 1920s white Americans and Australians began playing it. This band was called Muriel and the Redheads and they played in Sydney dance halls.

On the beach in Perth around 1925.

pumps. The women wore shorter and shorter skirts and hair.

In the cities there were spacious and stylish dance halls, and ten or twelve piece bands. Increasingly they played music from America, especially jazz. For many people the 1920s was the jazz age.

It was also the age of films – the pictures, or the 'flicks'. You could watch the flicks in seedy country and suburban halls where families often booked the same seats each week, or in the grand picture palaces in the city.

The picture palaces were another world – of luxurious carpets, marble staircases and statues, two thousand or so deep red velvet-covered seats under ceilings painted with stars and clouds.

The films were black and white and silent. The talkies were not invented until the end of the decade. In the dark of the theatre someone tinkled on a piano or thundered on an organ to provide the right mood for the films.

Australians liked to see films about their frontier history. The convict era and bushranging were favourite subjects. But soon Hollywood films were all the rage.

A dance hall in a Melbourne suburb. The tramway workers got out of the photographer's road, but the dog didn't.

Australian film makers found they could not compete with the rich American studios and their stars. A film starring cricket heroes was cheaper than employing actors.

DAISY BATES AND THE ABORIGINES

Daisy Bates was born in Ireland in 1863. Her family was rich and Daisy had a free and happy childhood. As a girl she was a bit of a rebel.

When she was still young she developed a chest complaint and to cure it she went to the warm climate of Australia. She arrived in Townsville, Queensland, in 1884. From there she went by Cobb & Co. coach to Sydney, where she met John Bates, a drover, horse-breaker and a man of action whom his friends called a 'wild colonial boy'. Daisy and John married in 1885.

The marriage was not happy and after ten years Daisy went back alone to Britain, where she worked as a journalist. In 1899 she sailed back to Western Australia to visit her son and never left again.

Daisy decided to report on the way Aboriginal people were living in Western Australia. She took a horse and a buggy and went off into the outback for six months. What she saw changed her life completely.

The Aborigines were badly clothed, poorly fed and there was a great deal of disease among them. Alcohol had become a major problem.

To protect white people from the diseases which were widespread among Aboriginal groups, the government had decided to keep the Aborigines apart. Those with diseases were taken to two islands off the coast of Western Australia – the Aboriginal men to one island, and the women to another.

In 1910 Daisy Bates visited the islands with two scientists. She was appalled by what she saw and decided that she would spend the rest of her life trying to help.

Like most Australians, Daisy Bates was convinced that the time was not far off when there would be no

Daisy Bates thought that the Aborigines were already a dying race when white people arrived in Australia. They were not, but without their land they became dependent.

Aboriginal women at Oodnadatta, South Australia, dressed as missionaries liked to dress them.

Aboriginal people left in Australia. Years later she wrote a book called *The Passing of the Aborigines*. Her task was to make their 'passing' – their dying out – as comfortable as possible.

There was no point in trying to understand the Aboriginal people because they would soon be gone, Daisy said.

In 1912 Daisy Bates shocked white Australians by going to live in a tent with an Aboriginal group at Eucla, a harsh and lonely place on the Great Australian Bight. This was considered most peculiar, even a disgraceful thing for a decent white lady to do.

Daisy did not care what other people thought. If white people were worried that she might have gone wild in the desert, they need not have been. Daisy Bates never failed to look as if she were on her way to church.

Daisy enjoyed her life among the Aborigines. She treated them as 'her children'. The Aborigines called her 'Kabbarli', or grandmother.

The Aboriginal people liked her because she cared for them. And she did not insist they work for her.

In 1919 she set up a new camp at Ooldea, a tiny place on the new railway line across the vast and empty Nullarbor Plain. Ooldea was hot and dusty and plagued with flies. But Daisy stayed, in her long dark dress buttoned up to the neck.

Daisy Bates became famous and highly respected throughout Australia and the Empire. In 1934 she was awarded a medal by the King.

But life for Aborigines did not improve. Had there been a hundred people like Daisy Bates working among them, little would have changed. It did not help to treat Aboriginal people as children. And telling white Australians that the Aborigines were going to die out only encouraged them to turn away from the problem, saying that there was nothing they could do.

Daisy Bates' kindness to the Aboriginal people was nothing in the face of the problems they had to face when the land was taken from them. In the north of Australia, Aborigines trying to keep their land were being shot by white settlers in the 1930s.

Not everyone agreed with Daisy Bates. One man, a professor from Melbourne, said she talked 'humbug'. The Aborigines were never a dying race, he said, until white men 'started to make them die'.

Daisy at her desk, well covered up. She wears gloves and a fly net on her hat.

FLYING MACHINES

Bert Hinkler's plane leaves Perth Oval.

People had always dreamed of flying. Towards the end of the nineteenth century it had at last begun to seem possible.

Huge balloons had been used to lift brave men and women into the air. This was exciting enough but it was not the bird-like flight they dreamed of.

In the 1890s men built machines with wings attached that could fly with someone in them. In Australia in 1909 Mr Colin Defries flew a contraption about one hundred metres in five seconds. At one point he was four or five metres off the ground and, as a newspaper said, 'There was every prospect of the aeroplane soaring aloft had not the engine worked badly.'

Of course at other times the engine worked well and the wings worked badly. Some thought these early airmen were very brave, many others thought they were mad. 'If God had meant us to fly he would have given us wings,' they said.

But during the war aeroplanes became faster and safer. Thousands of planes were built as fighting machines.

After the war many young pilots bought planes and travelled around the country putting on shows of clever flying. People paid to come and watch them twist and turn their little planes in the sky and swoop down so low the crowd would gasp and duck their heads. The pilots also offered 'joy-rides' to those who were game enough to leave the ground.

Soon it was realized that planes could be more useful. Planes were faster than trains, ships or motor cars. In a huge country like Australia they could carry mail and supplies and even passengers to isolated places. And planes might also reduce the time to America and Europe – from several weeks to a few days.

In 1919 the government offered a prize of £10,000 to the first Australians to fly from England to Australia. Ross and Keith Smith won the award after making

Twenty-six year old Amy Johnson and the plane in which she flew alone to Australia in 1930. She became as much a hero among Australians as she was in her native England.

the journey crammed into a little two-engined plane with two mechanics. It took them twenty-seven days.

The newspapers were much impressed. They had flown 'across mountains, deserts and several seas; through rainstorms, snowstorms and fogs; across the Equator where difficult air conditions were experienced, and . . . made many hazardous landings in places where no airman had landed before'.

The next twenty years saw many such races and competitions in Australia. Every year new records were set. Pilots like the Smiths and Bert Hinkler became popular heroes.

Bert Hinkler grew up in Bundaberg in Queensland. When the war started in 1914 Hinkler joined the British Airforce and became a pilot. He loved the flying but hated the war.

Hinkler's planes were tiny, with one small engine, but he set a number of records flying them, first in Europe and then in Australia. Then in 1928 he set out alone to fly from England to Australia. It seemed impossible in such a small plane but Hinkler made the journey in only fifteen days.

Bert Hinkler in suit and flying headgear. There was no protection from the wind in the early planes, and no weather forecasts. Yet these pilots flew at 160 km/h in all kinds of weather.

Bert Hinkler was famous. Crowds gathered wherever he went. Songs were written about him. He was given a medal by the King and money by the Australian government.

On a foggy night in January 1933 Bert Hinkler took off alone from an English aerodrome. He planned to reach Australia in eight days. Hinkler's wife had gone on ahead by ship. She never saw him again.

In a terrible snowstorm over the Italian Alps Hinkler lost his directions and flew into the side of a mountain. Four months later the plane was found with Hinkler's body beside it.

Hinkler was not the only Australian pilot to die in a plane crash. Two other famous Australian pioneers in aviation, Sir Charles Kingsford Smith and Charles Ulm, were both killed. But before their deaths they had made several historic flights in their plane, 'Southern Cross'.

The most famous of these flights was across the Pacific Ocean in 1928. Ten thousand people were at Eagle Farm aerodrome in Brisbane to watch her appear out of the clouds, circle three times 'like a giant blue hawk' and land with 'graceful precision, pulling up to a standstill in a remarkably short distance'.

THE BATTLER ON THE LAND

Bill Matthews and Frank Laffey were soldier settlers near Shepparton, Victoria. They worked for the water commission during the day and cleared their blocks for orchards at night. They shared a horse, and the spray pump behind them here. Frank was gassed and had his hip shattered in the war.

The Anzacs of World War I had been promised great rewards for their service to the country. One of them was land. Land would be available to any soldier who wanted to become a farmer.

The government divided some of the very big properties into small farms and made them available to returned soldiers.

Nearly forty thousand soldiers went on the land. In some places they tried to grow wheat. In others, they raised animals, planted orchards and vegetable crops, milked cows.

Very often life for these farmers was as hard as it had been for the selectors forty or fifty years before. Most of the land had to be cleared before it could be planted. The settler then had to fence his block and build a house.

The whole family had to work from morning to night. There was no money for clothes or anything but the most basic food. No one took holidays. For children there was little time for school work, no money for toys.

While many people in the cities were enjoying the advantages of electricity, gramophones and radios in their homes, very few soldier settlers could afford them. While the suburbs were getting sealed roads and sewerage these country people were not.

The soldier settlers preferred the independence of farming life to the comforts of the town. They saw themselves as carrying on the tradition of the pioneers. They were opening up the land, serving their country with their hard work and courage.

They needed courage. Like all farmers they sometimes had to battle droughts, floods and bushfires. They also had to struggle with poor soil, weeds, erosion and pests like grasshoppers and rabbits – millions of rabbits. Soldier settlers grew sick of trying to kill them, and sick of eating them – baked, stewed and boiled.

Australians in the 1920s liked to imagine the time when a vast population would be living in the interior of their country. Politicians spoke of Australia

A jinker with a very clean child in muddy country.

supporting fifty or even one hundred million people within fifty years.

Not only returned soldiers were settled on the land. English migrants were enticed to Australia with offers of small farms. It was believed that the English were a superior race and well-suited to pioneering, but like many Australian soldier settlers, they often failed to survive on the land.

Many of the settlement schemes were an expensive failure. Governments invested a lot of money dividing up the land and providing roads, railways and irrigation channels. But too often the settlers did not know enough about farming. In some places the soil was too poor, or the markets for products were too far away. Some of the blocks were simply too small – no one could have made a living off them.

Not all the farmers were defeated. Some were lucky such as the group of seven hundred families that settled at Red Cliffs, near Mildura on the Murray River. They changed a huge area of dry, scrubby land into good, green orchards.

The difference between success and failure for a settler was very often a year-round supply of water.

Farms in the vicinity of a large river could be irrigated. Channels were dug from the river or reservoir to carry water out into the countryside. Farming was made possible where once settlers would have given up in despair.

Alice Laffey washes the clothes in an outdoor copper on a new dairy farm near Wangaratta, Victoria.

BILLY HUGHES

Billy Hughes went to the meeting of world leaders in France when the war ended. He made headlines with his fierce arguments on behalf of Australia and the Australians who had fought in the war. Here the soldiers show their gratitude.

William Morris (Billy) Hughes was a Welshman. Born in 1862, he migrated to Australia at the age of twenty-two. He spent several years in Queensland and New South Wales at various times working as a shearer, stockman, fruit picker, sailor and school teacher.

Hughes got to know the working people of Australia. He learnt what their hopes were, what things they valued highly, what they wanted from their politicians.

In 1890 Hughes married Elizabeth Cutts and set up a small shop in a Sydney inner suburb. He was now taking an interest in politics. Having been a worker himself he naturally joined the Labor Party.

When the new Commonwealth parliament met for the first time in 1901, Billy Hughes was a member of it. He was still a member of it fifty years later.

Hughes was a gnome-like man with large ears and skin like baked leather. He was partly deaf and frequently unwell. But he was a tireless worker and ambitious. He never showed mercy to an opponent.

He had two deep beliefs. First, that the wages, working conditions and opportunities for Australian workers should be improved. Second, that Australia should always stay closely tied to Britain. Hughes loved Australia but he was also fiercely loyal to Britain.

When he became Prime Minister in 1915, Hughes was determined that Australia should fight to the end. The war must be won. He went to Europe and visited the troops on the battlefields. He promised the British that more Australians would be sent.

To provide these soldiers Hughes tried to introduce conscription – young men would be forced to join the army and be sent to the battlefields. Many people supported Hughes. Why should only some Australians fight for their country, they asked. Why not all?

Many others, however, opposed him. No man should be forced to die on foreign soil, they said. It must be a matter of choice. Some asked whether Hughes was going to fight until there were no young men left. The politicians should be trying to arrange a peace, they said, not fighting to the end.

Twice Hughes put his conscription idea to a popular vote. Each time the people voted NO.

Hughes left the Labor Party because it had opposed him. He started a new party with the people who had once been his enemies. The people in the Labor Party, the ones who had once been his friends, called him a 'rat'.

But the soldiers – 'the diggers' as they became known – loved him. He had fought the war to the end. They called Hughes the 'Little Digger'.

1930-1949

1930 Prices for Australian wool, wheat, meat and minerals fall, industry slows down. Unemployment rises rapidly.
Australia connected to London by telephone.

1931 One third of Australian workers unemployed.
Joseph Lyons, Prime Minister.

1932 Unemployment remains at thirty per cent.
Sydney Harbour bridge opened.
Phar Lap, great Australian racehorse, dies in California.

1933 Adolf Hitler becomes dictator of Germany.
Australians outraged at English 'bodyline' bowling in test matches.
Australian Women's Weekly begins publication.
Australia gains control of a sector of Antarctica.

1934 Greek, Italian and Yugoslav miners attacked by Australians at Kalgoorlie. Two killed.

1935 Italy invades Abyssinia (Ethiopia).

1936 Civil war in Spain.

1937 Ceremony at the crowning of King George VI in England is first world wide radio broadcast.
Tasmanian, Les Vaughan, invents Defender Slug and Snail killer.

1938 Germany invades Czechoslovakia.

1939 'Black Friday' in Victoria and New South Wales — bushfires devastate the countryside and more than one hundred people die.
Robert Menzies, Prime Minister.
Germany invades Poland. Britain declares war.
Australian Prime Minister declares war with Germany.

1941 John Curtin, Prime Minister.
Germany invades Russia.
(December) Japanese attack American fleet at Pearl Harbour, British at Singapore, and invade Philippines.
Fifteen thousand Australian soldiers defend Tobruk in Libyan desert — become famous as the 'Rats of Tobruk'.

1942 Japanese bomb Darwin, Broome and Townsville.
Japanese midget submarines enter Sydney Harbour.
United States navy defeats Japanese in the Battle of the Coral Sea.

1943 Italy surrenders.

1944 D Day. Allied forces, largely British and American land in France.
Liberal Party formed, Robert Menzies leader.

1945 War ends in Europe. Hitler commits suicide. Mussolini killed. Atomic bombs dropped on Hiroshima and Nagasaki, Japan. Pacific war ends.
John Curtin dies. Ben Chifley, Prime Minister.
United Nations created in San Francisco. All member countries declare that they are dedicated to international peace and freedom, and improved living conditions.

1946 Missile testing site established with British government at Woomera, South Australia.

1947 Eastern European countries become communist in alliance with the Soviet Union.
Forty hour week for Australian workers introduced.
Scheme assisting people from Europe to migrate to Australia launched.

1948 First Holden produced in Australia.
State of Israel created.

1949 Robert Gordon Menzies, Prime Minister.
Communists, led by Mao Tse Tung, take over China.

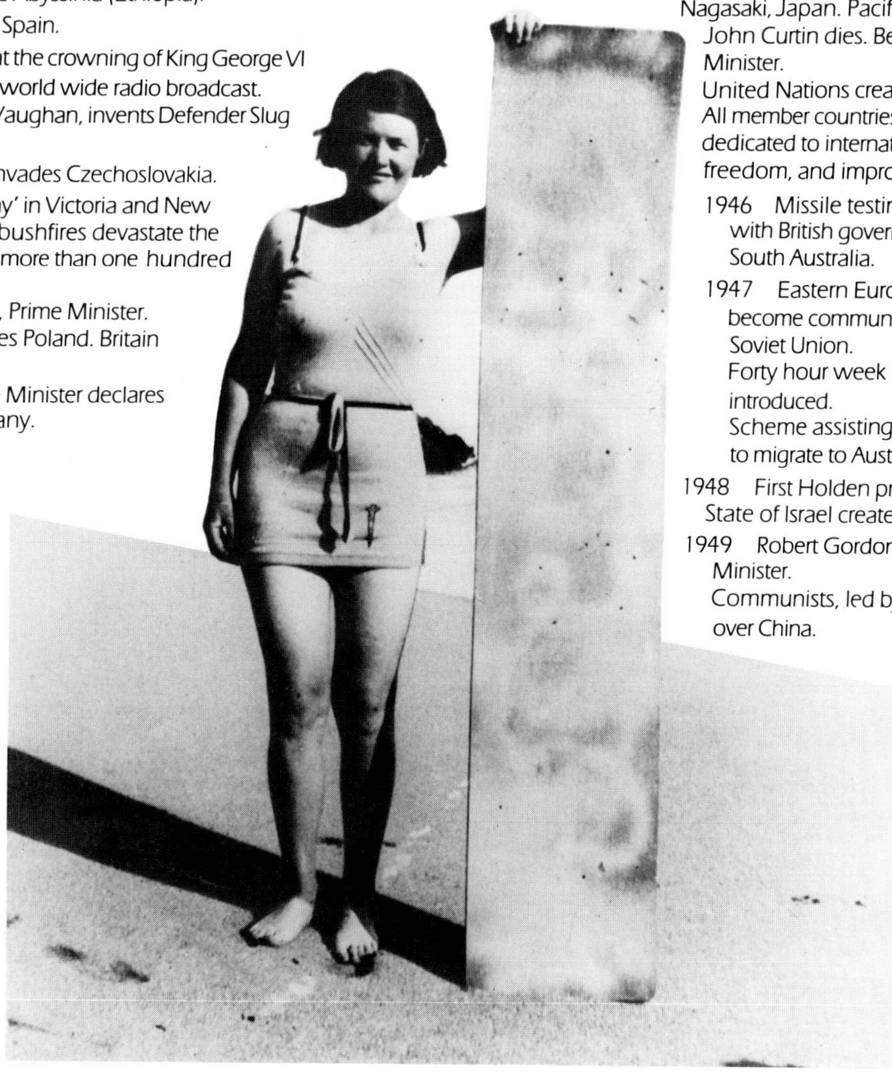

Surfer, 1930s.

THE GREAT DEPRESSION

Times had been hard for many people in the 1920s, but there had also been many signs of progress. The cities had grown. New roads and railways had been built for the new suburbs. New land was opened up. Huge irrigation schemes commenced. People talked about Australia's great future – 'Australia Unlimited' it was called.

But in 1929 Australia, like many other countries, found itself in trouble. Once again Australia was unable to sell its wool and wheat and metals overseas. There was no money to pay for the building works which had employed so many people in the previous ten years. The Australian government was heavily in debt to Britain.

With no money people stopped buying goods. The factories that made the goods stopped producing so many, or closed down altogether. So more people lost their jobs.

By 1932 about one in every three Australian workers was unemployed, and in some places the number was even higher. Australia was in the grip of a depression.

Governments seemed unable to solve the problem. Many people offered suggestions. Some said print more money. Others said print less. Some said give everyone free bread. Some said overthrow the rich and start a society like Russia. Some said pray.

A small 'dole' was paid to the unemployed but it was not enough to keep them – particularly if there was a family to feed. Soup kitchens were set up by local councils and the Salvation Army. Men and women trudged along to get their handouts of food.

Governments also established a system they called sustenance. The workers called it 'susso'. Unemployed people were given food and clothing in return for doing useful work, like building roads or clearing land. Not all the work was useful – much land they cleared grew back to bush within a few years.

The workers who did 'susso' hated it. They felt that they were being treated as inferior citizens – rather like convict labour even though they had committed no crimes.

This was the worst thing about unemployment for many people. Some could not bear to rely on charity. They wanted to really earn their living, to pay their own way. Instead they were humiliated by being treated as if they were a problem.

Of course not everyone was affected by the depression. Many continued to live very well. Letters from the well-off people appeared in the newspapers saying that they could not understand why there were so many unemployed people hanging

A bank manager and three young employees who knew they were fortunate to have a secure job.

Poisoned rabbits by the cartload. These farmers are pleased to be rid of them.

Life seems to be going on as usual for this 1930 tennis party.

about in the cities. If they really wanted to help themselves, they said, they should go to the country. They were sure that there was plenty of work there.

Perhaps these people disliked the sight of the poor. It was hard to avoid them. There were beggars in the streets. Whole families were living in the back lanes of inner suburbs. There were people with malnutrition, and skin diseases caused by bad diets. There were hundreds of people in the old army greatcoats handed out to them by charities. Long queues formed outside shops and factories every time a job was advertised.

And occasionally there were street marches by unemployed people who wanted to show the world that something should be done.

Unemployed people queuing in Adelaide for their share of extra rations provided by the government at Christmas.

A lot of men and women did go to the country. It was called going 'on the track'. These people wandered about in search of work by day and slept under the stars by night. There were often camps of unemployed people in country towns, as there were in the cities.

Some farmers and townspeople gave them jobs to do in return for food or a few shillings. Some who had no work to offer gave them food anyway.

There was not much farm machinery in the 1930s so farmers needed more workers at various times of the year. The unemployed could eke out a little money in the countryside, following the harvests of hay, vegetables and fruit. Or they picked up jobs clearing farms of rubbish and cutting wood. And there were rabbits in the country – rabbits to be trapped or caught with ferrets. Rabbits provided a meal and their skins and carcases were worth a bit.

But not everyone could go on the track. A man or woman needed to be pretty fit because the life was hard. For married people with children it was just not possible – although many married men did go, promising to send money home.

People suffered a great deal in many other ways. The depression ended the hopes of thousands of young people for a good education which would let them do the things they dreamed of. Some people got stuck in dull jobs for life – too afraid of being out of work. The depression was a waste of people.

But Australians coped as best they could. They could not buy clothes or furniture or toys, so they made them. They could not buy much food so they grew what they could in their backyards and swapped or shared it with neighbours.

They could not afford to pay much for their entertainment, so they went to football and cricket which were cheap. And they organized their own amusements – there were card nights, community singing, neighbourhood picnics and sports days.

Nothing much was done for people, so they made do.

THE *W*IRELESS IN THE LOUNGEROOM

Although they were very expensive, thousands of wirelesses had already been sold in the 1920s. A wrestling match had been broadcast in 1925.

Music to do the new American dance steps to was heard in some people's homes. Now the carpet could be rolled back and everyone could dance without having a squeezebox or a piano – or someone to wind up the gramophone every few minutes. You could dance in your loungeroom any time you liked.

In the 1930s wireless sets became cheaper so more people bought them. Some people bought the basic parts and put the wireless together themselves. Wirelesses had valves instead of transistors then. They were big. A wireless was a piece of the furniture. It took pride of place in the loungeroom.

In the 1930s many more radio stations were built. It was hoped that soon everyone would have a wireless. The Prime Minister, Joe Lyons, said that, with the wireless, 'The word "lonely" will be eliminated from Australian life.'

Sport on the radio was very popular – first racing, then football and cricket. In 1933 the ABC kept half the country up late at night broadcasting the cricket from England.

The commentators were all in the studio in Australia. They received telegrams describing each ball of the match and they broadcast what they imagined they would see. Sound effects were made by hitting a hollow piece of wood with a pencil. The roar of the English crowd heard by Australian listeners was actually a gramophone record played in the studio.

Radio serials had people tuning in at the same time every night to shows like *Dad and Dave*, made in Australia. Many other serials were bought from America.

Radio shows often did stunt programmes, like broadcasting from an aeroplane or from a cave.

And talent quests were often held. During the depression many parents entered their children in

Fox trotters and waltzers at a dancing competition in a country hall, 1935.

them, hoping to win the £2 prize money.

There were news broadcasts, school programmes, plays, popular and classical music and community singing. People gathered in local halls to join in, or they sang along in their own loungerooms.

The wireless relaxed people. One well-known doctor believed that if listened to long enough the wireless could cure stomach cancer.

It could also frighten people. In America a play about an invasion from Mars was broadcast. Thousands of listeners thought it was actually happening and ran out into the streets in terror.

In spite of the depression, people saved up for many other kinds of household machines that ran on electricity. These made a big difference to the way housework was done and food was prepared.

Electric irons were a lot easier to use than the heavy old flatirons that had to be heated on a wood stove. Electric stoves meant less time cleaning grates and chopping wood. Electric jugs and reading lamps were popular.

Life in Australia was starting to feel good again for those people with jobs and homes and gardens of their own. Many men, by 1936, had found work. Mothers usually were fully occupied looking after their families. A new magazine, *The Australian Women's Weekly*, was in great demand.

But as life improved for many people in Australia, the news from overseas got worse. War was approaching.

In September 1939 listeners heard an announcement from the Prime Minister, Robert Menzies. Britain had just declared war on Germany, he said, and as a result Australia was at war too.

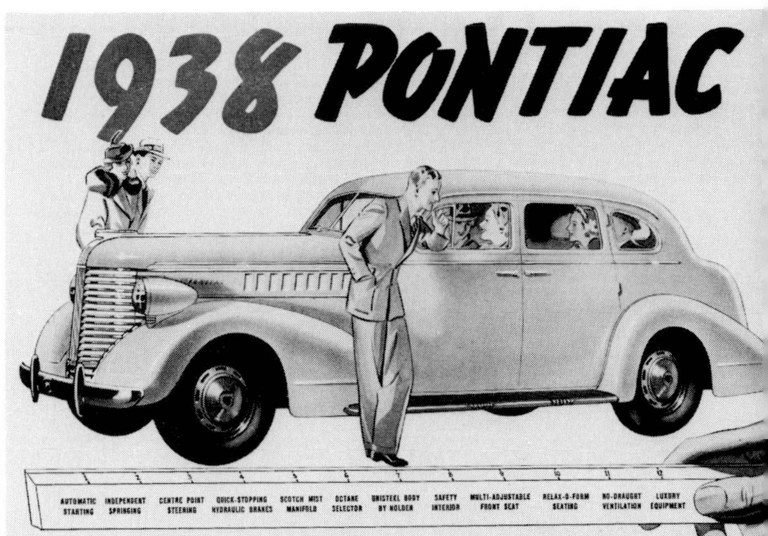

'FOR THEIR OWN GOOD'

Aboriginal reserves were large fenced-in places set up by governments in the 1920s and 1930s. There Aboriginal people were confined – 'for their own good, to protect them from mistreatment' the Aboriginal Protection Board said.

But people on the reserves were still mistreated. Aboriginal girls were taken from their parents and trained as maids. White women were giving up jobs as servants because the pay was very poor and the work was often humiliating. They preferred to work in factories. The pay for Aboriginal servants was even worse – sometimes they were not paid at all. Many of them soon ran away from the homes they had been placed in.

In many parts of Australia mission stations run by the churches also tried to protect the Aborigines. They provided housing, food, clothing and medicine. The children were given lessons in church schools.

But most missionaries treated Aborigines like children who would only 'grow up' when they became as much like whites as possible. And they too arranged for children to be taken from their families.

The big cattle and sheep stations in northern Australia employed Aboriginal men as stockmen and labourers, and the women as servants. Aboriginal workers received little money. Some received only their 'keep' – clothing, meat, flour, sugar, tea and tobacco.

An Aboriginal stockman in the Kimberleys, Western Australia.

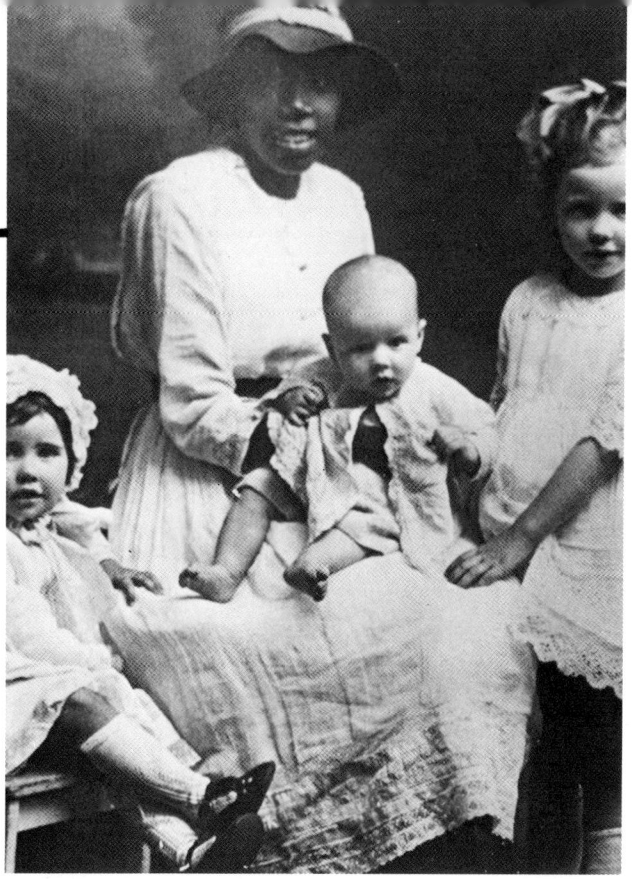

Aboriginal servant. Three white children.

It is not surprising that, despite the whites' talk of protecting them, Aboriginal people resented the whites. Sometimes they took violent action. And whenever they did, the whites inflicted terrible punishments.

The Warramullas were a proud, strong tribe about 320 kilometres from Alice Springs. In the 1920s they decided to drive the white settlers away once and for all. A war started.

In 1928 they met an old dingo hunter and killed him.

Constable Murray of the Northern Territory Mounted Police and Mr Strafford, the owner of Coniston Station, set out with three black trackers to find the men who had killed Brooks.

They went to a blacks' camp and began chaining up the men as they arrested them. Then, as Murray said, when one of them was being marched off

> He swirled the weighty chains above his head and came rushing for me. It was him or me. I drew my revolver and shot him between the eyes.

Next day the police moved off to another camp

> They were armed with spears, and when I shouted to them to put down their weapons they sat down in the long grass . . Firing broke out. I don't know who started it, but the whole seventeen of them – fifteen men and two women – were dead when it finished.

Further on, the following day the police found 'five blacks among a lot of women and children'. The constable wrote later

> They ran for cover in some rocks. I spurred my horse after them. As I reached them a shower of boomerangs came hurtling at my head. In the fighting, two blacks were shot dead and three taken prisoner, two of whom died on the way back.

Some days later Mounted Constable Murray and his men made yet another raid

> We rounded them up in a creek bed – fourteen men and a big following of women. The men gathered together threateningly and told the women to run. The blacks refused to put down their spears except by the nearby trees. One boy was holding his spear in a very threatening way . . . firing broke out. This time we took no prisoners.

Thirty-one Aborigines were dead by the time this police expedition was over.

In September 1932 five Japanese fishermen were speared at Caledon Bay, near the north-eastern tip of the Northern Territory. A patrol of four mounted police went out to investigate. They were ambushed by a group of Aborigines and Constable McColl was killed with a shovel-nosed spear through the chest.

The government announced that it was sending out an expedition to teach them a lesson.

Missionaries in the area believed that there would be another terrible massacre. They persuaded the government to wait. The missionaries sent out a small 'peace expedition' of three men – without guns. Many people thought they were mad and would all be killed.

The Aborigines were suspicious but friendly. The missionaries asked the men who had done the spearing to give themselves up. They did. There was no fighting.

The Aborigines believed that they were going to Darwin to talk things over. They would tell the white men that on their land they obeyed their own laws. The white man's law was not their law.

But they were put straight into jail, some of them for twenty years with hard labour.

WAR IN THE PACIFIC

Germany, Italy and Japan were governed by dictatorships in the 1930s. Each of them was controlled by a small group of fanatical and brutal men.

Each of them was determined to conquer other countries in their regions. Germany under Adolf Hitler and Italy under Benito Mussolini had invaded parts of Europe and Africa. Japan had invaded China and Manchuria. The dictatorships had built huge armies.

Britain and the other democratic countries did very little to stop them until September 1939 when Germany invaded Poland. Britain then declared war on Germany.

When the war began, Australia sent soldiers to fight against Germany and Italy in the Middle East and Greece. They fought in famous battles at Tobruk and El Alamein. They had victories and suffered defeats.

In the first week of December 1941 the Japanese bombed Pearl Harbour in the Pacific Ocean and began a rapid advance south. For Australians the war suddenly seemed a lot closer.

The Japanese army marched through the British and French colonies of South East Asia. Burma and Malaya were British colonies. The British were not prepared and the Japanese had easy victories.

Britain was sure that Singapore would not fall. It was too well defended by British ships and guns. But Singapore was captured in a few days.

There were Australian soldiers in Singapore and Malaya. Along with troops from Britain and her colonies they were captured and put in prison camps in Burma and Singapore. They were treated terribly and a great many died.

In March 1942 the Japanese reached New Guinea. It seemed that nothing could prevent them invading Australia.

In fact Japan had attacked Australia a few weeks before that. On 19 February nearly two hundred Japanese planes swept in over the sea to bomb and machine-gun Darwin. Eight ships in the harbour were sunk and many buildings were destroyed. Nearly six hundred people were killed or wounded.

Believing that the Japanese army was about to invade, some people in Darwin panicked. They grabbed a few clothes and anything else that they could easily carry and headed south in cars and on bikes.

In the next year Darwin and other towns from Broome in Western Australia to Townsville in Queensland were bombed. But there was never another panic like there was on the day of the first surprise raid on Darwin.

Within a few months of the attack at Pearl Harbour the Americans had organized a powerful army, navy and air force. Australia became the base for their campaign to drive the Japanese back. Their commander was General Douglas M. Macarthur.

In New Guinea the Japanese pushed across the Owen Stanley Ranges towards Port Moresby. Australian

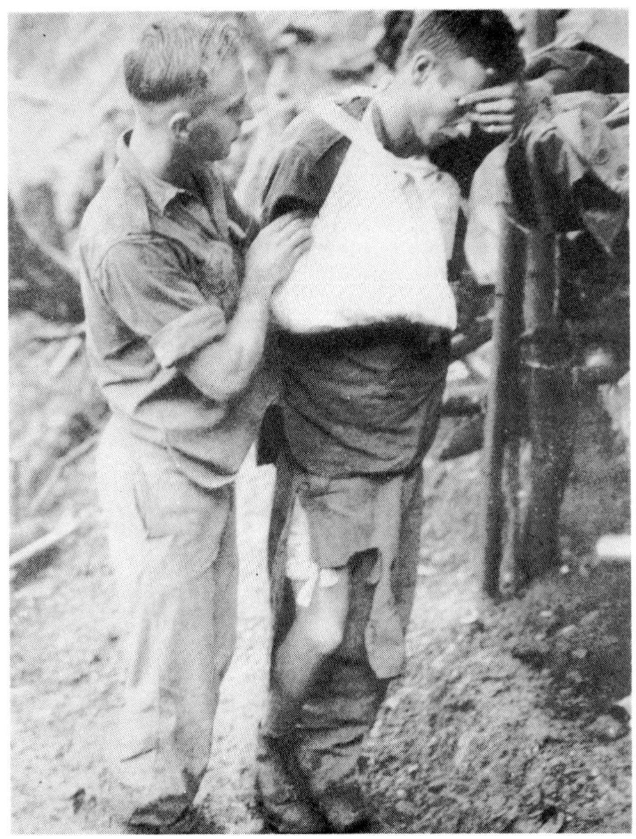

A wounded Australian comforted by a mate. The people of New Guinea often provided assistance carrying the wounded out of the battle lines.

Australian soldiers in the New Guinea jungle. Many of them had not long returned from the deserts of North Africa.

and American soldiers struggled to drive them back along the Kokoda trail.

The fighting in the New Guinea Highlands was tense and grim. Soldiers had to battle their way up steep mountain sides through dark and tangled jungle. Enemy snipers waited in trees.

Day after day heavy rain poured down. The men lived in slime and mud and steam. Malaria put many out of action. Thousands died in the fighting.

In May 1942 the American navy inflicted the first defeat on the Japanese in the Battle of the Coral Sea. In June they had another victory at Midway. Two months later Australian troops and airmen at Milne Bay in New Guinea had the first victory of land forces over the Japanese.

But it took another three years of bitter and bloody fighting to defeat the Japanese.

The 6 August 1945 was a fine, clear day in southern Japan. On that day the first atomic bomb was dropped by the Americans on the Japanese city of Hiroshima. There was a brilliant flash of fire. Then a huge pillar of smoke rolled high into the sky. The city was blasted flat, and its people killed. Three days later another nuclear bomb destroyed the city of Nagasaki.

The Japanese surrendered and the war was over.

Thirty-two thousand Australians died in the Second World War, a little more than half the number who died in the Great War of 1914-18. But the Second World War was the most terrible in history. More than fifty million people died.

The first bombing of Darwin in 1942 has been called Australia's Pearl Harbour. Next time the city was better prepared.

AUSTRALIANS PREPARE FOR INVASION

One night in May 1942 a fleet of five Japanese submarines surfaced ten miles off Sydney and launched three midget submarines. The three small but deadly craft glided underwater into the harbour. One was caught in a net and the Japanese crew blew it up. Another was detected, hunted and destroyed. The third torpedoed a small ship and then escaped back out to sea.

The submarine raid on Sydney and the attacks on Darwin were a great shock to Australians.

People in cities prepared themselves for attacks by sea and air. Should Australia be invaded there were plans to evacuate the population well away from the coast. Everyone knew the route to take. In each district there was a Volunteer Defence Corps of local men ready to organize evacuations and do what they could to defend the district. All farm stock was to be destroyed and houses and other buildings burnt before the Japanese arrived.

School playgrounds and parks were dug up to make trenches for people to shelter in case of air raids. There were trenches next to most bus, train and tram stops. Some families built shelters in their backyards.

Air raid practices were regularly held. A siren wailed and everyone had to go quickly into the nearest shelter. They stayed there until the siren started again to give the all clear.

At night no house was to show any light that might be seen from the sky. Windows were covered with thick black paper. Car lights had to be dimmed and screened by metal shields.

People were warned to be on the lookout for spies and not discuss the war in public places. German or Japanese agents might overhear. German-sounding names were regarded with great suspicion.

Mail was opened and read, and any remarks that the government thought could be useful to the enemy

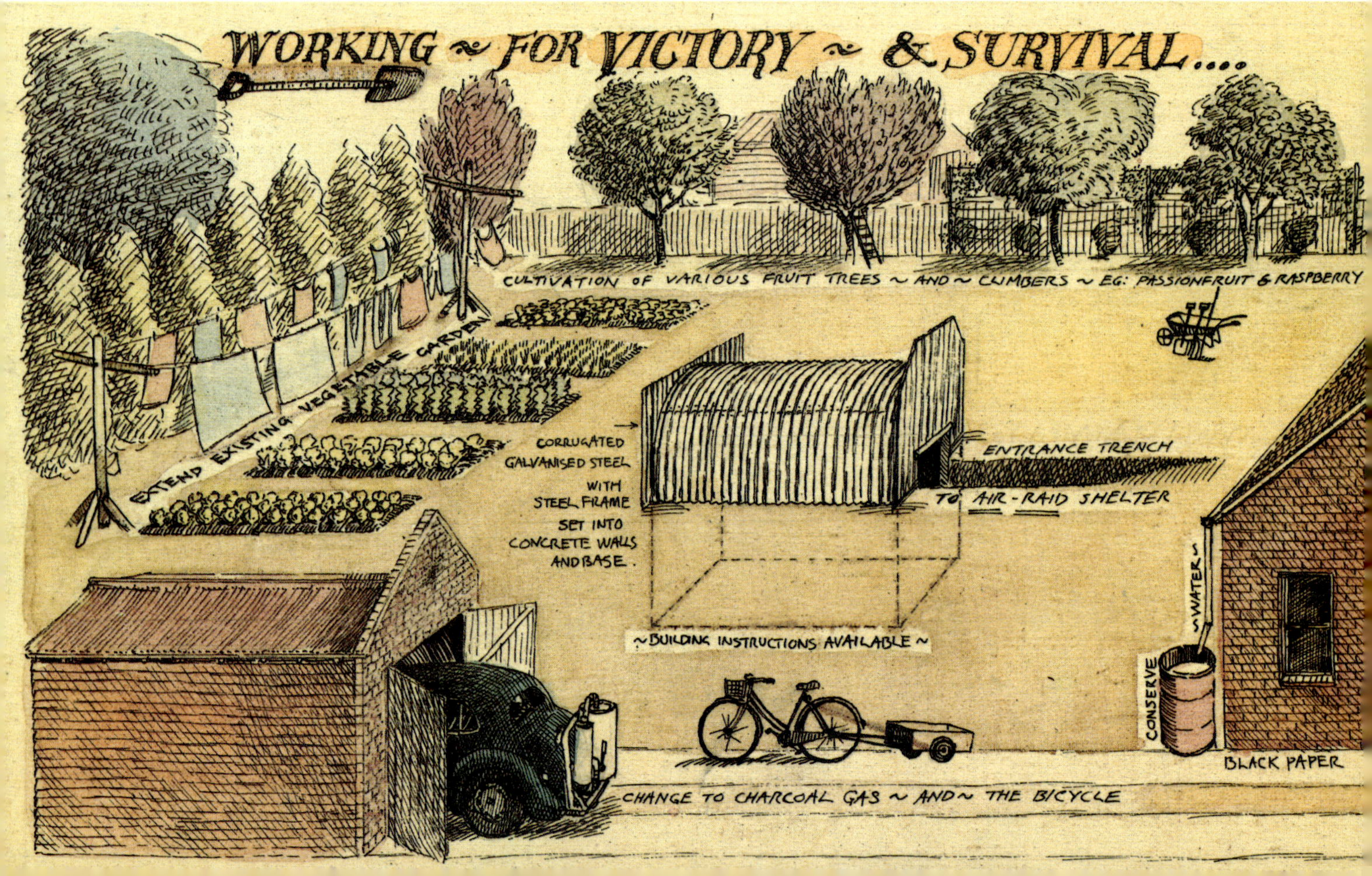

A warning for school children — loose talk could find its way to the ears of the enemy.

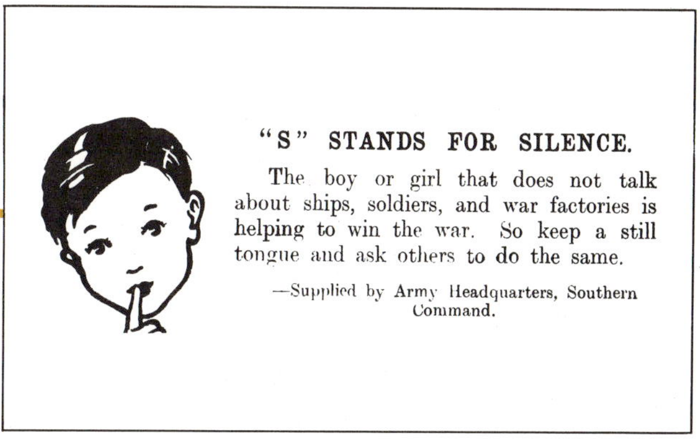
"S" STANDS FOR SILENCE.

The boy or girl that does not talk about ships, soldiers, and war factories is helping to win the war. So keep a still tongue and ask others to do the same.

—Supplied by Army Headquarters, Southern Command.

were cut out. Mail between soldiers and their families and friends was very carefully checked and censored.

Schoolchildren had to help with the war effort. They were asked to collect silver paper, old rubber tyres, newspapers and scrap metal, all of which could be reused. Old pots and pans, for instance, could be used to make guns and planes. Children who collected a lot of stuff were awarded badges and medals.

Everyone had a ration book with coupons in it. Coupons were a way of limiting how much people bought. Scarce things such as meat, petrol, butter, sugar and shoes could only be bought with coupons – and in small amounts.

Other things were not on sale at all or very hard to get. Furniture, blankets, radios, cigarettes and beer took a lot of finding.

The only people who had luxuries were the Americans. During the war American soldiers, sailors and airmen used Australia as a place for rest and relaxation. Sometimes they were resented, especially by Australian men.

The Americans had chocolate, Camel cigarettes, Coca Cola and nylon stockings to give away, and enough money for taxi fares and night clubs. Sometimes it seemed as if the real invaders were the Americans.

People grumbled about the Yanks, as they did about rationing. But both were essential. Australians were prepared to accept them in a war that could not be won without them.

WORK TO BE DONE

The boring side of war — women checking ammunition for defects.

Most Australian men and a lot of women still thought that the place for women was in the home – but by the 1930s thousands of women were in paid jobs.

Some were still servants but many more worked as shop assistants, waitresses, barmaids, stenographers, clerks, secretaries, and in such industries as food processing, clothing and textiles, rubber trades and confectionery.

Since the 1920s women had found a new kind of factory work, assembling household appliances like vacuum cleaners, toasters, refrigerators, radios, and washing machines. These were bought by well-off women to replace the work that servants used to do.

Some women were having less children in the 1930s. This worried a lot of community leaders who believed that having children was a woman's greatest duty.

When war came the politicians changed their thinking. Australia could not afford to have people at home. There was other work to be done. The country needed as many people as possible in the armed forces, and people to keep up the supply of arms and ammunition, food, tents and uniforms for the troops. This meant employing women in jobs most men had thought women could not or should not do.

But during the war women did them. They joined branches of the armed services and served in Australia and overseas. They worked as mechanics, truck drivers, anti-aircraft gunners, filled office jobs and, as the Women's Land Army, worked on farms.

They formed their own defence organizations, such as the Australian Women's Legion. They had no doubt that they could fight just as well as men, and

Making American flags to fly in Australian cities on 4 July, American Independence Day, 1942.

that they would be a vital part of the country's defence.

In heavy industry women operated the machinery which men had said would be too complicated for them. They welded, rivetted, operated cranes and trucks, filled cartridges and shells with explosive – as well as men had ever done.

People visiting the factories were amazed to see women 'behind mighty machines operating them with a skill and mastery that was little short of marvellous'.

When the day's work was over, most of these women went home to do housework and care for children. There were no child care centres provided and working women found friends or relatives to look after children during working hours.

But the government and other employers were not willing to pay women as much as men. Despite the efforts of women to get equal pay, in heavy industry they were paid only nine tenths of men's wages. In industries where women had always been employed they received just over half the male wage.

These low wages were one reason why some women were happy to hand over their jobs to men at the end of the war. Many others were told to leave by their returned-soldier husbands. Women's magazines and newspapers encouraged this. The 'ideal woman', they said, was again one who had babies, looked after the family – and was nice to come home to.

Bread and milk was delivered door-to-door from horsedrawn carts until the early seventies. Women bakers and 'milkies' were a familiar sight during the war.

PEACE

Australia's own car.

Jewish refugees arrive in Australia, 1948.

The Second World War had affected Australia little in comparison with the rest of the world. Unlike Russia, Britain, most of the other European countries and much of Asia, Australia had not been invaded. Australia numbered its dead in thousands. Other countries had lost millions, and their cities and farms lay in ruins.

On the day the war ended people all over the world celebrated. In Australia crowds gathered in the streets to sing and dance and drink to peace at last.

Many others on that day shed tears for the men and women they loved who had died in the war. And while all the celebrating was going on some must have wondered about the way the war had been brought to an end. What sort of peace would it be now that the world had atomic bombs?

In 1945 everyone hoped that the future would be better than the past. Not only did they want peace, they wanted something better than the 1930s.

Thinly stocked shelves in the corner store. Supermarkets were just a decade away.

The 1930s had meant unemployment and poverty. The aim now was to ensure that every man who wanted a job should have one.

The country needed more houses, hospitals and schools. People wanted better wages and working conditions. The government, which was led by Ben Chifley, did its best to make this happen.

Jobs were found for the men coming home from the war – new jobs and many of those done by women while the men were away. Returned soldiers were settled on the land in a number of places. Others were given training for new jobs. This time the scheme was more successful than the attempts of the 1920s.

Building an underground power station at Tumut in the Snowy Mountains.

The Australians were encouraged to buy more things now. A cheap family car was designed. Called the Holden, 'Australia's Own Car', it was made in Australia by the American company General Motors. The first Holden appeared in 1948. Within a few years it was easily the most popular car in Australia. Profits from sales of the Holden went to General Motors in America.

General Motors-Holden was one new industry. There were many others. And for industry to go ahead more electricity was needed.

In 1949 the Snowy Mountains scheme commenced. The plan was to divert the mountain rivers westward to provide more water for irrigation on the plains. There would be 130 kilometres of tunnels and nineteen dams.

At fifteen power stations high in the mountains the rushing water would be used to generate electricity for factories and homes hundreds of kilometres away.

Men and women from thirty different countries worked on the Snowy Mountains scheme. Some were refugees, people left homeless by the war in Europe. Many of them had engineering skills which were in short supply in Australia.

To Australians the project was an example of the marvellous things that could be done with imagination, science and energy in peacetime.

Australia did not get the fair and just society that many people hoped for. Nor did the peace last very long – by 1951 Australians were fighting a war in Korea, and people lived in fear of another world war.

But the terrible poverty of the 1930s did not return. In other ways as well Australia after the war was a very different place.

JOHN CURTIN

John Curtin began life as the son of a policeman in a small town, and ended it as Prime Minister and wartime leader of his country.

John Joseph ('Jack') Curtin grew up in Creswick, Victoria. He was not particularly clever at school, but he read everything he could lay his hands on.

By the time he reached his twenties Curtin was a socialist. He was convinced that there should be no rich or poor in Australia. The country's wealth, he believed, should be evenly shared among the people.

In Victoria and later Western Australia, Curtin worked for the trade unions and the Labor Party. He became a politician and was a member of the government during the Great Depression.

In these hard years Curtin became a heavy drinker, and it looked like his career was ruined. But he gave up drinking and in 1935 was elected leader of the Labor Party.

Young John and Elsie Curtin in 1917, shortly after they were married.

Prime Minister Curtin with the American who had pledged to drive the Japanese back, General Douglas Macarthur.

Just two months before Japan began the Pacific War, John Curtin became Prime Minister.

He rallied Australians together, insisting that everyone help in the country's defence. He also insisted to Britain that Australian troops be brought home from the Middle East to defend their country against the Japanese. And he formed a close friendship between the United States and Australia.

John Curtin was not the type of man you would expect to be a great war-time leader – he was a quiet, modest man. But he had a great love for his country and he was determined to do his duty as Prime Minister. He worked very hard.

It has been said by people who knew him that for long periods during the war Curtin could not sleep. He paced about for hours worried by decisions he had to make, and by the thought of what was happening to Australian soldiers.

He was not physically strong and the hard work and worry probably brought about his death on 5 July 1945, a few weeks before the war ended. Some people said that he was the greatest Prime Minister Australia ever had.

1950-1969

1950 War in Korea. Australia sends troops.

1952 Australian engineer and inventor, Mervyn Richardson invents the Victa Lawnmower.
Riot at Bonegilla, Victoria, over poor conditions in the migrant camp.
First hydrogen bomb tested in Pacific. British atomic bomb tests at Monte Bello off Western Australian coast.

1953 Elizabeth II crowned Queen of England.
Uranium mined at Rum Jungle, Northern Territory.
Oil discovered at Exmouth Gulf, Western Australia.

1954 Queen Elizabeth II and Prince Phillip visit Australia.
Vladimir and Evdokia Petrov, Russian diplomats defect to Australia, saying there are numerous Russian spies in Australia.

1955 Vaccine for polio — a disease which every year crippled hundreds of children — introduced.
Investigation into Petrov claims of spying finds no spies.

1956 Russia invades Hungary.
Olympic Games in Melbourne — Australia wins thirteen gold medals.
Television begins in Australia.
First atomic bomb testing at Maralinga, South Australia.

1957 Soviet Union launches first satellite, 'Sputnik', into space.

1959 Population of Australia reaches ten million.
Soviet Union puts two monkeys into space. Soviet rocket, 'Lunik', reaches moon.

1961 Discovery of huge iron ore deposits at Pilbara, Western Australia.
Yuri Gagarin, Soviet cosmonaut, orbits the earth in a satellite.

1962 Australian military advisers sent to train South Vietnamese soldiers.
World War close to breaking out during dispute between Soviet Union and United States over Cuba.

1963 United States establishes naval base at North-west Cape, Western Australia.
Russian woman, Valentina Tereshkova, spends three days in space.
Australian women begin to use the contraceptive pill.

1964 Australian aircraft carrier **Melbourne** collides with destroyer **Voyager** — eighty-two men drown.
World's most popular rock group, The Beatles, visit Australia — wild scenes in the streets.

1965 Battalion of Australian soldiers sent to South Vietnam.

1966 Oil and gas discovered in Bass Strait.
Robert Menzies resigns. Harold Holt becomes Prime Minister.
Conscripted Australian soldiers sent to Vietnam.
Northern Territory Aborigines appeal to United Nations for help in getting equal rights.
Pounds, shillings and pence replaced by dollars and cents.
Beginning of change to metric weights and measures.

1967 United States President Lyndon Johnson visits Australia.
President Saragat of Italy visits Australia — 300,000 Italians arrived in Australia since World War II. In same period 2½ million migrants from all countries have come.
Harold Holt disappears in the surf at Portsea.

1968 John Gorton, Prime Minister of Australia.
Russia invades Czechoslovakia.
Excavation at Lake Mungo in western New South Wales begins and produces earliest evidence yet discovered for human occupation in Australia (forty thousand years ago).

1969 Poseidon company announces discovery of nickel at Windarra, Western Australia — shares climb from fifty cents to $280.00.
American, Neil Armstrong, walks on the moon.
Increase in women in the workforce, but they continue to receive lower wages than men.
Women's Liberation Movement begins questioning the role of women in Australian society.

Sixteen year old country debutante who has just been presented to the Shire President and his wife at a Mechanics Hall, 1959.

A HOUSE, A HOLDEN AND A HILLS HOIST

In the 1920s and 1930s Australians had begun to watch American films, dance to American music and sing American songs. Australian films began to die out, and Australian songs seemed old-fashioned.

In the early fifties the first American rock and roll records were made. Rock and roll became a craze in Australia as it did in the rest of the world.

Teenagers not only danced to Elvis Presley songs, they went to see Elvis Presley films, and wore Elvis Presley clothes. Boys wore Elvis Presley haircuts and tried to keep them in place with endless combing and Brylcreem.

Australians formed rock and roll bands. No one thought they would ever be as good as the Americans, but Johnny O'Keefe, the Delltones, Judy Stone, and Johnny Devlin and the Devils were more than just good imitations.

When television came to Australia in 1956 teenagers could watch Australian singers doing their versions of American songs, and some of their own. On one channel there was a weekly Hit Parade in which some local actors mimed the top ten songs.

The Kool Kats show on television in 1959. A lot of the boys wouldn't dance.

The most popular of the rock and roll television shows was Johnny O'Keefe's *Six o'Clock Rock*. The show horrified a lot of parents who did not like to see young people throwing themselves around on the dance floor. The music was too loud too, they said. For many people rock and roll was a sign that things in Australia were going to the pack.

Older people saw some American films as another sign of decay. In some cases, the stories were just a weak excuse for the stars to sing their new songs.

But young Australians flocked to see American teenagers rebelling against their parents, teachers and police. There was *Blackboard Jungle*, Elvis in *Jailhouse Rock*, Marlon Brando as the leader of a motor bike gang in *The Wild One*, and James Dean fighting his father in *Rebel Without a Cause* and *East of Eden*. They often saw them at the new drive-in theatres, which worried their parents even more.

Older people preferred to go and see good old British soldiers beating the Germans in the Second World War, or American musicals by Rogers and Hammerstein such as *Oklahoma* or*The King and I*.

In the 1950s people had more money to spend and more things to spend it on. There was very little unemployment. People were confident of keeping their jobs. They were prepared to borrow money because they knew they would be able to repay it.

Australians wanted to own their own homes. The banks lent money to build them. The houses all looked much the same – brick veneer and tiled roofs with a Hills Hoist rotary clothes line out the back. The cities spread wider and wider. Farms and orchards became suburbs.

Once people had built their homes they bought all sorts of gadgets to put in them. They paid cash for the gadgets if they could afford to: if they could not they put them on hire purchase – the 'never-never' as it was called.

They got rid of their old ice boxes and bought refrigerators. They replaced their coppers with washing machines, their old eggbeaters with new mixmasters, their open fires with Warmray briquette 'space heaters', and their razors with Remingtons. They cleaned their new carpets with new vacuum cleaners and mowed their young lawns with new

Victa lawnmowers.

The iceman and the woodman did not come any more. Nor did the fishman and the nightman. People were buying frozen fish fingers, and they were flushing their newly sewered lavatories.

Australians became very proud of their new possessions. It was a bit embarrassing to have your neighbours see ice delivered to your house when you knew they had a refrigerator. It was even worse not to have a television.

But the proudest possession of all was a car. Australians bought thousands and thousands of cars in the fifties. They bought more Holdens than any other make.

Once you owned a car the next thing to do was to put a radio in it. Then you could listen to Elvis, some songs from *The King and I*, *Dad and Dave* or *Tarzan, King of the Apes* as you drove along.

The men drove to work in their new cars. They took their families for a drive on Sundays – to the seaside in summer, to the hills in spring and autumn to see the English trees and the views. Their teenage sons borrowed them on Saturday nights.

Laminex and wrought iron were the fashion in the fifties — and making every surface a different colour.

AUSTRALIA GOES WILD ABOUT THE QUEEN

Princess Elizabeth was crowned Queen of England in 1953, after the death of her father King George VI the year before. The Princess had been on the way to Australia when she heard of the King's death. She returned to England. Then, in 1954, she came as Queen – the first reigning monarch to visit Australia.

In every city thousands of Australians waited for hours in the streets to catch a glimpse of the young Queen as she passed by. In country towns people gathered in the street, outside town halls and war memorials, and at showgrounds to watch as Her Majesty was driven in an open Rolls Royce around the trotting track. They gathered along train tracks to see her pass by with her tall handsome husband in the royal train.

The people waved and cheered, flew flags, threw streamers and confetti. The Queen and the Prince waved and smiled.

For those lucky people who were going to meet the Queen there were important things to know. The government printed a set of instructions. The Queen was to be called 'Your Majesty' on first meeting her and 'Ma'am' after that, and no one was to ask for her autograph. People invited to garden parties she attended were told that Her Majesty did not want them to go out and buy expensive clothes for her sake. The instructions said that she preferred them to come in the best they had.

Robert Menzies who was Prime Minister from 1949 to 1966 loved the Queen. He loved England and the Empire. So did most Australians. Mr Menzies certainly wore his best clothes. On one occasion the Prime Minister quoted a few lines of poetry for the Queen.

> There is a lady sweet and kind,
> Was never face so pleased my mind;
> I did but see her passing by,
> And yet I love her 'til I die.

Hundreds of schoolgirls were carefully trained in maypole dancing to provide a spectacular display for Her Majesty and His Royal Highness at the Melbourne Cricket Ground.

These people have just seen the Queen pass by.

Mr Menzies was pleased about the Queen's visit because it made so many Australians happy. Heads of Government are always pleased when people have something to distract them.

And there were lots of things which Australians were happy to forget in 1954. Wars were being fought not very far away in South-east Asia. World leaders, as well as the Australian Prime Minister, were talking of a new world war – this time with Russia as the enemy. New kinds of weapons, much more powerful than the bomb dropped on Japan in 1945, had just been successfully tested in the United States.

The visit of the Queen also helped people to forget their daily worries – how much they owed the bank or hire purchase company for their new car, house or refrigerator.

The Queen reminded a lot of Australians of the good old days. She was young, pretty and perfectly behaved. She had 'brought goodness back into fashion', the *Women's Weekly* said. She reminded the people of the days when Britain ruled the world – or most of it – and how good and simple the world had seemed then.

The Queen loved horses and horse-racing. Here she meets a famous Australian jockey, Jack Purtell.

MILKING COWS AND LISTENING TO TARZAN

On the way to Timboon Consolidated School in Western Victoria in the 1950s.

Life in the country changed after the Second World War. For most small farmers the really back-breaking work was over. Much of the land was cleared. Farmers no longer had to walk behind horse-drawn ploughs and harrows. They rode on tractors. They used a lot more machinery. The work was still hard, but not as hard as it had once been.

The Commonwealth Scientific and Industrial Research Organisation (CSIRO) had done a great deal to help farmers. The most important of its discoveries was a virus called myxomatosis which was used to kill off rabbits.

Prices for farm produce were generally good. Farmers still worked hard but many of them could now hope to get out of debt.

Women in the country still did farmwork, but chores in the house got easier. Electricity and Porta-gas arrived and farmhouses became more like suburban houses. Radio and television kept country people in touch with the cities.

Electricity made life easier outside too. Sheep were shorn with electric shears, cows were milked with electric machines.

Most small farmers had left school early because in the depression of the thirties their parents could not afford to educate them. With more machinery to do the work for them, and more money, farmers were able to keep their children longer at school.

Schools throughout Australia had to grow in the 1950s because there were more children to educate. There had been a 'baby boom' after the war when husbands and wives were reunited and an unusually large number of young men and women married and started families. By the 1950s their children needed schooling.

In the country a lot of the little bush schools were closed down. Children went to bigger schools in the towns. They usually went on a school bus.

Venetian blinds came to schools and homes alike in the 1950s. There's a nature study display and pictures of Aborigines on the back wall.

Consolidated schools were set up for farmers' children. They taught children from the age of five to fourteen. As well as the usual subjects, consolidated schools taught farming skills.

The school usually had a plot of potatoes and one or two other vegetable crops. Students learnt about growing the crops and the school made money from selling them.

Every year there was a field day to which children brought their animals and anything else they had grown or made. There were prizes for the best calf, the best lamb, the best hen, the finest marrow, pumpkin or bowl of butter beans.

Hagley Farm Area school, Tasmania, 1954.

Field days were meant to teach children about farming and encourage them to take a pride in their animals. But like city children, kids in the country were often more interested in the local football or basketball team, the Hit Parade, Friday nights in the local hall watching films like *Davy Crockett* and, after 1956, watching television at home.

Like city kids, they also listened to the radio serials – the adventures of Tarzan in the African jungle, the Englishman Biggles in his aeroplane, and *Dad and Dave* who were still battling it out on an Australian farm. The local store sold comics which had nothing to do with country life and nothing to do with Australia. The comic heroes were American – Donald Duck, Goofy, Batman, Captain Marvel, Archie and Jughead.

The children at consolidated schools came from all sorts of families. Some of them had been in the district for many years. Some were descended from the pioneers. A lot of them were the children of soldier settlers – people who had been given blocks of uncleared land very cheaply as a reward for fighting in the war.

There were town kids too of course – children whose parents worked in the local butter factory, in the shops, the banks and the pubs, the shire council, the sawmill or the abattoirs.

Some children in these districts were only seen during school holidays. They had been sent to expensive private boarding schools in the city – some of them from the age of five. Their parents hoped this would give them better accents and a better start in life. It seemed important to make friends with other children whose parents could afford to send them there.

When they reached the age of fourteen, country children had the choice of leaving school for the farm or a job in the town, or going to the high school. Most went on to the high school. There were not enough jobs in the country to go around and a person needed a high school education to get a good job in the city.

Consolidated schoolgirls sit down to a meal they cooked themselves. They were also learning to make baby clothes like those pinned to the wall.

THE BEST IN THE WORLD

Opening day of the Games.

Perhaps because it had been a pioneering country where people needed to be strong, Australians had always encouraged and admired ability in sport. When their runners and swimmers and cricketers took on the world's best and beat them it seemed to prove that Australia really counted. A lot of Australia's national pride grew out of the achievements of her sporting heroes.

In 1956 the Olympic Games were held in Melbourne. It was the greatest thing to happen in that city since the Great Exhibition of 1880. For a fortnight the world's attention would be focused on Melbourne. The Games would put Australia on the map.

They turned out better than most Australians ever dreamed.

One hundred thousand people went to the Melbourne Cricket Ground on the sunny opening day. People who could not go to the ground listened to the descriptions on the radio or watched the action on the new television sets.

Ron Clarke, the Australian junior mile champion, carried the Olympic torch into the arena and climbed to a great bowl above the grandstands to light the Olympic flame. The flame burnt throughout the Games as a symbol of peace – the nations coming together in peaceful competition.

Some of the competition was not very peaceful. Hungary had recently been invaded by the Soviet

Television came in time for the Games but not in time for most people to buy one. Many watched sets in shop windows.

Union. There were Soviet tanks in the Hungarian capital, Budapest. A water polo match between teams from the two countries turned into a vicious brawl.

There was very little sympathy for the Soviet Union among Australians in the 1950s, but there was one Russian at the Games they took to their hearts. Vladimir Kuts proved himself a hero and a gentleman by winning both the 5000 metres and 10,000 metres, and waiting at the finishing line to shake hands with all the other competitors as they finished.

But Australian athletes stole the show. The swimmers, Dawn Fraser, Lorraine Crapp, Murray Rose and Jon Hendriks broke Olympic and world records. On the running track Shirley Strickland, who had won a gold medal at Helsinki four years earlier, won two more.

Betty Cuthbert, a shy eighteen year old from Sydney was the hero of the Games. Running with her mouth wide open she stormed down the track to win both the 100 metres and 200 metres. And she won a third gold medal for Australia and for herself when she ran the last leg of the 4 × 100 metres relay.

Betty Cuthbert became known as Australia's Golden Girl. Eight years later she won another gold medal in the 400 hundred metres at the Tokyo Olympics.

Australian athletes won thirteen gold medals at the Games. Only the United States and the Soviet Union won more. It was an extraordinary achievement for a country with such a small population, and Australians were very proud of themselves.

Betty Cuthbert starts the last leg of the women's relay on her way to her third gold medal.

WATCHING THE BOX

Television was invented by a Scotsman named James Logie Baird. He transmitted the first pictures in 1928. They were in colour.

A few sets were sold in Britain and America during the thirties, but it was not until after the Second World War that ordinary people had the chance to enjoy television.

The first television pictures beamed in Australian cities were in black and white. Chuck Faulkner read the first news on TCN9 in Sydney on 16 September 1956, just a few weeks before the Olympic Games opened in Melbourne. Chuck Faulkner was an American. Australians were going to see a lot more Americans on their television sets in future.

For many people it was a long time before they could afford a set, and an even longer time for many more before they had paid them off on hire purchase. People watched TV in store windows. Some took a rug, a chair, sandwiches and a thermos of tea and settled in for the evening.

When people got television sets their lives were changed. To begin with they re-arranged their loungerooms. The chairs and the couch now all had to face in one direction – towards the TV screen. The radio was put in a corner, or in the kitchen where it could be listened to in the morning. Soon very few people sat around listening to the radio at night.

They did not sit around playing cards much either. Or even talking. They watched television in the evening and talked during the day. Often they talked about what they had seen on television or what was going to be on television that night.

What Australians saw in the fifties was not so different from what they see now. There were variety shows, police shows, quiz shows, rock and roll shows, shows about families, sport shows, news, weather and advertisements. Television has always been very good at making people want to buy things.

Television advertising became big business in the sixties. Two of the television channels made a lot of

money by charging companies who wanted to advertise their products. Advertising agencies employed large numbers of people to write the words for advertisements and make the films. It was not long before some television viewers were saying that the advertisements were better than many of the shows.

For those who were irritated by commercial breaks or who preferred more serious television there was the ABC channel. The ABC was owned by the government. It had more news and more shows on politics and current affairs. A lot of ABC television was English television. It had English-sounding voices which most educated and well-off Australians preferred.

On all the channels there were shows for children. Some of them were Australian, like *The Happy Show* and *Mr Squiggle*. In Melbourne there was something called *The Tarax Show* – which encouraged children to buy the new Tarax soft drink.

But the most popular show by far – for children and adults – was *The Mickey Mouse Club*, which was made in Hollywood by Walt Disney. The kids in *The Mickey Mouse Club* were all very healthy looking Americans. As Australian children grew up *The Mickey Mouse Club* children grew up. The only difference was the American kids wore big plastic mouse ears.

It was not long before quite a few Australians began to wear mouse ears too, and they began to go about singing the *Mickey Mouse Club* song.

> Mickey Mouse. Mickey Mouse.
> Forever let us hold his banner high, high, high.
> M-I-C-K-E-Y
> Why? Because we like you.
> M-O-U-S-E.

After a while quite a lot of Australian parents began to wonder what television was doing to their children.

MIGRANTS FROM EUROPE

Migrants had to obey rules on board ship and stay in a specially roped-off area

The war left millions of people homeless. Many European and British cities had been destroyed. Housing was hard to find and so, for many people, was food.

Several thousand Jewish refugees had begun to arrive in Australia just before the war. They had been forced to leave Germany and other countries in Europe which Germany had occupied. The Nazis hated Jews. During the war they had set up extermination camps to kill them all.

In Australia the Jewish refugees worked in many different occupations. A lot of Australia's finest university teachers, writers and musicians in the last thirty years arrived as refugees from Nazi occupied Europe.

Australia had been on the brink of invasion during the war. It was believed that the country could only be safe in future if a lot more people lived here. 'Populate or perish' became the slogan. A great new immigration scheme was organized.

After the war, Australia also badly needed people to build houses, offices and factories, dams, roads and bridges. They were needed to work in old industries such as steel manufacturing and new ones, particularly the assembly lines which churned out cars, electrical appliances and all the new plastic goods which people were now buying.

Coming ashore.

The government advertised its plans in Britain and Europe. People heard that if they were willing to leave their old way of life they would find that there was work for everyone in Australia, plenty of good houses and plenty of food.

Seventy thousand migrants came in the first year of the scheme, 1948. The ships they came on were often old and run down. It was the women's job to clean the cabins, toilets and corridors, as well as to look after their families. The migrants were often crammed into very poorly ventilated dormitory cabins.

For migrants who had gone through the previous decade in Europe when meat was almost impossible to get, the sight of an Australian butcher's shop was amazing. But the jobs and the housing were often disappointing.

It was true that there were plenty of jobs, but migrants generally got the worst of them. Many skilled workers, and even people with high qualifications in science and engineering were sent to work at labouring jobs. Those without skills usually became 'factory fodder', which means that they were given the worst jobs in industry.

More migrants were brought in than the government could provide houses for. When they first arrived they were placed in special camps which were often no more than rows of old huts. They were cold in winter and terribly hot in summer. The water supply was poor and there were often no places for children to play. The migrants felt they had been dumped and forgotten – as if they had come to a country which did not want them.

The camp at Bonegilla in Victoria was one of the worst. There were thousands of migrants there, mainly from Yugoslavia and Italy. They had been there for months without getting a job. In July 1952 some of the migrants rioted. Huts were set alight. Four army tanks were sent in to stop the riot. But conditions did not improve very much and in 1961 there was another riot.

The migrants came from all over Europe. Many Australians were suspicious and hostile and called them by a variety of ugly names. The government decided that they should be called 'New Australians', which did nothing to make 'old Australians' welcome them, and nothing to stop people calling them 'dagos', 'wops', 'reffos', and 'spags'.

By the late fifties most of the migrants were coming from the countries of southern Europe – Italy, Yugoslavia and Greece. Australians knew nothing of these places. They knew only the Australian way of life which had largely come from Britain. They liked meat pies, breakfast sausages, stewed fruit, plum pudding, and spaghetti only if it was chopped up small, served on toast and came out of a tin. They were very suspicious of people who ate eggplant, chicken livers, capsicums and long spaghetti.

They were even more suspicious of people who didn't speak English. Who could know what they were saying? They might be saying Australians were mugs.

A lot of migrants left Australia believing that the government had misled them about the opportunities in Australia, and that Australians were ignorant and intolerant. In 1965, for instance, 14,000 went home.

But most migrants stayed. In the same year 140,000 migrants arrived. For a long time they had to put up with being treated as second class citizens. In the end most of them did make better lives for themselves, and in so doing they made the lives of 'old Australians' richer.

THE MINING BOOM

Lewis Harold Bell Lasseter believed that he had seen a fantastic reef of gold in the desert of central Australia. Back in Sydney in 1930 he told people about his discovery.

Lasseter led an expedition out towards the Petermann Ranges from Alice Springs. When they were near the place he believed he had seen the reef, Lasseter disappeared. Some months later his body was found in a shallow grave.

No one knows what happened to Lasseter but there was a frantic search to find his reef.

Theories and rumours spread.

Lasseter probably never saw a reef. But a lot of Australians wanted to believe that he had. That great empty inland had to be good for something, they thought. And in fact it was.

Since then, the remote corners of Australia have produced much of the nation's wealth – even though a lot of the profits, as well as the minerals, have gone overseas.

There was copper, in huge amounts at Mt Isa. Uranium and bauxite (for making aluminium) were discovered in the Northern Territory, iron ore in vast quantities in Western Australia, oil and natural gas at Moonie in Queensland, Bass Strait and the North-West Shelf, and immense black coal fields in Queensland. Right through the fifties and sixties there was a long mining 'boom'. Australia's wealth seemed to be limitless.

Near Laverton, one of the old goldfields of Western Australia, a small team of prospectors began drilling one day in September 1969. When the drill was down about seventy metres they noticed that in the sludge coming out of the hole there were traces of copper and nickel. It was nickel they were after. Nickel was in great demand for industry. It brought a very high price. For a while in 1969 and 1970 nickel was to Australians what gold had been to Lasseter.

The company which found these traces was based in

Operators shout their orders at the stock exchange. Investors watch the action from the gallery above.

Adelaide and called Poseidon. At the time of the discovery a share in Poseidon cost about one dollar. Then the company announced that it had found not just traces of nickel but a great lode of it.

Suddenly a Poseidon share cost $10, then people bid $25, then $50, then $100.

Some people had already made fantastic amounts of money. A person who had bought just $100 worth of shares in Poseidon in July 1969, could have sold them for $25,000 by Christmas. Within a month that figure had doubled, within another month, it had almost trebled. The price of a share in Poseidon in February 1970 was $280.

Poseidon had created a frenzy. People who had never given a thought to buying shares, and who could not have told the difference between nickel and basalt, started investing.

The newspapers, radio and television were full of Poseidon. All around the world the news was the astonishing events on the Sydney, Melbourne and Adelaide stock exchanges.

Dozens of new companies were started. Men set off into the desert in light planes, helicopters and jeeps to stake out a claim and start drilling. Poseidon's little claim was now valued on the stock exchange at $700,000,000.

But it was worth nothing like that amount. And nine out of ten of the other new mining companies found nothing. People with shares soon began to realize this and sell them. The prices suddenly crashed. People who had paid $200 for each share in Poseidon suddenly found that they could only get $100 for them, then $50, then $10.

ALBERT NAMATJIRA

Albert Namatjira was born in 1902 and grew up on a mission near Alice Springs. He was taught the ways of white people and to believe in the Christian God. Then, at the age of thirteen, his own people took him away from the mission. Now Albert Namatjira was taught Aboriginal laws and Aboriginal religion.

At eighteen he married Ilkalita. They had several children.

Albert's life at this stage had been little different to other Aborigines living around Alice Springs.

But Albert Namatjira had a talent for painting the Australian landscape. He painted landscapes as he'd been taught by white people – in water colours, usually with a white gum tree in the foreground, and a backdrop of a dry, rocky ravine.

White Australians who travelled to the centre liked to bring home mementos of their visit. A Namatjira painting was frequently one of them along with a plywood boomerang.

Namatjira's paintings became famous. They brought high prices. Thousands and thousands of prints of his were hung in loungerooms of Australian homes. Most of the people who owned them had never seen the Australian desert – a good many of them had never seen an Australian Aborigine.

But for them a Namatjira painting was a pleasant link with both. It was Aboriginal art that white people found acceptable – because it was like white art.

Albert Namatjira became quite wealthy. He mixed with important white Australians. He met the Queen. White Australians admired him as a man who had quit his own people, learnt a white skill, and done well in the world.

Albert Namatjira, however, had not broken away from his own people. He spent a good deal of his time with them, and shared his earnings with them.

But one thing separated Namatjira from his people. The law said that only Aboriginal people who had shown that they were 'capable' of living in the white community would be made citizens of Australia.

Albert Namatjira had been granted full citizenship. An Aborigine who was a citizen of Australia had all the rights whites had. He could travel freely, vote, earn equal wages for equal work – and buy and consume alcohol. Namatjira had these rights but his friends did not.

In 1958, in Alice Springs court, Namatjira was sentenced to six months jail for supplying alcohol to a friend of his who was not a citizen of Australia.

A lot of Australians – white and black – thought that this was unfair. There should be one law for all Australians, they said. Namatjira's sentence was reduced.

He died shortly after his release, in 1959.

1970 - to the present day

1970 Moratoriums against the war in Vietnam in Australian capital cities. In Melbourne, 100,000 people fill the streets.
The Pope visits Australia.

1971 William McMahon, Prime Minister.
Neville Bonner, the first Aboriginal elected to the Australian parliament.

1972 Women's Electoral Lobby set up to force politicians to reveal their attitudes to women's issues so that women can vote accordingly.
Labor Party wins election. Gough Whitlam, Prime Minister.
Australian troops brought home from Vietnam.
Conscription ended.

1973 Sydney Opera House opened.
Land given back to Gurindji people at Wave Hill.
Elizabeth Reid appointed first advisor to the government on women's affairs.

1974 Cyclone Tracy destroys much of Darwin.
Whitlam Labor government returned at election.

1975 Papua New Guinea granted independence from Australia.
Colour television introduced.
Saigon, capital city of South Vietnam, falls to North Vietnamese and Viet Cong armies. Last Americans withdraw.
Governor General dismisses government.
Liberal and Country parties win election.
Malcolm Fraser, Prime Minister.
Indonesia invades East Timor.

1976 Earthquake in China kills estimated 700,000 people.

1977 Liberal Government returned to office after election.
Refugee boats from Vietnam arriving in Darwin.

1980 Ronald Reagan, former Hollywood actor, elected President of the United States.
Liberal Government returned to office after election.
Massive earthquake in Naples area, Italy.

1981 North-eastern South Australia returned to Pitjantjatjara people by South Australian government.
Population of Australia: 14,922,300. Males 7,448,300; females 7,474,000.
Unlike the census of 1901, Aboriginal people were counted in with all other Australians. There were 159,600 Aborigines in Australia in 1981.

1982 Britain and Argentina at war: Britain recaptures Falkland Islands in south Atlantic ocean after they are seized by Argentina.

1983 Labor wins election. Robert Hawke, Prime Minister.
Australia II wins America's Cup.
Ash Wednesday — bushfires kill eighty people in South Australia and Victoria.
End of long drought in eastern Australia.
Uluru (Ayers Rock) returned to Aboriginal people by Commonwealth Government.

PICTURES OF AUSTRALIA

By the 1960s Australians had forgotten a lot of their own history. It was often said that Australian history was too short to be history at all. Nothing very important had happened in Australia.

At school Australians learnt a lot of English history, and when they did learn Australian history at secondary school it was called British history anyway.

People knew more about the American wild west than they knew about their own pioneers. They saw a lot more of American Indians than they saw of Australian Aborigines, more American and British comedy than their own, more British and American soldiers winning wars.

In the late sixties an English film director came out to Australia to make a film about Ned Kelly. The director thought no one would come to see an Australian play Ned. So Mick Jagger of the Rolling Stones was chosen instead. The Australian bush looked just right in the film, but Mick Jagger looked wrong.

Towards the end of the sixties a lot of Australians grew tired of the way the country seemed to depend on America and Britain for ideas. Britain seemed less and less important to Australia, especially now that so many Australians came from southern Europe. Many people blamed the United States for the war in Vietnam, and no longer wanted her as an ally.

For a growing number of people it was time for Australia to stand on its own feet. There was plenty in Australia's past and present society to write about, and plenty of Australian subjects for films and television shows. There were Australian voices and Australian jokes – and there were plenty of different kinds of Australians.

A lot of new books and plays were written in the 1970s. More and more Australian film and television shows were seen. The writers of the seventies were

Helen Morse as **Caddie**. The film was based on a book about a woman's struggles during the depression.

The Irishman was one of many films made in the seventies set in Australia's pioneering days.

The makers of **Mad Max**, 1979, imagined a violent world of the future, perhaps after a nuclear war.

rather like the writers of the 1890s – they wanted to say something about what it was like to live in this country. It was like no other country on earth. And the Australian public wanted to read and see what they had to say.

Quite a few of the films were about men and women struggling to make a living from the land. As the painters of the 1890s had, filmmakers began to show how beautiful the Australian landscape was. The people who made *Picnic at Hanging Rock* also realized that it was a mysterious place. Filmmakers seemed to discover what the Aborigines knew a long time ago.

Through film, Australian history has been held up for Australians to see. Some of the films have been critical of the way Australians have acted in the past. In *Wake in Fright*, which was made early in the 1970s, Australians seemed a pretty brutal, drunken lot. And of course some of the films have made the past seem more glamorous than it really was.

Australians have seen films and television shows about the convict era, the gold rush, bushrangers, Australia in the wars and the depression. They have seen the city and the country, ordinary Australians and famous ones. They no longer think their history or their films are second rate.

Australian films have also become popular in the United States, Britain and other parts of the world. It seems that once Australians got interested in their own country they were able to make it interesting for people in other countries as well.

VIETNAM YEARS

In the 1950s and 1960s Australians lived in fear of a third world war. The United States and the Soviet Union were testing more and more nuclear weapons. Each side accused the other of wanting to dominate the world. This was called the Cold War. Australians also lived in fear of invasion.

Communism seemed to be spreading through South-east Asia towards Australia. The old colonial powers – Britain, France and the Netherlands – were pulling out of those countries. Civil wars were fought to decide what sort of government should take their place.

In every case America and the Soviet Union stepped in. They wanted to see governments set up that were friendly to them. So they gave arms and money to the competing sides.

Vietnam is a very small country in South-east Asia. The French had ruled there for many years. In 1954, after a long struggle, the French were driven out.

A peace treaty drawn up in 1955 divided the country in two. North Vietnam had a government supported by the Soviet Union and China. In the south a government backed by the United States was set up.

In the south many Vietnamese opposed both the division of the country and the new government. A civil war started. North Vietnam supported the opponents of the South Vietnamese government who were known as the Viet Cong.

Early in the 1960s America started to send troops to Vietnam to fight the Viet Cong and North Vietnam. They were sure they would soon defeat the communists.

In 1964 Australia joined the Americans. The Prime Minister, Mr Menzies, sent troops, saying that unless North Vietnam and the Viet Cong were defeated, Australia would not be safe. If Australia did not help America in Vietnam, he said, America would not help us when we needed help.

Australian troops in action in Vietnam. It seemed impossible that a country as powerful as America could be defeated.

People blocking the streets as a way of telling the government that they want American and Australian troops brought home from Vietnam, and the war brought to an end. Hundreds of people were arrested in demonstrations against the war.

Mr Menzies also introduced conscription – or National Service. It was like a lottery. Every twenty year old male had to register for National Service but only those who were born between certain dates were called up. The dates were drawn out of a barrel.

The Americans sent just a few troops at first. Then they sent more and more. Eventually they had 500,000 men there. They also sent B-52 bombers, helicopter gunships and almost every other deadly weapon they had. To everyone's relief they did not send nuclear weapons.

But the Americans could not win the war. Every night Americans and Australians saw the war on television. Many of them began to feel not only that the war could not be won but that their soldiers should not be there.

In Australia thousands of people marched through the streets urging the government to stop the war. More and more young men refused to be called up. The people of Australia – and America – were divided about the Vietnam war. There were those who said that Australian troops must stay. But the numbers opposed to the war grew larger every year.

There were bitter arguments. The marches became larger and there were frequent fights with police.

In 1972 a new government was elected. It had promised to bring the Australian troops home, and it did. In 1975 the war ended. North Vietnam had won and America withdrew.

Almost 60,000 Americans had been killed and 300,000 wounded. Australia had lost nearly 400 troops and more than 2000 had come home wounded.

Hundreds of thousands of Vietnamese were dead and the country lay in ruins.

When the war ended many thousands of Vietnamese people who did not want to live under communism left the country – most of them in small and flimsy boats.

In Vietnam a great deal of rebuilding has been done, but the country is still recovering from the war.

IT'S TIME

Gough Whitlam explains the Labor Party's policies during the election campaign of 1972. The audience liked everything it heard.

In more than fifty years as a politician Billy Hughes made thousands of speeches – from balconies, platforms and soap boxes, often without even the help of a microphone. But in 1972 many more people saw politicans William McMahon and Gough Whitlam in two hours of television than all Hughes' audiences from 1901 to 1951. And the audience of 1972 saw them in close up.

Gough Whitlam was a good television performer. He looked as if he knew what he was talking about and believed what he was saying.

The Labor Party won the election. Gough Whitlam's better television image was only one of the reasons. A majority of Australians really did think it was time for a change.

Since 1949 Australia had been governed by the Liberal and Country parties. For sixteen of those years the Prime Minister had been Robert Gordon Menzies. Mr Menzies did not like change. He was a clever politician and a lucky one – he had to be to stay Prime Minister for so long.

For some time after Menzies resigned the majority of Australians went on believing that Australia was a lucky country and no one should complain. They went on believing that Australia should remain loyal to Britain and America, keep all Asian people out, have nothing to do with China, send more troops to Vietnam, and, at home, alter things as little as possible. They wanted the Menzies years to last forever.

But a growing number of Australians wanted a change. They particularly wanted an end to the war in Vietnam and conscription. And they also believed that major changes were needed at home. Education and health services had been neglected for years. For too long, they said, the government had favoured the rich. They also wanted Australia to be a more independent country, owning its mineral wealth, making its own decisions, and taking pride in its own way of doing things.

Gough Whitlam made these kinds of promises. He talked about creating a fair and just society, one that the world would look up to. He spoke of taking Australia out of the past and into the future.

In the first few months the new government seemed to be rapidly carrying out its promises. The troops were brought home from Vietnam. Land rights were granted to some Aboriginal groups. The White

Television had become the key to success in politics. Like a television compere William McMahon, the Prime Minister in 1972, is using an autocue to address an audience. The trick is to read the words without it being obvious.

Australia Policy was officially abolished. A friendly relationship was established with the communist government of China.

Money was poured into education, housing and health care – especially for poorer sections of the community. Schemes were drawn up to make sure wealth from the new mines would stay in Australia.

Whitlam offended Australia's old friends. He criticized the United States government for bombing North Vietnam. 'Advance Australia Fair' replaced 'God Save the Queen' as the Australian national tune. The Queen's portrait, which had always hung in every Australian post office, was taken down and her insignia, 'ERII', on mail boxes was painted out. A lot of Australians were horrified.

A feeling grew that the new government was changing too much too fast. Increasingly, people blamed the government as unemployment and prices rose. In 1975 the press found out that a loan from the rich Arab countries was being arranged. Labor wanted the money to pay for its plans to change Australia. The newspapers and those who disliked the government said the secret loan was a scandal. Others said it was a terrible bungle.

Towards the end of 1975 the Liberal and Country parties, led by Malcolm Fraser, voted to block the government's supply of money in the Senate. Whitlam would be unable to govern. His opponents hoped that he would be forced to call an election. They knew that they would win it.

For weeks the Whitlam government held out. The country waited to see which side would be the first to give way.

Then, on 11 November 1975 the Governor-General, John Kerr, dismissed the Whitlam government and made Malcolm Fraser Prime Minister.

For days the country seemed to be in chaos. Many Australians were outraged that the elected government had been dismissed by the Queen's representative in Australia.

Some believed it was a put-up job arranged by overseas banks and the American government anxious to keep control of Australia. Thousands marched in the streets of the major cities, protesting at what Kerr and Fraser had done.

But when an election was held in December that year a lot of the rage had gone. Malcolm Fraser easily won the election. The people seemed to have had enough of changes.

Seven years later they had had enough of Malcolm Fraser's government. At an election in 1983 the Labor Party, led by Robert (Bob) Hawke, was returned to power.

LIVING IN THE CITIES

Usually, when people think about Australia, they think of the bush. They think of pioneers and explorers in the outback, koalas and kangaroos, the Southern Cross in the night sky and on the flag.

But most Australians have never seen a kangaroo or a koala, except in the zoo, have never seen the outback except on television, and could not point to the Southern Cross on even the clearest night.

Most Australians live in cities. They always have. By 1900 two out of three people were living in towns or cities with a population of a thousand or more. This was a much higher proportion of city dwellers than most other countries, including the United States. And ever since then the proportion has steadily grown.

People who plan cities often make the wrong decisions even though they mean well. In the 1950s and 1960s it was decided that poor people would be better off in 'high rise' blocks rather than their old houses in the inner suburbs. Instead of fixing up the houses they knocked them down. But the new buildings were not only ugly, the people who lived in them often felt as if they were trapped in cells. In some parts of the world 'high rise' buildings are being knocked down – not because they are old and falling apart, but because they are miserable places to live.

Cities are forever changing. With the exception of Sydney, Australian cities used to be famous for closing down at night and on Sundays. The streets may still seem quiet on a Sunday but until the 1960s they were almost ghostly. All you could hear was the occasional sound of church bells and, in Melbourne, the rattle of a tram every hour.

European and Asian migrants have done a lot to make Australian cities livelier and more interesting. Their restaurants, coffee bars and shops changed Australian eating habits. They did a lot to create a night life in the cities.

Two kinds of working class housing. Very few workers' cottages like these remain.

Within a year huge high rise flats will block out the view for the terraced cottages on the other side of the road. Life will be very different for everybody in this area of Melbourne, especially for the people living in the new flats.

People used to live in the heart of cities, but they made way for shops and offices. Now they are starting to come back. Changes to the city were not always welcomed by the people. A new freeway might help traffic to move faster, but for those who live in its path a freeway means the demolition of their houses or constant noise and air pollution from cars. And freeways often destroy communities by cutting suburbs in half.

Cars have drastically changed Australian cities. Because most people wanted to drive their cars to and from work, governments felt that it was necessary to build more and better roads and freeways. While a great deal of money was spent on roads public transport became dilapidated. People in the seventies sat in traffic jams in their brand new cars while train carriages built before the first World War clanked along the rails.

A lot of fine old buildings were destroyed in the sixties and seventies. Companies bought them and knocked them down to put up office blocks. There was a lot of money to be made from letting and selling office space.

A lot of old buildings were familiar landmarks. When they were pulled down it seemed to many people that they were losing the city they knew and liked. In some cases trade unions refused to work on demolition and building jobs. These union actions were called 'green bans'.

The inner suburbs used to be home for working people who needed to live close by the factories where they worked. In recent years a lot of working people have left their old homes for the newer suburbs. They now shop, not in the city, the markets, or at a corner shop, but in huge new shopping complexes which have everything they want – and piped music. They drive to the shops and they drive to work.

Young middle class people have moved into the old workers' homes and renovated them. The inner suburbs used to be the cheapest places to buy a house. Now they are among the dearest.

Residents have their say on a wall in Sydney.

A FAMILY IN THE SEVENTIES

In the 1970s eight in every ten Australians were living as part of a family and most of them were living in comfortable suburban houses.

Australians had never been so keen to get married as they were in the seventies, and they married younger. They had fewer children than couples used to have – two or three was average, whereas five or more was still common in the 1930s. An increasing number of couples decided not to have children at all in the seventies – and an increasing number got divorced.

In about sixty per cent of families the man was the only breadwinner. He worked, and his wife looked after the house and the children.

With the man in a steady job – maybe as a bricklayer, a primary school teacher or a factory worker with plenty of overtime – a couple had just enough to put a deposit on a block of land and build a house. It would take them twenty years or more to repay the loan from the bank or finance company. The family car and the furniture would probably also have to be paid off. The loans could have been repaid faster if the wife also had a job.

Just about everything in these houses was new. People prized things that made life easier – a dish washer, a vacuum cleaner, a stereo, a wall-to-wall carpet. There might be some prints of old Tom Roberts' paintings on the walls. On the mantle piece above the new gas heater might be an old photo or two – their wedding of course, and perhaps one of his parents or hers outside their house back in Italy or Greece, Liverpool or Brisbane.

Their brick veneer house might have been about twenty kilometres from the city where trains didn't go. The house had three bedrooms, a loungeroom, kitchen and diningroom and a carport to the side. The kitchen and diningroom were not separated by a wall. The lavatory was in the bathroom. There was a good deal of glass.

The family looked out into the backyard where there

Greg and Sandra got engaged in 1973,

and worked and saved to build a house so that

Greg and Sandra's baby.

stood a paling fence, a rotary clothes line, a young gum tree, a silver birch and a barbecue.

There was a shed in one corner which was used as a workshop by the man of the house. He dreamed in there perhaps of buying a little boat for himself, or a block of land by the sea. One of his wife's dreams might have been about doing something more with her life than housework.

Television and advertisements seemed to say that housekeeping and raising children were the only things for a woman to do.

But some popular magazines, best-selling books and many women themselves were questioning what women's lives had become.

Probably one or two of her friends had by now separated from their husbands and were raising their children alone. They may have taken a part time or full time job to support themselves.

A lot of women decided to go back to work in the 1970s. An increasing number of others went back to school. The schools, colleges and universities had begun to take in adults who had missed out on higher education when they were young. Child-care centres helped to make it possible.

Many women who took jobs had no choice. It was the only way to keep up with the loan repayments and rising prices at the supermarket. Other women wanted a different kind of life from the one they had been told was the best – the one the advertisements displayed. A whiter wash was not the most important thing in anybody's life. Women wanted the same chance to take part in the world that men had.

Husbands often found this difficult to understand. Some could not put up with the idea of their wives working – it seemed unmanly to have a wife who earned money. They were not keen to mind the children while their wife studied history, bookkeeping or law. Men liked their tea on the table when they got home. Their wives had broken tradition.

after the wedding — and the honeymoon — they could move into a place of their own.

THE RIGHT TO THE LAND

Members of the Pitjantjatjara Land Council face an invasion of their lands in the Gibson Desert from the Shell Company. The company was drilling for oil.

For a hundred years in northern Australia Aborigines had been working on cattle stations owned by white people.

In June 1966 at Wave Hill station, which was owned by a huge British company called Vestey, a group of Aboriginal workers from the Gurindji tribe refused to work any more. They walked off the station, set up a camp on the Victoria River, and demanded that a large part of the station be handed back to them.

Elsewhere in Australia at this time the majority of Aboriginal people were living much as they had ever since the whites had come and taken their land from them. In the cities they lived in the poorest suburbs, in the country in camps on the fringes of towns.

They did not have the rights that white Australians had. In many places they were banned from swimming pools, hotels, and other public places. And they did not receive the same medical care as whites. The chance of an Aboriginal child dying was almost eight times higher than it was for a white child.

Since then the Aboriginal people have been trying to improve their position. They have organized themselves to demand legal rights, better housing and medical care. They want to be in charge of their own affairs.

Their most important demand has been land rights. White people have often said that if Aborigines want land they should buy it, just like everyone else. But

Camp flying the Aboriginal flag.

Talking about the best way to win back the land.

Aboriginal people point out that the land was not bought from them, it was taken by force.

Everywhere Aboriginal people live on the land, they want white people to acknowledge that they have a right to it. Aborigines want to be the people who decide what happens to the land – whether it will be mined or visited by white tourists for instance.

They also want their sacred sites protected. These places mean nothing to white people but they are part of the Aboriginal Dreaming. Aborigines know the story of these rocks and waterholes. They know how they were created and their religion tells them that they must never be destroyed.

For a long while the Australian government was unwilling to listen to these arguments. In 1972, a group of Aborigines set up a tent embassy outside Parliament in Canberra. They were determined to stay there until land rights were won.

For a lot of white people in the 1970s what was happening to the land also became very important. Farming, mining, logging, dam building and the spread of cities and towns had destroyed much of the natural environment. Conservation groups began attracting people who wanted to stop further damage being done. White Australians were starting to realize that they should care for the land.

In 1973 the Whitlam government announced that it would buy two cattle stations in the north and hand them back to the Aboriginal people. Four thousand square kilometres would be taken from the company which owned Wave Hill and returned to the Gurindji tribe.

Since then Aborigines have lost land to mining companies in several parts of Australia. But they have also had victories.

A lot of white Australians have been forced to remember that the land was not always theirs. And they have also learnt what the Aborigines always knew – that the land needs understanding and careful treatment.

Pitjantjatjara people at Ernabella, South Australia, celebrating the government's decision to return a large part of their tribal lands to them in 1981.

MORE HAIRDRESSERS THAN $TEELWORKERS

In the 1970s Australians found that not everything in their country was as it seemed. They read, for instance, that about two and a half million Australians did not earn enough to buy their basic needs.

The poor were to be found in high-rise flats, in parts of the inner suburbs of the major cities where they'd always been, in the sprawling outer suburbs, in country towns, and on small farms. They were factory workers, people whose disabilities made them unable to work, farm workers, migrants, single mothers, widows, pensioners, Aborigines, students.

Most of them needed assistance from the government, the churches, or from organizations like the Brotherhood of St Laurence and the Smith Family. The medical attention available to them and the schooling their children received was much worse than that of other Australians. They had few chances in life and very little choice about how they lived.

For men and women with good jobs in the seventies life got better and better. Incomes rose and there were more things to spend money on – colour televisions, holidays in Asia, restaurants, expensive haircuts. It was hard to believe that in this rich country so many people were poor.

The same people also found it hard to believe that unemployment was a serious problem when the numbers began to swell in the early seventies.

Places like this, paid for by the government, provide young unemployed people with a regular meeting place and sometimes the chance to learn arts and crafts. But they cater only for the needs of a few. By 1984 there were well over half a million unemployed people in Australia.

Inside the factory fence are men who still have their jobs. Outside are men who have just been sacked.

There had been so little unemployment since the second World War that most Australians were convinced that the problem would never arise again. When they read that a hundred thousand Australians were out of work they were inclined to say that most of them were 'dole bludgers' – meaning people who preferred the unemployment benefit to working.

Some young people did prefer to live in poverty on the 'dole'. It was better, they thought, than working in a lousy job. They argued that if such a rich society as Australia could not provide rewarding jobs for everyone it could not expect everyone to work. They wanted a different kind of society.

Most people felt as they did in the thirties – often humiliated, resentful and angry.

The number of unemployed grew steadily through the seventies, as it did throughout the world. It became clear that while a few people were dropping out of work, many more were being thrown out. By the end of the seventies the number of unemployed had reached half a million. People had to admit that it

Cheap meat for people without jobs. Few shopkeepers and no supermarkets are as generous as these two butchers.

was not bludging that was causing the problem, it was the lack of jobs.

In recent times some unemployed people have got together to work out ways to live on very little money. They share cheap houses, teach themselves music and skills in making things that they can sell. They go busking in the streets and selling in the markets.

Some find temporary jobs renovating the homes of wealthier people, cutting their lawns, baby-sitting their children, washing their cars, cleaning their loungerooms, kitchens and bathrooms. Many watch television, play pinball and apply for job after job.

These days there are fewer regular jobs which involve making things. Computers, robots, fully-automated assembly lines have already changed the way people work.

Despite the efforts of trade unions, ordinary Australians have had little say in this. Companies, most of them owned overseas, decide whether new technology will be useful or destructive.

New technology can create jobs by making new projects possible and encouraging inventiveness. It can do much to make life easier and more rewarding. It can reduce the hours people have to work, save them from tedious and dangerous tasks, improve their health – and entertain them.

But meanwhile those people who get jobs are increasingly finding them, not in making goods or inventing them, but in performing services for those who can afford them – in restaurants, tourism, hotels and hamburger chains, hairdressing and so on. There are now more hairdressers than steelworkers in Australia.

People make their own history, even in a world that is often not of their making.

PICTURE SOURCES

3 Sketch by Henry Galiano; **4** Photograph by Reg Morrison; **5** *top* Drawing by Shane McGowan; *bottom* Drawing by Peter Schouten; **6** Victorian Archaeological Survey; **7** *top* Map by Shane McGowan *bottom* Drawing by Shane McGowan; **8** Drawings by Shane McGowan; **9** Victorian Archaeological Survey; **10** Australian Heritage Commission, photograph by Alan Thorne; **11** Painting by Giovanni Caselli, from *The Evolution of Early Man*, Cassell, 1977; **12** Painting by William Blake, 'Elohim creating Adam', Tate Gallery, London; **13** *left* Drawing by Shane McGowan after Giovanni Caselli; *right* After J. Peter White & John Mulvaney; **14/15** Painting by Ron Brooks; **15** *top* Victorian Archaeological Survey; **17** *top & bottom* Victorian Archaeological Survey; **18** George French Angas, *South Australia Illustrated*, private collection; **19** Donald Thomson Collection, Museum of Victoria; **20** Donald Thomson Collection, Museum of Victoria; **21** Photograph by the late W. MacDougall, 1958; **22/23** Painting by Ron Brooks; **23** George Taplin, *The Folklore, Manners, Customs and Language of the South Australian Aborigines*, 1979; **24** Photograph by the late Charles P. Mountford, 1940; **25** *top* Photograph by the late Charles P. Mountford, 1940; *bottom* Photograph by Noel Wallace, 1966; **26** *top* Painting by Robert Darling, Queen Victoria Museum and Art Gallery, *bottom* Painting by Charles Alexandre Lesueur, *L'Atlas Historique*, private collection; **27** *top* From an engraving after Nicholas Martin-Petit, *L'Atlas Historique*, private collection; *bottom* From *Plates to Cook's Third Voyage*, private collection; **28** *top* From George Grey, *Journals of Two Expeditions of Discovery*, private collection; *bottom* Title page of Cornelis de Jode's world atlas, *Speculum Orbis Terrae*, Flanders, 1578; **29** *top* Donald Thomson Collection, Museum of Victoria; *bottom* From bark painting, Museums and Art Galleries Board, Northern Territory; *margin* Museum of Applied Arts and Sciences, Ultimo Watercolour; **30** by Joseph Lycett, National Library, Canberra; **31** *margin* From *Dampier's Voyages*, Vol. III private collection; *bottom* From *Plates to Cook's Third Voyage*, private collection; **32** Mitchell Library, Sydney; **33** *top* National Library, Canberra; *bottom* Engraving attributed to Captain James Wallis, National Library, Canberra; **34** *bottom* British Museum; *top* Professor J. Mulvaney, Australian National University, Canberra; **35** Drawing by Juan Ravenet, Mitchell Library, Sydney; **36** From an engraving by Gustav Dové; **37** *top* From an engraving by Gustave Dové; *bottom* National Library, Canberra; **38** Drawing by Shane McGowan; **39** *top* Drawing by Thomas Rowlandson, National Library, Canberra; *bottom* From the *Historical Journals* of Hunter, private collection; **40** Detail from sketch attributed to F. Fawkes, 1788, Rex Nan Kivell Collection, National Library, Canberra; **41** From *James Reid Scott's Scrap book*, National Library, Canberra; **42** Etching from *Historical Journals of Hunter*, 1793; **43** *top* From *L'Atlas Historique*, 1800, private collection; *bottom* Rex Nan Kivell Collection, National Library, Canberra; **44/45** Painting by Ron Brooks; **45** Filmco; **46** James Bonwick, *The Last of the Tasmanians*, 1879, La Trobe Library; **47** *top* From J.B. Hirst, *Convict Society and its Enemies*, La Trobe Library; *bottom* From *The Voyage of HMS Rattlesnake*, La Trobe Library; **48** Channel Seven; **49** *top* National Library, Canberra; *bottom* Mitchell Library, Sydney; **50** *top* From a painting by A. D. Colquhoun, National Library, Canberra; *bottom* From an etching by Julian Ashton, National Library, Canberra; **51** From Backhouse, *A Narrative of a Visit to the Australian Colonies*, 1843, private collection; **52** *top* Engraving, 1792, private collection; *bottom* Mitchell Library, Sydney; **53** Channel Seven Publicity; **54** Drawing by Shane McGowan; **55** *top* Photograph by the New South Wales Department of Leisure, Sport and Tourism; *bottom* Painting by Augustus Earle, Rex Nan Kivell Collection, National Library, Canberra; **56** Painting by Ron Brooks; **57** Drawing by Morton Herman; **58** Mitchell Library, Sydney; **59** *top* From J.R. Elder, *Letters and Journals of Samuel Marsden*, 1932; *bottom* National Library, Canberra; **60** *top* Beattie Album, National Library, Canberra; *bottom* Port Arthur Historical Project; **61** *top* Archives Office of Tasmania; *bottom* La Trobe Library, Melbourne; **62** Dixson Gallery, Sydney; **63** *top* Drawing by Shane McGown; *bottom* Drawing by Joseph Lycett, National Library, Canberra; **64** Painting by J.W. Huggins, National Library, Canberra; **65** *top* Watercolour, Mitchell Library, Sydney; *bottom* National Library, Canberra; **66** *top* From Calvert, *The Exploration of Australia*, 1895, private collection; *bottom* From David Collins, *An Account of the English Colony in New South Wales*, 1798, private collection; **67** Royal Historical Society, Perth; **68** Rex Nan Kivell Collection, National Library, Canberra; **69** *top* Rex Nan Kivell Collection, National Library, Canberra; *bottom* From T. Pennant, *A Tour in Scotland*, 1773, private collection; **70** National Library, Canberra; **71** *top* National Library, Canberra; *bottom* National Library, Canberra; **72** Painting by W. Macleod, La Trobe Library, Melbourne; **73** *top* Etching, from *Australasian Sketcher*, La Trobe Library, Melbourne; *bottom* Painting by W. F. E. Liardet, Library Council of Victoria; **74** *left* Penguin Books collection; *right* Painting by W.A. Cawthorne, 'The Fight on the Murray', Mitchell Library, Sydney; **75** Australian Institute of Aboriginal Studies; **76/77** Painting by Ron Brooks; **78** Engraving, *Sturt's Expeditions in Australia, Vol. II*, private collection; **79** Etching by George Hamilton, National Library, Canberra; **80** From James Bonwick, *The Last of the Tasmanians*, La Trobe Library, Melbourne; **81** Painting by Benjamin Dutterau, 'The Conciliation', Tasmanian Museum and Art Gallery; **82** *top* Rex Nan Kivell Collection, National Library, Canberra; *bottom* Wood engraving, National Library, Canberra; **83** La Trobe Collection, State Library of Victoria; **84/85** Painting by Ron Brooks; **86** Photograph from the Holtermann Collection, Mitchell Library, Sydney; **87** *top* Drawing by Shane McGowan; *bottom left Illustrated Sydney News*, 1854; *bottom right* Penguin Books collection; **88** *top* 1984 Postcard; **89** *top* National Library, Canberra; **88/89** Channel Seven Publicity; **90** *top* La Trobe Library; *bottom* Don Whyte Picture Library; **91** *top* La Trobe Library, Melbourne; *bottom Illustrated Sydney News*, 4 September 1880; **92** From *Illustrated London News*, February 1861, National Library of Australia; **93** From *Illustrated London News*, February 1861, National Library of Australia; **93** From *Voyage autour de monde parle Compte de Beauvoir* Paris 1878, National Library of Australia; **94** *top* Detail from an engraving by C. Hutchins, Rex Nan Kivell Collection, National Library, Canberra; *bottom* From *Illustrated Sydney News*, 1855; **95** *top* Drawing by Shane McGowan; *bottom* From *Illustrated Melbourne Post*, 25 January 1866; **96** Watercolour, National Library, Canberra; **97** *top* Wood engraving, National Library, Canberra; *bottom* Archives Office of Tasmania; **98** *top* State Library of Victoria; *bottom* Penguin Books collection; **99** State Library of Victoria; **100** *top* From Ross Fitzgerald, *From the Dreaming to 1915*, University of Queensland Press, 1981; *bottom* From Ross Fitzgerald, *From the Dreaming to 1915*, University of Queensland Press, 1981; **101** From Ross Fitzgerald, *From the Dreaming to 1915*, University of Queensland Press, 1981; **102** From Max Kelly, *Plague Sydney 1900*, Doak, 1981; **103** *top* Gundagai Collection, National Library, Canberra; *bottom* From *Australian Ironmonger*, Diary and Textbook, 1888; **104** Painting by S.T. Gill, 'The Desert Interior', National Library, Canberra; **105** *top* Don Whyte Picture Library; *bottom* Photograph by Alphonse Chargois, 1894; **106/107** Photographs, BHP collection; **108** Victorian Public Records Office; **109** *top* Drawing by Shane McGowan *bottom left* La Trobe Library, Melbourne; *bottom right* From the *Australian Sketcher*, 1880; **110/111** Painting by Ron Brooks; **111** From *Australian Illustrated News*, 1880, La Trobe Library; **112** Etching, National Library, Canberra; **113** *top* From B. Kingston, *My Wife, My Daughter and Poor Mary Anne*, Nelson, Melbourne, 1975; *middle* Penguin Books collection; *bottom* Photograph, John Oxley Library, Brisbane; **114** Watson family collection; **115** Photograph by Walter C. Hume, Fryer Library, Brisbane; **116** *top* From *London Graphic*, 13 June 1891; **117** *top* Watson family collection; *bottom* La Trobe Library, Melbourne; **118/119** Painting by Ron Brooks; **120** Photograph from the Holtermann Collection, Mitchell Library, Sydney; **121** *top* Photograph by Charles Kerry National Library, Canberra; *bottom* Education Department, Victoria; **122** Photograph from Brotherhood of the Good Shepherd album, National Library, Canberra; **123** *top* Penguin Books collection; *bottom* Photograph from *Australia Today*, 1907; **124** Painting by William Ford, 1875, National Gallery of Victoria; **125** Painting by Arthur Streeton, National Gallery, Canberra; **126** *top* Cartoon, *Punch*, 2 June 1888, National Library of Australia; *bottom* From C. Pearl, *All Our Yesterdays*, Angus & Robertson, 1956; **127** *top* La Trobe Library, Melbourne; *bottom* From *Descent*, Vol. 4, 1969; **128** *top* From Inson and Ward, *The Glorious Years*, Jacaranda, 1971; *bottom* From Max Kelly, *Plague Sydney 1900*, Doak, 1981; **129** Painting by Tom Roberts, Department of Home Affairs and Environment; **130** *top* National Library, Canberra; *bottom* National Library, Canberra; **131** Watson family collection; **132/133** Painting by Ron Brooks; **134** *top* Watson family collection; *bottom* private collection; **135** *Australia Today*, 1916; **136** Photograph by Frank Hurley, National Library, Canberra; **137** Painting by George Lambert, Australian War Memorial, Canberra; **138** Don Whyte Picture Library; **139** *top* National Library, Canberra; *bottom left* Don Whyte Picture Library; *bottom right* Australian Film Institute; **140/141** Don Whyte Picture Library; **140** *bottom* La Trobe Library, Melbourne; **141** *bottom* La Trobe Library, Melbourne; **142** West Australian Newspapers Limited; **143** *top* Don Whyte Picture Library; *bottom* Don Whyte Picture Library; **144** Laffy family collection; **145** *top* Laffy family collection; *bottom* Laffy family collection; **146** National Library, Canberra; **147** Don Whyte Picture Library; **148** *left* Watson family collection; *right* McPhee family collection; **149** *top* National Library, Canberra; *bottom* National Library, Canberra; **150** Drawing by Shane McGowan; **151** *top* Postcard, Watson family collection; *bottom Walkabout*, 1 April 1938; **152** National Library, Canberra; **153** Ronin Films; **154** From *Jungle Warfare*, Australian War Memorial, 1944; **155** *top* Watson family collection; *bottom* Australian War Memorial; **156/157** Painting by Ron Brooks; **157** *top School Paper*, August 1942, Education Department, Victoria; **158** Australian War Memorial; **159** *top* Australian War Memorial; *bottom* Australian War Memorial; **160** *top* General Motors Holden, Melbourne; *bottom* National Library, Canberra; **161** *top* History Department, La Trobe University, Melbourne; *bottom* Snowy Mountains Hydro-Electric Authority, Cooma; **162** *top* From Lloyd Ross, *John Curtin*, Macmillan, 1977; *bottom* Australian Information Service; **163** Watson family collection; **164** *Cinema Papers* collection; **165** *top* private collection; *bottom* Drawing by Shane McGowan; **166** Herald & Weekly Times Ltd; **167** *top* Herald & Weekly Times Ltd; *middle* Education Department, Victoria, *bottom* Herald & Weekly Times Ltd; **168** Education Department, Victoria; **169** *top* Education Department, Victoria; *bottom* Education Department, Victoria; **170** Herald & Weekly Times Ltd; **171** *top* Drawing by Shane McGowan; *bottom* Herald & Weekly Times Ltd; **172/173** Painting by Ron Brooks; **174** Lillie Reeves collection; **175** Herald & Weekly Times Ltd; **176/177** Painting by Ron Brooks; **177** *top* Herald & Weekly Times Ltd; **178** Herald & Weekly Times Ltd; **179** Photo by Ruth Maddison; **180** *left and right Cinema Papers* collection; **181** *Cinema Papers* collection; **182** Tony Frederick collection; **183** The *Age*; **184** Australian Information Service; **185** *top Canberra Times; bottom* Ross Lansell collection; **186** Herald & Weekly Times Ltd; **187** *top* Ministry of Housing, Victorian State Government; *bottom* McPhee Gribble collection; **188/189** Gary Smith collection; **190** *top* Phillip Toyne collection; *bottom* Herald & Weekly Times Ltd; **191** *top* Phillip Toyne collection; *bottom* Phillip Toyne collection; **192** *top* Herald & Weekly Times Ltd; *bottom* Herald & Weekly Times Ltd; **193** *top* Photograph by Ruth Maddison; *bottom* Photograph by Ruth Maddison; **194** Photograph by Ruth Maddison.

SELECT BIBLIOGRAPHY

Australian Dictionary of Biography, (9 volumes to date), Melbourne University Press, Melbourne

Geoffrey Blainey, *The Triumph of the Nomads*, Macmillan, Melbourne, 1975

A Land Half Won, Macmillan, Melbourne, 1980

Michael Cannon, *Who's Master? Who's Man?*, Nelson, Melbourne, 1971

Life in the Country, Nelson, Melbourne, 1973

Life in the Cities, Nelson, Melbourne, 1975

Manning Clark, *A History of Australia*, (5 volumes to date), Melbourne University Press, Melbourne

Select Documents in Australian History 1788-1901, Angus and Robertson, Sydney, 1955

A Short History of Australia, Macmillan, Melbourne, 1981

R. W. Connell and T. H. Irving, *Class Structure in Australian History*, Longman Cheshire, Melbourne, 1980

F. K. Crowley (ed.), *Modern Australia in Documents 1901-70*, (2 volumes), Wren, Melbourne, 1973

A New History of Australia, Heinemann, Melbourne, 1974

David Denholm, *The Colonial Australians*, Penguin, Melbourne, 1979

K. S. Inglis, *The Australian Colonials: An Exploration of Australian History 1788-1870*, Melbourne University Press, Melbourne, 1974

Beverly Kingston, *My Wife, My Daughter and Poor Mary Ann*, Nelson, Melbourne, 1975

Kenneth Gordon McIntyre, *The Secret Discovery of Australia*, Picador, London, 1977

Michael McKernan, *All In! Australia During the Second World War*, Nelson, Melbourne, 1983

Humphrey McQueen, *A New Britannia*, Penguin, Melbourne, 1970

Social Sketches of Australia 1888-1975, Penguin, Melbourne, 1978

John Mulvaney, *The Prehistory of Australia*, 2nd edition, Penguin, Melbourne, 1975

Henry Reynolds, *The Other Side of the Frontier*, Penguin, Melbourne, 1982

Geoffrey Serle, *The Golden Age*, Melbourne University Press, Melbourne, 1963

From Deserts the Prophets Come, Heinemann, Melbourne, 1973

Anne Summers, *Damned Whores and God's Police*, Penguin, Melbourne, 1975

Robert Tonkinson, *The Mardudjara Aborigines. Living the Dream in Australia's Desert*, Holt, Rinehart and Winston, New York, 1978

Russell Ward, *Australia Since the Coming of Man*, Lansdowne, Sydney, 1982

J. Peter White and James F. O'Connell, *A Prehistory of Australia, New Guinea and Sahul*, Academic Press, Sydney, 1982

INDEX

Aborigines, *see* burial practices, Dreaming, fire-stick farming, hunter-gatherers, massacres, mud lumps, rock art, sacred sites, Tasmania, tools, *passim*
Abrahams, Esther, 52
Adelaide, 79, 92, 106, 113, 117
aeroplanes, 137, 138, 142-3
agriculture, 30-31, 40-41, 44-5, 74, 79, 96-7, 114
Alice Springs, 153, 176, 178
Anzacs, 136-7, 138, 144
archaeologists, 9, 12, 16
Arnhem Land, 191
Arthur, Governor George, 80-81
atomic bomb, 155, 160, 167
Australian Broadcasting Commission, 150, 173
Australian Women's Weekly, 151, 167

Backhouse, James, 76
Bakery Hill, 88
Ballarat, 85, 88, 98
Barcaldine, 117
Barton, Edmund, 128
Bass, George, 50, 54
Bates, Daisy, 140-41
Bathurst, 49, 84
Batman, John, 72-3
Baudin, Nicolas, 60, 79
Baynton, Barbara, 125
Benalla, 108
Bendigo, 85, 112
Bennelong, 32, 43, 50
Black Caesar, 48
Black Line, 81
Blaxland, Gregory, 54
Bligh, Governor William, 47, 49, 52, 63
Boake, Barcroft, 125
Bonegilla, 175
Bowen, 105
Bradman, Donald, 138
Brady, Matthew, 61
Brahe, William, 92-3
Brisbane, 112, 130, 143
Britain,
attitudes to Australia, 30
Australian attitudes to, 124-5, 126, 128, 132-3, 134-5, 167, 180
life in, 36-7
see also, British Empire, British government
British Empire, 110, 126, 132-3, 134, 141, 154, 166
British government, 36-7, 39, 40-42, 46, 60, 62, 64-5, 66, 84, 154
Broken Hill, 106-7, 117
Broken Hill Proprietary Co. Ltd, 106-7
Broome, 154
Bryant, Mary, 48-9
Buckley, William, 60, 72
Bulletin, The, 125
Bundaberg, 143
burial practices, 10, 15, 16-17, 18, 20
Burke, Robert O'Hara and Wills, William John, 92-3, 104
Burra Burra, 79
bushranging, 48-9, 60-61, 72, 76, 80
Byrne, Joe, 108

Callaghan, Eliza, 72
Camden, 49, 62-3
Canberra, 191
Cape Barren Island, 81
Cape York, 29
Carboni, Raffaello, 98
Castle Hill, 49, 89
Catholics, 49, 59, 82, 114
Charlton, Andrew 'Boy', 138
Ch'eng Ho, 28
Chifley, Ben, 161
China, Chinese, 28, 37, 54, 85, 90-91, 100-101, 126-7, 133, 154, 182, 184
Chisholm, Caroline, 68, 77, 82
Church of England, 49, 56, 58
Clarke, Ron, 170
Colbee, 43
Collingwood, 118-19
Collins, David, 60, 72
conscription, 146, 183, 184-4
convicts, 36-7, 38-9, 40-41, 42-3, 44-5, 47, 48-9, 54-5, 56-7, 58, 60-61, 70, 76, 79, 84, 89
see also, first fleet
convict women, 47, 52-3
Cook, Captain James, 28, 30, 37
Cooper Creek, 92-3
Country Party, 184-5
Crowley, Catherine, 54
Creswick, 162
cricket, 94-5, 138-9, 149, 150, 170
CSIRO, 168
Curtin, John, 162
Cuthbert, Betty, 171

Daly River, 105
Dampier, William, 30-31, 64
dancing, 138-9, 150
Darling Downs, 70, 97
Darling, Governor Ralph, 64, 78
Darling River, 70, 78, 117
Darwin, 105, 113, 153, 154, 156
Deakin, Alfred, 127, 128
Depression, 148-9, 151, 162, 168
dingoes, 14-15, 153
Diprotodon, 10
disease, 41, 43, 69, 74, 77, 78, 97, 101-2, 106-7, 118, 140, 149
Donohue, Jack, 49, 76
Dreaming, 6, 20, 30, 191
droughts, 14, 32, 54, 77, 96
Dutch, 28, 37

East Indies, 27, 28
Echuca, 113
Edward VII, King of England, 133
Elizabeth I, Queen of England, 37
Elizabeth II, Queen of England, 166-7, 178
emancipists, 41, 44-5, 59
England, English,
attitudes to Australia, 30
Australian attitudes to, 124-5, 132, 166-7, 180
emigrants, 41, 61, 94, 188-9
equal pay, 159
Eucla, 141
Eureka Stockade, 88-9, 98, 117
excavations, 16-17
exclusives, 44

Faulkner, Chuck, 172
Fawkner, John, 73
Federation, 128-9
Female Factory, 53
films, 139, 180-81
fire-stick farming, 20, 25, 30
first fleet, 37, 38-9
Fisher, Andrew, 135
Flinders Island, 81
Flinders, Matthew, 50, 79
floods, 77
football, 94, 138, 149, 150
France, 37, 38, 39, 62, 64, 98, 110, 134, 136-7, 154, 182
Franklin, Miles, 125
Fraser, Dawn, 171
Fraser, Malcolm, 185
Fremantle, Charles, 64
Fromm's Landing, 15,
Furphy, Joseph, 125

Gallipoli, 136-7
gambling, 95
Geelong, 73, 85
George III, King of England, 43
George VI, King of England, 166
Germans, Germany, 79, 85, 88, 110, 126-8, 134-5, 137, 151, 154, 156, 174
Giles, Ernest, 25
Gilmore, Mary, 125
Gippsland, 73, 97, 114
Gipps, Sir George, 74-5
Glenrowan, 108-9

gold, 84-5, 86-7, 88-9, 90-91, 98
Goulburn, 49, 76-7
Gray, Charley, 92
Great Exhibition, 110, 170
Greece, 110, 175, 188
Green Bans, 187
Greenway, Francis, 57
Gregory, A.C, 104
Guildford, 91
Gurindji, 190-91

hangings, 40, 42, 49, 59, 61, 76, 109
Hargraves, Edmund, 84
Hawke, Robert, 185
Henty brothers, 72
Hinkler, Bert, 143
Hitler, Adolf, 154
Hobart, 60, 80
Holden, 161, 164
Hotham, Charles, 88
Howe, Michael, 61
Hughes, William Morris, 146, 184
Hume, Hamilton, and Hovell, William, 72, 78
Hungary, 134, 170-71
Hunter, Governor John, 47, 50, 57
hunter-gatherers, 20, 22, 27, 30-31, 40

Indonesia, 29, 41
Ireland, 36, 49, 59, 61, 69, 88, 94, 108, 118, 126, 140
irrigation, 145, 148
Italy, 85, 88, 98, 126-7, 134, 154, 175, 188-9

Jagger, Mick, 180
Jansz, William, 28
Japan, Japanese, 153, 154-5, 156, 162, 167
Jerilderie, 108
Jews, 174
Johnston, George, 52
Johnston, William, 49

Kanakas, *see* Pacific Islanders
Kelly, Ned, 108-9, 139, 180
Kerr, John, 185
Kimberleys, 29, 30
King George III's Sound, 64-5
King, Governor Phillip Gidley, 39, 47, 60, 62
King, John, 92-3
Kokoda Trail, 155
Korean war, 161

Labor Party, 117, 162, 184-5
Lachlan River, 70
Lake Alexandrina, 79
Lake Disappointment (Gumbubundil), 24
Lake Mungo, 10, 18
Lalor, Peter, 88-9
Lambing Flat, 91
Lane, William, 130
La Perouse, Jean-Francois, 39
Lasseter, Lewis, 176
Launceston, 72, 80
Lawson, Henry, 120, 125
Lawson, William, 54
Leichhardt, Ludwig, 92
Leichhardt River, 104
Liberal Party, 184-5
Lone Pine, 136-7
Lord, Simeon, 59
Lyons, Joseph, 150

Macarthur, Elizabeth, 49, 62-3
Macarthur, John, 47, 49, 62-3, 66
Macarthur, General Douglas M., 154
Macassans, 28-9
McCubbin, Frederick, 125
Mackay, 104
McKenzie, Farquhar, 71
McKinlay, John, 104-5
McMahon, William, 184
Macquarie, Elizabeth, 66
Macquarie, Governor Lachlan, 49, 56, 59, 66
Macquarie Harbour, 61
Mahogany ship, 28
Mallee, 112
Marsden, Samuel, 59, 66
Marsh, Rosetta, 44
massacres, 74-5, 80, 153
Melba, Dame Nellie, 138
Melbourne, 60, 73, 85, 92-3, 94, 98, 109, 110-11, 112-13, 114, 117, 154, 170, 186
Melville Island, 29
Menindee, 92-3
Menzies, Robert Gordon, 151, 166-7, 182-3, 184
Methodists, 118
Meyrick, Henry, 75
Mickey Mouse Club, 173
migrants, 41, 68-9, 70, 79, 82, 84, 126, 174-5, 186
Mildura, 145
mining, 79, 84-5, 86-7, 88-9, 90-91, 106-7, 113, 176-7
missionaries, 25, 77, 105, 152-3, 178
Mitchell, Thomas, 70
Monaro High Plains, 70-71
Moonie, 176
Mt Isa, 176
mud lumps, 10
Murray River, 16, 34, 70, 78, 112-13, 145
Murrumbidgee River, 70, 78
music, 138
Mussolini, Benito, 154
Myall Creek, 74-5

Namatjira, Albert, 178
Native Police, 75
Nepean River, 54
Neptune (ship), 41
New Australia, 130
Newcastle, 49, 107
New England, 70
New Guinea, 4-5, 6, 14, 100, 154-5
New South Wales, 10, 68, 84, 90, 112, 117, 122
New South Wales Corps, 46-7, 49, 62
New Zealand, 31, 50, 126, 130, 136
Norfolk Island, 37, 39, 41
Northern Territory, 4, 105, 153, 176
North-West Shelf, 107

O'Dowd, Bernard, 125
O'Keefe, Johnny, 164
Olympic Games, 138, 170-71, 172
Ooldea, 141

Pacific Islanders, 31, 100-101
painting, 33
Parkes, Henry, 128
Parramatta, 41, 49, 53, 62
Paterson, A.B. 'Banjo', 125
Pearl Harbour, 154
Peel, Thomas, 65
Perth, 92, 138
Phillip, Captain Arthur, 38-9, 40-41, 42-3, 45, 46, 50-51
Pitjantjatjara 24-5
Poland, 85
Port Arthur, 61
Port Kembla, 107
Port Phillip, *see* Victoria
Port Pirie, 106
Portuguese, 28-9, 37
Poseidon, 177
Presbyterian Church, 114
Presley, Elvis, 164
prickly pear, 124

Queensland, 97, 100-101, 112, 117, 124, 140, 154, 176, 191
Quinn, Ellen, 108

Rabbits, 124, 133, 144, 149, 168
Rasp, Charles, 106
Red Cliffs, 145
Reiby, Mary, 53
Religion, 6, 20, 30, 37, 39, 58, 74, 82, 96, 132, 191

Robe, 91
Roberts, Tom, 125, 188
Robinson, George Augustus, 81
Robinvale, 16-17
rock art, 8, 29
Rockhampton, 104-5
Royal Marines, 38, 40-41, 52
Ruse, James, 44-5
Russia, 134, 148, 160, 167, 170-72, 182

Sacred Sites, 20, 30, 191
schools, 120-21, 124, 134, 156-7, 168-9, 189
Scotland, Scots, 30, 61, 66, 69, 71, 114, 118
selectors, 96-7, 108, 114
sheep, 54, 62, 69, 70-71, 74-5, 79, 104-5
Singapore, 154
slavery, 37, 101
Smith, Ross and Keith, 142-3
Smith, Sir Charles Kingsford, 143
Snowy Mountains Scheme, 161
soldier settlers, 144-5
Solomon Islands, 100
South Australia, 15, 78-9, 112
Southern Cross, 88-9, 117, 143, 186
Spain, 37
squatters, 70-71, 73, 84-5, 90, 96-7, 100, 108, 126
Stirling, Captain James, 64-5
Streeton, Arthur, 125
strikes, 116-17, 127
Stuart, John McDouall, 92-3
Sturt, Charles, 78-9, 92, 106
Supply (ship), 41
Sutherland, John, 104-5
Swan River, 64-5, 72, 84
Sydney, 32-3, 39, 40-41, 42-3, 48-9, 52, 54, 56-7, 66, 76-7, 94, 102, 112, 138, 140, 156, 176-7, 186

Tasman, Abel, 27
Tasmania, 6, 10, 14, 26-7, 50, 53, 60-61, 62, 68, 72-3, 80, 108
technology, 193
television, 164-5, 170, 172-3, 180-81, 184, 189, 192-3
Tenterfield, 128
Terry, Samuel, 44
Thompson, Andrew, 59
Thylacines, 14, 18
tools, 6, 8-9, 10, 12-13, 14, 22-3, 25, 27, 45, 56, 70, 85, 86, 87, 97, 106
Townsville, 140, 154
Trade Unions, 116-17, 123, 130, 162, 187
transportation, *see* convicts
trepang, 29
Truganni, 81
Turkey, 134, 136-7

unemployment, 130, 135, 148-9, 161, 185, 192-3
United States of America, 37, 41, 85, 88, 110, 139, 150, 154-5, 157, 162, 167, 169, 171, 172-3, 180-81, 182-3, 184-5, 186

Vancouver, George, 64
Van Diemen's Land, *see* Tasmania
vegetation,
  after white settlement, 65, 71, 107
  before white settlement, 10, 14, 32-3
  conservation, 191
Victoria, 10, 28, 71, 72, 82, 85, 88-9, 94-5, 97, 108, 110, 175
Victoria, Queen of England, 113, 132-3
Victoria River, 105, 190
Vietnam, 182-3, 184-5
volcanoes, 10
voyage out, 38, 41, 69

Wakefield, Edward Gibbon, 78-9
Wales, 37
Waltzing Matilda, 125
Warramullas, 153
Warrnambool, 22
Wave Hill, 190-91
Wentworth, D'Arcy, 54
Wentworth, William, 54-5
Western Australia, 24, 28, 84, 107, 112, 140, 154, 176, 191
whalers and sealers, 41, 60
White Australia, 101, 126-7
Whitlam, Gough, 184-5
Whyalla, 107
Wooraddy, 81
World War I, 107, 133, 134-5, 136-7, 138, 144, 146, 155
World War II, 154-5, 156-7, 158-9, 160, 162, 168, 172, 174, 192
Wright, William, 92-3

Yarra River, 73, 118-19
Yemmarrawanie, 43
Yugoslavia, 175

Thomas Nelson Australia
480 Latrobe Street, Melbourne Victoria 3000
First published 1984

Originated and produced by
McPhee Gribble Publishers
Typeset in Plantin by Bookset, Melbourne and
made and printed in Hong Kong by
South China Printing Co.

National Library of Australia
Cataloguing-in-Publication data
The Story of Australia.
For children.
Includes index.
ISBN 0 17 006349 6.
1. Australia – History – Juvenile
literature. I. Watson, Don, 1949-
994